The Narrow Way

The Narrow Way

Samael Aun Weor

GLORIAN

The Narrow Way
A Glorian Book / 2017

Originally published in Spanish as "Mensaje de
Navidad 1967-1968" (1968) and later published under
various names given by students, such as "The Solar
Bodies" and "The Doomed Aryan Race."

This Edition © 2017 Glorian Publishing

Print ISBN 978-1-943358-02-1

Glorian Publishing is a non-profit organization. All
proceeds go to further the distribution of these books.
For more information, visit our website.

gnosticteachings.org

Contents

Illustrations

Chapter 1

Atlantis

Beloved gnostic brothers and sisters, on this Christmas night of 1967, we are going to start our Christic message by remembering the very ancient, submerged continent of Atlantis.[1]

The priests of Sais in the ancient Egypt of the Pharaohs told Solon that Atlantis had been destroyed 8,000 years before having that conversation with him.

On a Mayan manuscript preserved in the British Museum, the following can literally be read:

> "In the year 6 Kan, in the 11th Mulac, in the month Zac, there occurred terrible earthquakes, which continued without interruption until the 13th Chuen. The country of 'The Hills of Mud,' the Atlantean land, was sacrificed; being twice upheaved, it suddenly disappeared during the night, the basin being continually shaken by volcanic forces. Being confined, these caused the land to sink and rise several times and in various places. At last the surface gave away and ten countries were torn asunder and scattered; unable to stand the force of the convulsions, they sank with their 64 million inhabitants 8,000 years before this book was written."
> —How I Found the Lost Atlantis, The Source of All Civilization by Dr. Paul Schliemann [1912]

The famous Dr. Heinrich Schliemann, who had the high honor of discovering the ruins of ancient Troy, found within the treasure of Priam a strange jar with a peculiar shape upon it. Upon it appears a phrase written with Phoenician characters, which textually says, "From King Cronos of Atlantis."

It is interesting to note that jars very similar to those found in Priam's treasure were also found amongst the unburied objects in Tlahuanaca, Central America. Certain coins were found within these mysterious jars, when they were intentionally broken "for scientific purposes." Upon these coins the following phrase could easily be read, "Emitted in the Temple of the Transparent Walls."

---

1 "...Atlantis... was an island greater in extent than Libya and Asia..." —Plato, Critias

Esoterically speaking, we must state that any temple of mysteries, any gnostic Lumisial,[2] is in fact a Temple of Transparent Walls with the starry infinite as its ceiling. However, the cited temple mentioned upon the mysterious coins was the National Atlantean Treasury's Office.

In the archives of an ancient Buddhist temple of Lhasa, a very ancient Chaldean inscription can still be read, one that was written 2,000 years before Christ. It states:

> "When the star Bal fell on the place where is now only sea and sky the Seven Cities with their Golden Gates and Transparent Temples quivered and shook like the leaves of a tree in storm. And behold a flood of fire and smoke arose from the palaces. Agony and cries of the multitude filled the air. They sought refuge in their temples and citadels. And the wise Mu, the hieratic of Ra-Mu, arose and said to them: 'Did not I predict all this?' And the women and the men in their precious stones and shining garments lamented: 'Mu, save us.' And Mu replied: 'You shall die together with your slaves and your riches and from your ashes will arise new nations. If they forget they are superior, not because of what they put on [materialism], but of what they put out [generosity, serving others], the same lot will befall them!'"
> —How I Found the Lost Atlantis, The Source of All Civilization by Dr. Paul Schliemann [1912]

Tradition states that the flames and the fog choked the words of Mu. In a few months, the country and its inhabitants were smashed and swallowed in the abysms of the ocean.

Our boastful modern civilization has not yet surpassed the Atlantean civilization. The Atlanteans also knew about atomic energy and utilized it in times of peace as well as in times of war.

Atlantean science had a tremendous advantage, because it was united with magic.[3] Therefore, with such knowledge, they were able to create extraordinary mechanical robots that the Atlanteans endowed with certain types of superior elementals[4] in order to control them. Thus, this is how these robots were in fact converted into intelligent androids that looked like human beings and who devotedly served their masters. Any robot could inform its owner about all the dangers that were

2   "A place of light." A name for gnostic temples.
3   The word magic comes from magi, priest. See glossary.
4   The intelligence or soul of non-human creatures. See glossary.

threatening him/her; in general, these robots could inform about multiple things dealing with everyday life.

The Atlanteans had such extraordinary and marvelous machines. There was one that could telepathically transmit wonderful intellectual information into the mind of any human being.

Atomic lamps illuminated the Atlantean palaces and Temples of Transparent Walls.

The maritime and aerial ships from that ancient submerged continent of Atlantis were propelled by nuclear energy.

Atlanteans learned how to de-gravitate bodies at will. They could levitate any given body, as heavy as it might be, with a small device that fit in the palm of a hand.

The God Neptune governed Atlantis wisely. The very sacred temple of this holy god was dazzlingly admirable. The stockade or silver-coated walls of this temple were amazing with their remarkable beauty. All of its pinnacles and ceilings were made out of the best quality solid gold. All of the royal splendors of ancient times, the ivory, silver, gold, and brass, radiantly glowed within the Temple of Neptune. The gigantic sacred sculpture of the God Neptune was made completely of pure gold. The minds of his Atlantean devotees were infused with profound veneration by the mysterious, ineffable, golden statue, which was mounted on a beautiful chariot and pulled by exotic winged steeds, with a respectable court of one hundred gleaming sea nymphs around him.

While its inhabitants remained loyal to the religion of their forefathers, fulfilling the precepts of the God Neptune and not violating law and order, the Atlantean cities flourished. Yet, when they profaned sacred things, when they abused sex, when they stained themselves with the seven capital sins, then they were punished and submerged with all of their wealth into the bottom of the ocean.

The priests of Sais said onto Solon, "All bodies moving in the heavens around the Earth suffer perturbations that cause great conflagrations of things upon the Earth; this recurs after long intervals. Of the many destructions of mankind arising out of many causes, the greatest have been brought about by the agencies of fire."

The Atlantean continent extended and oriented itself towards the austral regions and the most elevated areas towards the septentrional ones. In grandiosity, elevation, and quantity, its mountains exceeded all those that presently exist.

The history of the Universal Flood can be found within the traditions of all human races, and all are just simply recollections of the great Atlantean catastrophe.

All of the religious teachings from primeval America (such as the sacred cults of the Incas, Mayans, and Aztecs, as well as the gods and goddesses of the ancient Greeks, Phoenicians, Scandinavians, Hindustanis, etc.) have Atlantean origins.

It is urgent to know, it is necessary to comprehend, that the gods and goddesses cited by Homer in his *Iliad* and *Odyssey* were heroes, kings, and queens of Atlantis.

All of the ancient populaces venerated and worshiped those holy gods who lived in Atlantis, and who now inhabit the Empyrean.[5]

America was geographically united with the Old World (Europe and Africa) through Atlantis. The ancient Indo-American civilizations have an Atlantean origin.

The Egyptian, Incan, Mayan, etc., religions were the primeval religions of the Atlanteans.

The Phoenician alphabet, father of all the famous European alphabets, has its origin in an ancient Atlantean alphabet. The latter was correctly transmitted from the Atlanteans to the Mayans. All the Egyptian and Mayan symbols and hieroglyphs come from the same Atlantean source. This is the only way that the similitude of these alphabets can be explained; indeed, the similarity is too enormous to even consider that it is an outcome of chance.

Ancient traditions affirm that the Atlanteans had a metal more precious than gold; this was the famous orichalcum.

The catastrophe that finished Atlantis was frightful. Undoubtedly, the outcome of the violation of the law is always catastrophic.

5   The highest heaven, related to Neptune and the sephirah Kether of the Tree of Life.

Chapter 2
The Aryan Root Race

The epoch of Atlantis's submersion was indeed an era of many geological changes. During that time, other landmasses surfaced from within the profound bosom of the immense sea to become new islands and new continents.

Some Atlantean survivors sought refuge on the small continent of Grabontzi (present-day Africa). This continent increased in size and extent because other landmasses (that had surfaced from within neighboring seas) were added onto it.

In ancient times, the Gulf of Mexico was a beautiful valley. The Antilles Islands, Canary Islands, and Spain are pieces of the now-submerged Atlantis.

Today, the ancient Kolhidius Sea is known as the Caspian Sea. It was situated in the northeast of the then newly-formed continent of Ashhartk, which is present day Asia. The coasts of the Caspian Sea were formed by those lands that surfaced from within the ocean and joined the continent of Asia. Asia, the Caspian Sea, and the entire block of that land together, is presently known as the Caucasus. That block of land, in those times, was named Frianktzanarali and later on Kolhidishssi; however, in this day and age, as we already stated, it is the Caucasus.

In those times of yore, a great river that fertilized the whole rich land of Tikliamis flowed into the Caspian Sea. The river at that time was known as Oksoseria. This river still exists; however, it no longer flows into the Caspian Sea due to a secondary tremor that deviated it towards the right. The rich volume of water from this river violently precipitated itself through the most depressed zone of the Asiatic continent, thus originating the small Aral Sea; however, the very ancient river bed of that old river, which is currently named Amu Darya, can still be seen as a sacred testimony of the flow of the centuries.

Atlantis passed through terrible and frightful catastrophes before it totally disappeared. The first catastrophe happened more or less 800,000 years ago. The second catastrophe occurred 200,000 years ago. The third catastrophe took place about 11,000 years ago. People have more or less befuddled memories of this latter catastrophe and its deluge.

After the third great catastrophe that finished off Atlantis, all of the cities and towns of the ancient country of Tikliamis, with its formidable capital situated on the shores of the river that flowed into the Caspian Sea (which later originated the Aral Sea), was covered by sand, and today remains only as a desert.

During those epochs unknown to Cesare Cantù and his universal history, there was another beautiful country, known as Marapleicie. This country traded with Tikliamis and there was a very strong commercial competition between them.Later on, the country of Marapleicie changed its name to Gobland, due to the great city of Gob. Gobland and its powerful city were swallowed up by the sands of the desert. So, within the sands of the Gobi desert, many wealthy Atlantean treasures are hidden, as well as powerful machines that are unknown by the populaces of this Aryan root race.[6] Once in a while, the sands leave all of those treasures exposed; yet nobody dares to touch them, because the one who tries is instantaneously killed by the gnomes who guard them. Only the human beings of the future sixth root race will know of these treasures, based upon the condition that they behave upright.

Many pearl tradesmen from Atlantis were saved by taking refuge in Pearland, a country that is known in this day and age as India.

The Atlanteans were the ones who built the pyramids of the Egyptians and Aztecs. The Atlanteans were the ones who founded the Inca civilization, the ones who established the mysteries in India, China, Egypt, Yucatan, etc.

The Atlantean root race disappeared, swallowed up by the sea. That race had seven subraces; the last of these subraces,

---

6   Contemporary humanity, regardless of color. See glossary.

the seventh subrace, corresponds to the survivors of the great tragedy.

The seed of our Aryan root race is Nordic. When the Nordics mixed themselves with the Atlantean survivors, they gave origin to all of the subraces of our Aryan root race.

The first Aryan subrace flourished in Central Asia.

The second Aryan subrace flourished in India and the entire south of Asia.

The third Aryan subrace created the powerful civilizations of Babylon, Chaldea, Egypt, etc.

The fourth Aryan subrace developed in Greece, Rome, etc.

The fifth Aryan subrace is made up of the Anglo-Saxon and Teutonic populace.

The great authors of modern anthropogenesis, such as H.P.B., Rudolf Steiner, Max Heindel, and others, committed the very lamentable mistake of supposing that in their epoch they were in the fifth Aryan subrace of the Aryan (fifth) root race, as if the Latin-American people did not exist, as if the Latin-Americans were also Anglo-Saxon or Teutonic, or something of the sort.

It is an absurdity to ignore the racial phenomenon of Latin America; by all means, it is logical to see that from the mixture of the Spanish Conquistadors with the Indo-American tribes, we get, as a matter of fact and by its own

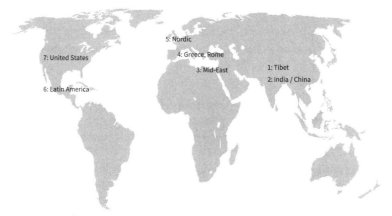

SIGNIFICANT REGIONS AND TIMES IN THE HISTORY OF CONTEMPORARY HUMANITY, ALSO KNOWN AS THE SUBRACES OF THE ARYAN ROOT RACE.

right, a new Aryan subrace, that is, the sixth branch of the
Aryan trunk.

The labor of forming the sixth Aryan subrace in the
native, red-skin territory (USA) was more difficult, because
instead of mixing themselves with the native, indigenous people, the English conquerors destroyed them; they assassinated
them. Thus, in North America, an insignificant amount of
blood mixing was performed between the two peoples, causing enormous difficulty for the formation of the sixth Aryan
subrace. Therefore, the esoteric fraternity who governs the fate
of the world foresaw the necessity of converting the North
American territory into the melting crucible of all races. This
is why all of the races of the world are integrating within the
United States.

The authors of anthropogenesis and esotericism should
not ignore that the sixth Aryan subrace was easily formed in
Latin America.

The seventh Aryan subrace is the last to exist. The seventh Aryan subrace will exist until the end and will be among
the survivors of the great new cataclysm that will very soon
destroy this Aryan root race.

There were powerful spiritual civilizations from the first
Aryan subrace in those kingdoms of Central Asia, in the
countries of Gobland, Marapleicie, etc., which were situated
in the heart of Asia and that presently have vanished. In the
Himalayas, around the country of Tibet, only their ruins exist.

Formidable esoteric cultures and tremendous civilizations
existed in Pearland (the sacred land of the Vedas, the ancient
Hindustan), as well as in the entire regions of Southern Asia
where the second Aryan subrace developed.

Babylon (before its decadence), Chaldea and its ancient
mysteries, Egypt and its pyramids, were all scenarios of very
rich and powerful civilizations created by the third Aryan subrace.

Athens, the great city founded by the Goddess Athena,
Rome (before its degeneration and destruction), were the mar-
velous scenarios where the powerful civilizations of the fourth
Aryan subrace developed.

The First and Second World Wars, with all of their barbarism and moral corruption, aimed their accusatory fingers at the men and women of the fifth Aryan subrace.

South America is the scenario of the sixth Aryan subrace, since their cousins, "the gringos" from North America, are still extremely Anglo-Saxon by majority.

Presently, instead of evolving, the Aryan root race has devolved, and its corruption is worse than that of the Atlantean root race. The Aryan root race's malignity is so great that it has "reached unto heaven."[7] Therefore, this Aryan root race will be destroyed so that Ra-Mu's prophesy (which he uttered before the submergence of Atlantis) will be fulfilled: If these people forget that they should not amass material things, not only for their own progress, but also for generosity towards mankind, the same fate will surprise them.

---

7   "For her sins have reached unto heaven, and God hath remembered her iniquities." —Revelation 18:5

Humanity is suffering.

Chapter 3
The New Catastrophe

Beloved gnostic brothers and sisters, on this Christmas of 1967, it is urgent that we all very judiciously study and analyze this tremendous moment in which we are living.

It is indeed impossible to deny that we presently live in moments of global crisis; in the history of our Aryan root race, there have never been such terrible moments.[8]

Woes and weeping are heard everywhere; executions are occurring the world over; unhappy people remember their beloved relatives with supreme anguish as they waste the last moments of their life in hard labor camps; widows with children who die of starvation, etc.

The entire Earth is filled with armies and wars; rumors of wars are heard everywhere.

The present chaos is awful; nonetheless, the tyrants, while seated on their blasphemous thrones, uselessly intend to establish a "New Order" based upon blood and drugs.

Paris, as a great harlot, continues wallowing in its filthy bed of pleasures. London has become a new Sodom; it even intends to establish the legal bond of matrimony between homosexuals. The United States of America has fallen into a collective madness, because they have not only destroyed other countries, but moreover, they are also destroying their own. China, the venerable China of Confucius and Lao-Tse, has fallen as a prostitute in the arms of Marxism-Leninism. China has imported a corrupted doctrine from the Western world; nonetheless, they have declared themselves "enemies of the West."

8   "'Unprecedented' 65 million people displaced by war and persecution in 2015: The number of people displaced from their homes due to conflict and persecution last year [2015] exceeded 60 million for the first time in United Nations history, a tally greater than the population of the United Kingdom, or of Canada, Australia and New Zealand combined, says a new report released on World Refugee Day today... Distressingly, children made up an astonishing 51 per cent of the world's refugees in 2015, with many separated from their parents or travelling alone..." — The United Nations, 20 June 2016

The Third World War is inevitable, because the ones who planned and performed the First and Second World Wars are already working very actively in order to make the Third World War a reality. The Third World War will be millions of times more horrible than the two former World Wars.

Any sense of pity has disappeared. Today, it is considered a luxury to have a heart of stone, a flint stone heart.

Many schools and colleges teach their pupils that charity is weakness and that they must never give alms. This is how the students become perverse and cruel while sitting at their desks in school.

The moral epidemic of the so-called "rebels without a cause" fell upon the entire humanity after the Second World War; these rebels are the children of the "New Age" who, without God and without law, go around organizing gangs. Everywhere and anywhere, they go about killing, hurting, raping, getting drunk, etc., and the governments cannot control them. The gravest part of these "rebels without a cause" is their state of absolute moral irresponsibility. When they are taken in front of the tribunals, they do not know why they have killed, why they have hurt others, and worst of all is that they do not even care to know why.

The sublime world of art... has reached the maximum degree of degeneration. The temple of art has been converted into a whorehouse; it has become a brothel where homosexuals, drug addicts, alcoholics, harlots, assassins, thieves, etc., search for refuge.

Human corruption is so great that even homicide has become an art form.[9] Moreover, the breaking point of madness is the fact that there presently exist organizations for assassins and an abundant amount of literature on the art of assassination.

All branches of present day art encourage lust, alcoholism, drugs, homosexuality, blood, horror...

---

9   "By the time the average U.S. child starts elementary school [ie. age five or six] he or she will have seen 8,000 murders and 100,000 acts of violence on TV." —New Scientist, 2007. Note that violence in media has dramatically increased since 2007.

In this day and age, classical composers are seen with infinite despise. To play Beethoven or Mozart in any modern festivity causes the general withdrawal of the guests.

The four blasphemous clowns (the Beatles) from the degenerated music of England were endowed with the mark of distinction by the Queen of that Empire. The idiotic multitudes even kissed the ground that they walked upon.

Everywhere there are abundant assassinations, robberies, infanticides, matricides, parricides, uxoricides, assaults, rapes, genocides, prostitution, hatred, vengeance, sorcery, merchants of souls and merchants of bodies, greed, violence, envy, pride, arrogance, gluttony, love of luxury, slander, etc.

Indeed, the Aryan root race is a rotten fruit, a fruit that will fall from the Tree of Life by the weight of its own rottenness.

The students of esotericism are filled with infinite horror when they examine the history of Atlantis in the Akashic records of Nature; however, the Atlanteans had religion, in that sense they were less degenerated than the henchmen of Marxism-Leninism who hate any religious principle to death.

The initiates are filled with an unutterable psychic terror when they remember that woman with the seductive and malignant beauty, the Queen Katebet of the gloomy destinies from ancient Atlantis; with sovereignty, she governed the South States and the powerful City of the Gates of Gold of that submerged continent.

Indeed, even in the Borgia and Medici's family history there is no perversity like that of Queen Katebet. She captivated with her malignant beauty and necromancy. She fascinated and seduced princes and kings with her enchantments. In her honor, many maidens and children were immolated to the tenebrous entities of the inner underworlds.

In those times, the Atlantean sacerdotal medicine discovered what in this day and age we would scientifically call human opotherapy, that is, the infusion of glandular juices from the pituitary, thyroid, adrenaline, etc., to sick and caducous organisms. The priest-physicians utilized not only the chemistry of the endocrine glands as hormones and juices, but moreover, they also utilized the hyper-chemistry of those glands, or the psychic, vital fluids of the chakras or magnetic centers of the human organism, which are intimately related with the endocrine centers.

After having taken their immolated victims away from the sacrificial stones, the cadavers were transferred to certain secret chambers where the priest-physicians extracted the precious endocrine glands that were so indispensable in the preservation of the fatal Queen's body. Her youthful beauty with all of her enchantments lasted for many centuries.

The most frightening of all of this was the moment in which the priests—after having secretly extracted the glands from the cadaver—would toss the rest of the cadaver to the fanatical and corrupted crowds who would devour it hungrily; this is how the Atlantean populace became anthropophagi.

When we reflect upon all of these things, we feel terrified, horrified; however, all of these barbaric acts are minor, even ridiculous, when compared with the atrocities of the First and Second World Wars. Atlantean barbarity seems comical when compared with the monstrous explosion of the atomic bomb in the Japanese cities of Hiroshima and Nagasaki.

All of the Atlantean barbarities are insignificant when we compare them to the gas chambers where millions of men, women, children, and elders were stripped of their clothing and died with the most frightening desperation.

We felt horrified by Atlantean bestiality, but the bombarding of the martyred city of London, the concentration camps, the wall-shootings, the hangings, the cities destroyed by criminal bombs, sicknesses, hunger, and desperation, were all millions of times worse.

Never in the history of the centuries was such great perversity felt than that of this caducous and degenerated Aryan root race.

The breaking point of all of this evilness is that now the Tower of Babel has been lifted in order to conquer the infinite space. If that which is divine does not interfere with what we call "the conquest of outer space," then in a short time, the terrestrial hordes will assault Mars, Venus, Mercury, etc., and all of the crimes (such as those performed by Hernan Cortes in Mexico or by Pizarro in Peru) will be repeated again on those inhabited planets.

If that which has no name, if that which is the reality, the divine, does not interfere now, then That will become an accomplice of the crime.

This Aryan humanity is symbolized in the Book of Revelation as the great human harlot, a woman dressed in purple and scarlet colors, whose number is 666.[10] So, in the world of absurdity, there is nothing more absurd than to suppose, for at least a brief moment, that this great human harlot would conquer other inhabited planets with her famous rockets and would crown herself queen and sovereign of the infinite space.

Therefore, the new catastrophe that will doom this Aryan root race is totally just and absolutely indispensable.

---

10 Revelation 13:18

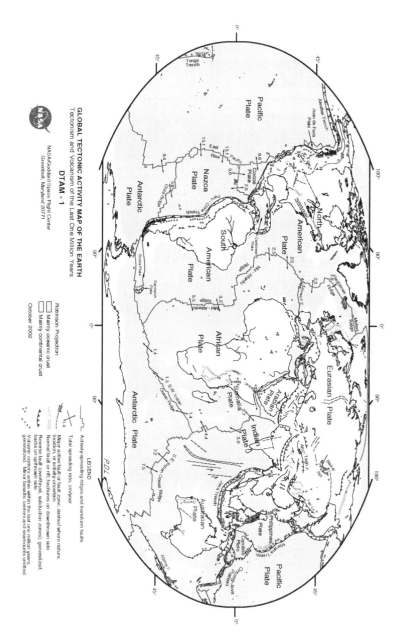

GLOBAL TECTONIC ACTIVITY MAP OF THE EARTH

Tectonism and Volcanism of the Last One Million Years

DTAM - 1

NASA/Goddard Space Flight Center
Greenbelt, Maryland 20771

October 2002

Robinson Projection

Mainly oceanic crust

Mainly continental crust

LEGEND

Actively-spreading ridges and transform faults

Total spreading rate, cm/year

Major active fault or fault zone; dashed where nature, location, or activity uncertain

Normal fault or rift; hachures on downthrown side

Reverse fault (overthrust, subduction zones); generalized; barbs on upthrown side

Volcanic centers active within the last one million years; generalized. Minor basaltic centers and seamounts omitted.

OCEANIC FAULTS MAPPED BY NASA

Chapter 4
Dangerous Symptoms

Eminent people of science from the famous Columbia University have made available to the world the alarming news that the fatal source of the diverse telluric commotions of former years are monstrous faults at the bottom of the seas.

The people of science calculate that these oceanic faults form a fissure about 90,000 kilometers in length, with a middle width of forty kilometers and an average profundity of two and a half kilometers.

We were told that an elder Tibetan Lama, before dying, warned a certain gentleman about those oceanic cracks. Without a doubt, the Lamas do not ignore this fact.

Scientific information states that these oceanic faults stretch from the Atlantic Ocean to the Indian Ocean and from the Antarctic Ocean until the Arctic Ocean. These faults surround the American continent as well as the Asiatic continent, thus leaving (in the center of such frightening ring of submarine faults) the entire Pacific Ocean.

The last investigation performed by scientists has demonstrated that these oceanic cracks depart from Antarctica and continue on very close to Cape Horn, where they diverge into two principal fissures: one that goes towards the east and the other which goes towards the west.

The Pacific Ocean's fissure follows a very sinuous trajectory, almost bordering the American continent along the coastlines of Chile, Peru, Ecuador, Nicaragua, El Salvador, Guatemala, Oaxaca and Guerrero, Mexico, the Californian Gulf, Seattle, USA, Vancouver, Canada, and Alaska.

This oceanic fissure splits in Alaska and continues its course along the Aleutian Islands. Another crack seems to pass through Alaska; the earthquakes in Fairbanks (situated in the center of that peninsula) have been very strong such as the one that occurred in March, 1964.

The oceanic fissure of the Aleutian Islands goes towards Tokyo, Japan, dangerously touching the islands of Sapporo, Hokkaido, Oahu, Waohua, Kawailoa, and some others.

A wise author states that some secondary fissures depart from Japan and go towards Hawai'i. There is no doubt that the main crack goes towards the Philippines and New Zealand, and from there it returns to its point of departure situated in Antarctica. Thus, in this way, a tremendously dangerous magic circle is closed.

There is no doubt that the fissure that goes towards the eastern world starts in mysterious Antarctica and then passes in front of the Cape of Good Hope, Madagascar, and the Arabian Sea in order to end in some unknown place in the Indian Ocean.

Men of science state that the Atlantic fault seems to have its origin in the Norwegian Sea. The extremely enigmatic course of this Atlantic fault passes by the coastline of Spain, Portugal, and part of Africa, and then ends close to the Portuguese Guinea.

By all means, it is clear that the most dangerous oceanic fault that inevitably will generate a tremendous cataclysm is the Ring of Fire in the Pacific Ocean. The news that constantly circulates in the newspapers around the world has confirmed that the lands which are most punished by earthquakes are precisely in the Pacific Ocean.

These cracks in the maritime floor are dangerous symptoms that, without a doubt, are warning us of the proximity of a great tragedy.

The times of the end have arrived and we are in them. The sword of cosmic justice menacingly weighs over the head of the great harlot (humanity).

It is urgent to know that there is a vast system of cracks in the profundity of the seas, and that these are the concrete outcome of a totally defined planetary type of geological action. Already, some of those cracks are so deep that they even have made the exterior waters of the oceans contact the interior fire (magma) of the Earth.

In this moment of global crisis, water vapor is being produced under such intense pressure within our planetary organism that indeed the day will come in which some mountain, no matter how powerful it may be, will not resist this pressure and will burst asunder, snatched in the air and made to dust, as has already been prophesized by Mohammed in the Qur'an.

A series of earthquakes have already begun and will only become more and more intense. The cities, like houses made out of a deck of cards, will fall and turn into dust. Earthquakes will swallow up this entire humanity.

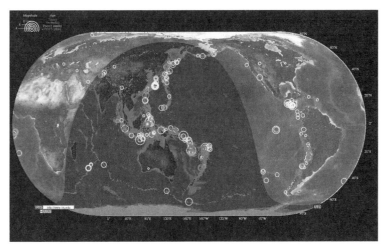

EARTHQUAKE ACTIVITY JUNE, 2016. IMAGE: DS.IRIS.EDU

We must recognize the fact that this humanity is doomed. There is no remedy for this humanity; therefore, it must perish.

For the moment, as a testimony of this imminent great catastrophe, it is already undeniable that the coast of Chile is sinking and that other diverse lands from this afflicted and martyrized planet are similarly sinking.

Experts know very well that the sea has lost profundity in diverse parts of the Atlantic and Pacific Oceans. This is due to the fact that the bottom of the ocean floor has been continuously rising up towards the surface as a result of the internal swelling of the marine floor created by the steam's pressure. Scientists know very well that while the mountains sink, the sea's floor is rising.

Without a doubt, great volumes of water are now in contact with the liquid fire (magma) that runs through the interior of the Earth; thus, the outcome will happen without delay. The steam's pressure has inevitably produced an intensive volcanic activity, in conjunction with terrible and frightening earthquakes and seaquakes. The pressure of the interior of the Earth is horrific, and worst of all, as each minute passes the pressure increases.

The culminating moment is approaching, the moment when the internal pressure reaches its maximum limit. The catastrophe is about to happen; any exterior phenomenon can generate this culminating doom: an atomic explosion, a body from outer space passing extremely close to the Earth, an appropriately combined solar and lunar attraction phenomenon, etc.

The explosion in the bottom of the seas will be frightful. The Sun will become as "black as a sackcloth of hair," and the Moon will become as red as blood[11] due to the reflection of the fire (magma) that will surface upon the face of the Earth.

The terrible sword of Damocles menacingly appears over the head of the great harlot, whose number is 666.

The sins of the great harlot have reached unto heaven, and the flaming sword of cosmic justice will wound this humanity to death.

Babylon the great (this present humanity), mother of all types of fornication and abominations of the Earth, will fall...

> "...for all nations have drunk of the wine of the wrath of her fornication, and the kings of the earth have committed fornication with her, and the merchants of the earth are waxed rich through the abundance of her delicacies." —Revelation 18:3

This perverse civilization of vipers, this great Babylon, will burn with fire, because it has become millions of times more corrupt than Atlantis.

---

11 Revelation 6:12

This great Babylon, this abominable modern civilization, has "become the habitation of devils, and the hold of every foul spirit, and a cage of every unclean and hateful bird."[12]

The world is now shaken by earthquakes; these are dangerous indicators of a great tragedy that announces a worse catastrophe and various other catastrophes thousands of times worse than those that finished off Atlantis.

---

12 Revelation 18:2

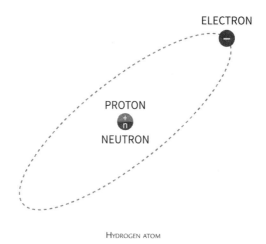

ELECTRON

PROTON

NEUTRON

HYDROGEN ATOM

Chapter 5
Atomic Science

In itself, the atom is a miniature universe. All of the mechanical processes that are performed within the depth of the atom are also performed within our solar system.

Atomic investigations have verified that in the exterior regions of the atom there is a cloud of electrons with an authentic negative electrical charge, which when dissociated from the atoms, agglomerate in dense floods in order to form all of the electric currents.

The atom has been abundantly investigated and its marvels are astonishing. The nucleus, positively charged, is the vital center of this small, spherical world. As the planets gravitate around the Sun, likewise electrons gravitate around that mysterious nucleus.

Without a doubt, the atomic nucleus possesses a considerable electrical charge that the nucleus utilizes in order to retain the whole cortege of peripheral electrons under its domain, yet at a respectable distance.

The nucleus is the very heart of the atom, and it is already foreseen that within that basic, fundamental, nuclear corpuscle, a vital mechanism must exist that is still up for discussion and further investigation.

The whole reason for the existence of the atom (miniature universe) is found within its nucleus. The whole inheritance of the atom and its potential resides precisely in its nucleus; the atom can explode, or on the contrary, it can be changed into other types of atoms, thanks to this central corpuscle.

At this moment, physicists admit two fundamental constituents of the nucleus: the proton and the neutron.

By all means, it is absolutely clear that the proton is the hydrogen's basic nucleus, in other words, it is the most central part of the hydrogen, which is the lightest and simplest of all known elements.

The scientist Prout admitted in his time that the different elements of nature are condensations formed by the simplest of elements, hydrogen.

There are twelve fundamental types of hydrogen; they correspond to twelve categories of matter that are contained in the universe from the Absolute down to the infernal worlds. The infernal worlds are symbolized in *The Divine Comedy* of Dante; they are situated within the submerged mineral kingdom in the interior of the Earth.

It is also interesting to study the second constituent of the atomic nucleus; this is the neutron that has the same weight of the proton; in other words, it has the same weight of the nucleus of the hydrogen. Nonetheless, until now it differs from all of the particles known by conventional science. It is indeed intriguing that it has no electrical charge, since it is a neutral corpuscle; this is why it is called neutron.

We, the gnostics, after having discovered the three aspects of electrical energy, and after having classified those three modes of electricity with the following terms: positive (+), negative (-) and neutral (N), have considered the neutron as a corpuscle with neutral electrical charge.

Our statement about the neutron charged with electricity in a neutral and static state might not appear very clear for modern scientists, but sooner or later they will prove it.

One of the greatest enigmas for modern atomic science is the enigma of the electrons. If the intimate mechanism of the atomic nucleus is still unknown, much less known is the intimate mechanism of the electron.

There are positive and negative electrons; this is no longer a secret for scientists. Nevertheless, they do not know anything about the intimate mechanism of the electron.

The intellectual animal mistakenly called a human being has achieved the fractioning of the atom in order to liberate energy; yet, fortunately, they still do not know the internal mechanism of the electron, within which resides tremendous power.

It is estimated that each time a positive electron is absorbed while penetrating platinum, it produces two photons of half of a million volts each. This corresponds to a production of one million volts of photonic energy per positive electron.

The active element of the Sun is hydrogen, and indeed, this is very interesting because the atom of the hydrogen (with a single electron rotating around a nucleus) is found at the border between matter in an electronic state and matter in a molecular state.

When hydrogen combines with denser and other matter, atoms combine with atoms for the construction of molecules. The superior rarefaction of hydrogen in a superior state releases free electrons, or matter in an electronic state: light, magnetic waves, etc.

By making use of the coveted uranium, modern scientists have separated one electron from one atom whose density is not natural, which is almost pathologic; they have had an indisputable success. Thus, it is logical to state that in this way, they have liberated an incomparably superior power of atomic energy that before now the human mind could not have conceived. Thereafter, by combining atoms of hydrogen, the scientists cunningly managed to form atoms; through this process, they thus produced frightful energy of practically unlimited power.

Undoubtedly, the atomic bomb is millions of times more terrible than dynamite; however, it is less horrific than the hydrogen bomb.

The hydrogen bomb is a prostitution of solar energy; this is the worst quality of black magic, whose outcome will be the total devastation, decline, and lifelessness of all living material on a totally new scale.

If a hydrogen bomb were to explode in the superior regions of the atmosphere (where the deposit of pure hydrogen is found), then the whole planet Earth would be burned by living fire and every creature would perish, as would every other form of life.

By wanting to use atomic energy (by intending to discover the entire science of the transmutation of atoms or the way and manner in which one atom is changed into another) the

On July 9, 1962, the U.S. blew up a hydrogen bomb 250 miles above the Pacific Ocean, because they wanted "to see what would happen." It was called project Starfish Prime, and in Hawai'i people hosted "viewing parties" to watch the explosion. It produced a yield equivalent to 1.4 megatonnes of TNT. It was the largest man-made nuclear explosion in outer space.

intellectual animal longs to enter into the world where matter has all possibilities. However, he wants to enter through a false door. The intellectual animal wants to use the scientific laws without any code of ethics, without having an awakened consciousness, without having reached true spirituality.

We, the gnostics, have legitimate procedures in order to enter into the mysterious world [where matter has infinite possibilities], into those atomic, molecular and electronic regions where all of the processes of universal life are gestated.

At this present moment, atomic radiation has altered the superior layer of the terrestrial atmosphere. If atomic explosions continue, soon the atmosphere will not be able to filter and analyze the solar rays in order to transform them into light and heat; thus, we will see the Sun as "black as a sackcloth of hair."

Earthquakes will intensify as long as the superior layer of the atmosphere continues to be altered due to atomic explosions, because on our planet Earth, this atmospheric layer is the provider of life.

The air that we breathe and the water that we drink is already charged with atomic radiation, and instead of being improved, this situation will only go from bad to worse. Therefore, when the atomic war explodes, we will see Dantesque scenes everywhere. People will lose their minds due to the abuse of atomic energy, hospitals will be filled with sorrow, and there will be no relief.

From under the surface of the Earth, atomic explosions are liberating from the infernal worlds—the submerged mineral element—infernal matter, abysmal atoms, such as the following: neptunium (93), plutonium (94), americium (95), and curium (96). The outcome of this blasphemy is already before our eyes.

Inside every atom there is a trio of matter, energy, and consciousness. Therefore, there is a diabolic consciousness or a terribly malignant intelligence within these types of already mentioned abysmal atoms.

These atomic demons are already poisoning the weak minds of people; this is why life in the great cities has become frightfully criminal, monstrous, horrible, chilling, and terribly malignant. Soon, everywhere in our neighborhoods and streets, we will hear wailing, howling, whistles, neighs, squeaks, bellows, gaggles, meows, barking, snorts, snoring, and croaks. We are in the times of the end.

MAGNETIC
NORTH POLE

GEOGRAPHIC
NORTH POLE

EQUATOR

ECLIPTIC

ε

EARTH

MAGNETIC AND GEOGRAPHIC POLES OF THE EARTH

Chapter 6
Nature's Warnings

In these moments of global crisis, scientists have discovered with astonishment that the magnetic pole of the
compass does not coincide with the physical north pole of
the Earth. One thing is the magnetic pole and another is the
physical pole.

Without a doubt, the axes of the Earth are now modifying
their inclination; consequently, every minute the poles are
consecutively deviating towards the equator.

These very remarkable geological changes have an exclusively cosmic origin; however, these can be accelerated by the
scientific madness of the intellectual animal through his
atomic experiments or through the frightening explosions of
the hydrogen bomb.

Thus, in the manner that this impending doom is pro-
gressing, it is reasonable to be familiar with the idea of the
revolution of the axes of the Earth as an inevitable catastrophe that will convert the poles into the equator and the latter
into the poles. Where today there are only enormous icebergs,
tomorrow there will be enormous and profound equatorial
jungles, and vice versa. The present equatorial lands will be
the icebergs of the future.

The revolution of the axes of the Earth is a natural cosmic
phenomenon that can be accelerated by the scientific madness
of the intellectual animal.

In a very abrupt way, the revolution of the axes of the
Earth finished off the infamous Atlantis.

It is very intriguing and significant that rain is falling on
the Sahara desert and in many other places where rain has not
fallen before.

It has been confirmed that the ice of the North Pole is
melting, and the consequence of this phenomenon brings
upon the terrible hurricanes and cyclones that are presently
lashing out at the world. Let us remember the hurricanes
that lashed out against the coast of Sonora, Mexico, and

Manzanillo in the Pacific Ocean, and all the other hurricanes that have devastated Japan, the United States, etc.

Earthquakes are now occurring in a continuous manner; these earthquakes are showing us that within the interior of this afflicted planet in which we live, the planetary fire has entered into terrible agitation. As soon as Turkey trembles, so does India; today North America trembles, and tomorrow Italy, Central America or South America, etc.

Ancient volcanoes are like dormant lions that are beginning to awaken from their millenarian dreams and are beginning to roar. Let us call to mind Fuji in Japan, Etna, and many other volcanoes that exist. Let us remember how Vesuvius finished off Pompeii.

Most intriguing of all is that the "Old Lions" are not the only ones that are awakening; besides them, new volcanoes have been born, some with a fleeting life, others with a life more powerful. Let us mention for instance Paricutin in Mexico and the other one in the cold and martyred land of Siberia.

With infinite astonishment, explorers have found lakes with warm water in the South Pole, lakes that are getting bigger and bigger as each day passes. Without a doubt, the growth of these lakes is due to very intense subterranean activity, whose development stretches far away.

Three volcanoes are now erupting in the South Pole; in Antarctica, they are spewing a very special type of rare lava; nonetheless, some nations have now hurriedly placed their flags on that continent. How imprudent humanity is!

All of these phenomena of Antarctica invite us to think. There is no doubt that the recent earthquakes of Chile (which also shook the bottom floor of the Pacific Ocean all the way to Japan) are intimately associated with the catastrophic processes of the South Pole. The final outcome of all of this has to be frightful.

It has been proven in a definite way that in the Gulf of Guinea (which is located over the equator) there are certain water currents coming from the Atlantic Ocean that have been uncommonly warmed; these water currents flow in the well-known "Gulf Stream" towards the north. Here they have been secretly undermining the ice, fracturing the icebergs, which then travel in chunks towards the equator (in expedient urgency) in order to fill the emptiness left behind by extreme evaporation.

There is no doubt that this creates a current inverse to the "Gulf Stream." This inverse current is very cold and fundamentally alters the climate of the coastlines that it flows by. Thus, life is given to cyclones, hurricanes, terrible windstorms, torrential rains, and every type of climatological disturbance that are presently causing great alarm to the whole human race.

Profound investigations allow us to logically deduce that these uncommon waters that are being warmed near the equator are intimately related with the volcanoes of Antarctica.

By all means, it is clear to comprehend that the warm currents of the Pacific Ocean, as a final resort, come from Antarctica. These waters arrive at the Gulf of Guinea and create an elevation in the temperature of the equator.

Common sense (as someone once said, "should be the most common of the senses") allows us to comprehend that these currents of warmed water (when arriving at the North Pole) will undermine and crack enormous icebergs, thus reducing (in the already mentioned "Gulf Stream") those previously compact icebergs.

The enigmatic volcanoes of the South Pole will intensify their igneous activities; thus, consequently, the lakes with warm waters from Antarctica will grow excessively.

Each day, the marine currents will become even hotter, and this will allow them to penetrate more and more powerfully within the solemn icebergs of the North Pole, until eventually achieving the total meltdown of the ice.

It is an absurdity to suppose that the South Pole with its erupting volcanoes will remain in an unmodified state. It is clear that its ice will melt just as the ice of the North Pole, thus the outcome will be an apocalyptic horror.

Logic makes us comprehend that when the polar ice has melted, the maritime waters will increase in volume, and that if the receptacle, the cup, the marine floor, is not deep enough, then the waters shall have to spread out, to overflow, to inundate the lands, thus, swallowing up entire countries. This is obvious.

Let us remember what we already stated in this 1967 Christmas Message. The sea has lost profundity in diverse parts of the Atlantic and Pacific Oceans, and the bottom of the ocean floor has been continuously rising up towards the surface, in other words, the profundity of certain seas has decreased.

Without even the tiniest amount of fear of being found mistaken, we can asseverate with complete solemnity that the cause of this formidable marine crack is found in the volcanic activity of the South Pole.

Based on what we have already stated in this chapter and former chapters, we can be certain that the Earth will return again to a primeval age where the existence of any kind of animal life will be impossible.

The Nahuas (Aztec masters) said that the children of the first sun (the first root race, the protoplasmic polar race) were devoured by tigers.

The Aztecs said that the children of the second sun (the second root race, the Hyperboreans) were cleared away by strong hurricanes and converted themselves into apes or monkeys.

The Aztecs said that the children of the third sun perished by the sun raining fire upon them and they transformed themselves into birds. The children of the third sun were the Lemurians whose continent, situated in the Pacific Ocean, was destroyed by earthquakes and volcanoes.

The Aztecs said that the children of the fourth sun (the fourth root race) were swallowed up by the waters and they converted themselves into fish.

The Aztecs said that the children of the fifth sun (we, the Aryan root race) will perish by that which is called movement: earthquakes.

The sacred scriptures of the Aztecs did not give any symbol to the degenerated humans of our present fifth root race, as they did for the previous four root races. However, the Christian gospel gives the symbol of sheep for the saved ones, and goats[13] for almost all of the human beings of the Aryan root race.

The Aztecs said that in the epoch of the children of the sixth sun (the future sixth root race) the gods will resurrect.

The Nahuas (Aztecs masters) have prophesized ineffable things for the seventh root race, for the children of the seventh sun.

---

13 Matthew 25

THREE FACES OF HEKATE, THE DIVINE MOTHER

Chapter 7
The Great Judge

The Hindustani sages cite the "Prakriti" in all of their
sacred books. The Prakriti is that primordial substance from
which the twelve basic, fundamental hydrogens (that serve as
foundations to the seven cosmoses) emerge by successive condensations or crystallizations.

Variety in its very depth is a unity, since tattvas, senses,
mind, and all of the other multiplicities of beings and things
become diverse modes of crystallization of the primordial
substance.

The fire that blazes, the air that not a single living creature could exist without, the waters of the boisterous sea,
and the perfumed earth are condensed Akash, materialized
Mulaprakriti, and densified Prakriti.

Mother space is therefore the primordial substance, the
raw matter of the great work.

Space as mother is the fertile bosom from which everything emerges and everything immerses.

Let it be definitively declared in this chapter: mother space
is the same Prakriti of the Hindustani: the Divine Mother.

During the pralaya (cosmic night), the Prakriti is one,
unique, indivisible, and integral.

Yet, during the mahamanvantara (cosmic day), as a consequence of the activity of the first, second and third Logoi,[14]
the Prakriti expands and builds up from herself in three
aspects.

The three modes of the Prakriti are: first, the
Unmanifested Prakriti; second, the Prakriti in nature; third,
the Prakriti as queen of the infernos and death.

The Unmanifested Prakriti has no symbol amongst the
Aztecs.

The Manifested Prakriti (nature) has the Aztec symbol of
Tonantzin, the adorable mother. The Greeks symbolized this
second aspect of the cosmic mother as the chaste Diana.

14 Plural of the Greek *logos*, "word." See *Logos* in the glossary.

Among the Aztecs, the third aspect of the Divine Mother is the terrible Coatlicue; among the Egyptians she is Proserpina, and among the Greeks she is the tremendous Hekate, lady of enchantments and death.

Mother-space herself is the same Roman Apia, the Nordic Urwala, the Scandinavian Erda, the chivalrous Urgada, the primeval Sibyl of the Earth.

Any of the three aspects of the Prakriti can (if she wishes) take on a feminine shape in order to communicate something to any illuminated mystic.

One summer night, I was in that state which is known in the eastern world as Nirvi-Kalpa or Samadhi[15]; what happened to me during that meditation was very profound; it was something marvelous.

Before me, the third aspect of Prakriti took on the frightful and terribly divine shape of Proserpina or Hekate, and then she spoke to me in a language with apocalyptic significance: "This perverse civilization of vipers, this great Babylon, will be destroyed, and in all of its cities, not one stone upon another will remain. The evil of the world is so great that it has even reached unto heaven. There is no remedy for this humanity; it is totally lost."

Then, overflowing with great terror, I uttered, "Oh mother of mine, we are on a dead-end street."

Then with a parable, Proserpina asked me, "Do you want to make a covenant with me?"

"Yes, mother of mine, I am willing to fulfill that covenant," with great decisiveness came this answer from my lips.

Then Proserpina, the queen of the infernos and death, took the floor again with a parable and told me, "Open the dead-end street, and I will kill them."

I immediately answered, "I accept, mother of mine, my lady."

Then, certain upper class ladies passed by in front of us. These ladies had achieved the Second Birth; thus, the solar light emanated splendorously from within their solar bodies.

---

15 A state of experience usually accessed through meditation in which the consciousness is temporarily liberated from conditioning factors like physicality, ego, desire, etc. See glossary.

Unfortunately, these ladies had not dissolved the pluralized "I," nor had they eliminated their lunar bodies. I saluted them; yet they did not answer, and full of pride they did not even prostrate themselves with reverence before the Divine Mother.

"They still have pride and this is because they still carry within themselves the remnants of the great harlot, whose number is 666." This was the only thing that occurred to me to say.

The Divine Mother answered, "I have to examine all of them." Evidently, she was referring to the Twice-born of this epoch in which we live.

Certain gentlemen also dressed with solar bodies passed by in front of us, yet contrary to the former ladies, they inclined themselves and were filled with profound reverence and respect for the Divine Mother and my insignificant person who has no value.

"These are children of the Sun," exclaimed the cosmic mother.

Afterwards, I entered into a period of profound reflection. If some of the Twice-born must still be rigorously examined, then what fate lies ahead for the great harlot? What then would be the fate that lies ahead for this lunar race?

It is obvious that all confessional religions are awaiting the Final Judgment of this humanity, of this degenerated and perverse lunar race. Yet, according to the chronology of the Great Pyramid of Egypt, the Last Judgment already occurred between the years 1946 and 1953.

We, the gnostics, know by illumination and direct, transcendental experience that the judgment of all nations occurred in the year 1950.

The holy gods judged the great harlot (humanity) and they considered it unworthy; the sentence of the gods was: "To the abyss! To the abyss! To the abyss!"

It is interesting that during the epoch of the judgment of the nations, 1946 to 1953, (according to the measurements of the Great Pyramid of Egypt) an enigmatic subterranean chamber ends in a rocky, obscure, dead-end chamber. Obviously, through this dead-end chamber, the wise constructors of the Great Pyramid of Egypt wanted to tell us that after the Final Judgment, humanity will enter into the infernal worlds (which Dante found within the interior of the Earth).

The Apocalypse of Saint John (Revelation 20:11-15) refers to the great judgment:

"And I saw a great white throne, and him that sat on it, from whose face the earth and the heaven fled away; and there was found no place for them.

"And I saw the dead, small and great, stand before God; and the books were opened: and another book was opened, which is the book of life: and the dead were judged out of those things which were written in the books, according to their works.

"And the sea gave up the dead which were in it; and death and hell delivered up the dead which were in them; and they were judged every man according to his works.

"And death and hell were cast into the lake of fire. This is the Second Death.

"And whosoever was not found written in the book of life was cast into the lake of fire."

All the symbolism of the Great Pyramid of Egypt starts when one treads upon "the great step." Afterwards, the first low passage becomes clear when you begin walking, and the remarkable date August 4-5, 1914[16] appears. This symbolism continues until one reaches the entrance of the King's Chamber; the date September 15-16, 1939 is marked with complete precision. It is overwhelming to find that these two terrible dates (related with the First and Second World Wars) are found in the geometry and chronology of the Great Pyramid.

What is most intriguing about all of this is that due to their construction and form, it is not possible to pass through these cited passages standing on the feet; in order to walk through it is necessary to use the four limbs (like the quadruped animals). This reminds us of the soldiers who walk on their hands and knees or who drag themselves (like animals) in the fields of battle.

---

16   The date Great Britain declared war on Germany.

According to the Great Pyramid, our epoch has to pass through three periods: death, preoccupation, and chaos.

> *"When ye therefore shall see the abomination of desolation, spoken of by Daniel the prophet, stand in the holy place...*
>
> *"For then shall be great tribulation, such as was not since the beginning of the world to this time, no, nor ever shall be.*
>
> *"And except those days should be shortened, there should no flesh be saved: but for the elect's sake those days shall be shortened."*
>
> —Matthew 24:15, 21, 22

Since the First World War, the former prophecy is being fulfilled in a dramatic way. The geometrical measurements of the Great Pyramid point towards the First World War, towards the interval between the First and the Second Wars, towards the year 1939 with the dates of September 15-16 (marking the beginning of the Second World War), and it also tells of the duration for each one of these great wars.

Finally, in the Chamber of the Judgments of Nations, the Great Pyramid places humanity in front of the great judge. The King's Chamber ends on the date 19-20 of August 1953. Now, the doom that lies ahead is work for Proserpina. She will terminate this entire humanity.

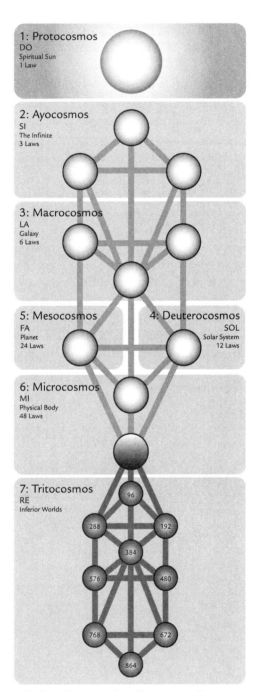

1: Protocosmos
DO
Spiritual Sun
1 Law

2: Ayocosmos
SI
The Infinite
3 Laws

3: Macrocosmos
LA
Galaxy
6 Laws

5: Mesocosmos
FA
Planet
24 Laws

4: Deuterocosmos
SOL
Solar System
12 Laws

6: Microcosmos
MI
Physical Body
48 Laws

7: Tritocosmos
RE
Inferior Worlds

96
288 192
384
576 480
768 672
864

THE RAY OF CREATION AND SEVEN COSMOSES ON THE TREE OF LIFE

Chapter 8
The Submerged Mineral Kingdom

The ray of creation begins in the Absolute[17] and ends in the inferno. The latter word comes from the Latin infernus, which means "inferior."

An author (whose name I do not wish to mention) stated that the inferior place is this physical world, this cellular world in which we live. Lamentably, that author was mistaken, because the infernus is the underworld, the submerged mineral kingdom.

Dante discovered the inferno within the interior of the Earth, the underworld of the Earth.

The descent towards the profound interior of our planetary organism is a descent into places of extreme density, of extreme materiality. Indeed, this is the wise idea expressed by Dante in his *Divine Comedy*.

Dante sees the underworld, he analyzes it, he comprehends it, and he formidably describes it. Dante talked about spheres (or circles) of increasing density that lead (in his own words)...

"...toward the middle, at whose point unites all heavy substance... That point to which, from every part, is dragged all heavy substance."

At the threshold of a door in hell, Dante saw (written in black letters) the following terrible worlds:

"Through me you pass into the city of woe: Through me you pass into eternal pain: Through me among the people lost for aye. Justice the founder of my fabric moved: To rear me was the task of power divine, Supremest wisdom, and primeval love. Before me things create were none, save things Eternal, and eternal I endure. All hope abandon, ye who enter here."

The subterranean layers of the Earth represent the kingdom of minerals (lithosphere). The kingdom of metals is the

---

17 The abstract space, emptiness, or voidness from which all things emerge. See glossary.

barisphere that envelops a heart of incredible density and frightful inertia.

We must make a clear distinction between the mineral kingdom and the kingdom of metals.

Among minerals, the group of metals is a cosmically separated group. A little beyond the kingdom of metals, there exists a certain very rare type of matter that has closer contact with the Absolute.

We must comprehend profoundly that the almighty holy one abides behind the kingdom of metals.

The ray of creation begins in the Absolute and ends in the inferno; but what is beyond the inferno? It is clear that beyond the inferno, behind the kingdom of metals, the Absolute is found.

Music clarifies all of this. As a complete process of life, the ray of creation is a descending octave, in which DO passes to SI and SI passes to LA, etc.[18]

With one law, the Absolute vibrates within the note DO of the musical scale.

From the great scale, the note SI resounds in all of the worlds of the infinite with their three laws.

The note LA vibrates in all the suns of the galaxy with their six laws.

The note SOL resounds in the Sun that illuminates us with its twelve laws.

All the planets of our solar system vibrate with the note FA that resounds in all of nature with their twenty-four laws.

On Earth, the microcosm vibrates with the note MI and its forty-eight laws.

The under-earth or underworld vibrates with the note RE.

The ray of creation ends in the underworld. Beyond the kingdom of metals is the Absolute with its note DO vibrating eternally.

Therefore, the inferno with its ninety-six laws and its note RE is the end of the ray of creation.

Within the ray of creation there are seven orders of worlds; the inferno is the seventh, the last one.

18   From DO-RE-MI-FA-SOL-LA-SI-DO. See "octave" in the glossary.

Happiness and spirituality increase in worlds that are governed by a small number of laws; yet the complication of life, the mechanization, the materiality and grief, increases in worlds governed by a large number of laws.

The inferno, governed by ninety-six laws (which multiply according to the law of three), is frightfully materialistic, horrible, and painful.

The submerged mineral kingdom is Dante's inferno with its nine circles or regions; in the last circle the nucleus of the Earth is found, where Dante (the good disciple of Virgil) discovered the foundation of Dis, the demon of treason.

Indeed, the world is triple: the world, the underworld, and the supra-world exist. The epidermis of the Earth, this cellular region in which we live, is just the intermediate zone, since the underworld (the Roman Averno, the Greek Tartarus, the Hades, Hellas, the inferno of Dante or the infernal worlds) is underneath the terrestrial crust.

The Elysian Fields of the supra-world, molecular and electronic kingdoms, the heavens, Deva, Amenti, paradise, etc., are all found above the cellular regions.

Such is the beautiful Pythagorean symbolism of the two dried circles: the circle above or supra-world, and the circle below or underworld; a third region is created, where the two intersect: this is the cellular world in which we live.

The Sun, as the gigantic cosmic heart of our solar system, illuminates not only the cellular region in which we live, but also the underworld and the supra-world.

The king star (the Sun) emits not only the luminous waves that we perceive with our eyes, but millions of other waves of different vibratory tonality that become, as a fact, an effective black light that human eyes cannot perceive.

Fine laboratory devices inform us that above the violet color there are seven ultraviolet colors (whose obscure and spectral rays are clearly perceived by photospectography). Undoubtedly, some large amounts of chemical and even hyper-chemical vibrations are above the ultraviolet colors, as those which belong to our imagination, or those which belong to our mind, willpower, and feelings.

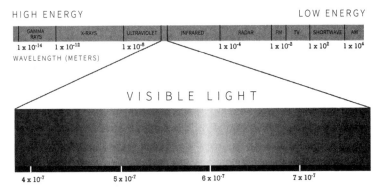

HIGH ENERGY   LOW ENERGY

| GAMMA RAYS | X-RAYS | ULTRAVIOLET | INFRARED | RADAR | FM | TV | SHORTWAVE | AM |

1×10^{-14} 1×10^{-12} 1×10^{-8} 1×10^{-4} 1×10^{-2} 1×10^{0} 1×10^{4}

WAVELENGTH (METERS)

VISIBLE LIGHT

4×10^{-7} 5×10^{-7} 6×10^{-7} 7×10^{-7}

THE VISIBLE SPECTRUM IN CONTEXT WITH WHAT WE CANNOT SEE

On the other hand, scientists know very well that red (below the Sun) emits calorific waves of the x-rays, electro-magnetic, etc., that as a fact and without a doubt, would be clear light if human beings had developed the third eye of the Limnoscelis Lacertidae, a third eye that is also cited by Homer in *The Odyssey*.

Creatures that inhabit the profound depth of the oceans and the obscure caverns of the Earth have developed that third eye, that sixth sense.

It has been widely proven that ants and other insects can see very well in the light of the infrared rays, but on the con-trary, they are in complete obscurity in the light of the vio-let-colored rays.

The outer darkness, mentioned by the four gospels of Christ, are indeed black light, another mode of light. Therefore, it is not exaggerated to affirm that the infernal worlds are illuminated by infrared light.

It is not necessary to be absolutely perverse in order to enter into the infernal worlds. Those who enter into the underworld are the ones who lived without deserving any type of praise or vituperation from their fellowmen; also those who were never rebellious or loyal to God, the lukewarm who are as numerous as the sand of the sea; they are the unhappy ones who only live for themselves, those crowds who were never interested in the realization of their innermost Self, the Being.

Into the underworld enter the multitudes that walk behind the flag of Esau, the vindictive ones, who changed their birthright for a pottage of lentils; those who say, "First, I am going to make money, and then, if I have time, I will dedicate my life to God."

Into the infernal worlds enter the lustful ones and those who hate sex, the homosexuals and the ignorant abstinent people who do not reach the Second Birth. Heaven reproves usury, incontinency, maliciousness, and insane bestiality.

Devolution in the infernal worlds is a descent into lower states, passing through animal and pseudo-vegetal states and ending in the mineral kingdom, with the fatal epilogue of the Second Death. Thus, and only thus, can the failed souls become liberated, and return into the primeval chaos. Thereafter, they reenter into a new evolving ascension, passing anew through the mineral, plant, and animal kingdoms towards the human state.

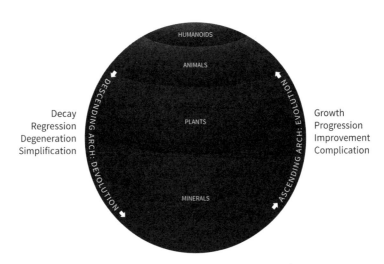

Decay
Regression
Degeneration
Simplification

DESCENDING ARCH: DEVOLUTION

HUMANOIDS

ANIMALS

PLANTS

MINERALS

ASCENDING ARCH: EVOLUTION

Growth
Progression
Improvement
Complication

EVOLUTION AND DEVOLUTION IN THE KINGDOMS OF MECHANICAL NATURE

Chapter 9
The Protoplasmic Bodies

Men of science have proven that metals also are vulnerable to sickness and death. Certain types of poison can produce sickness and death in metals.

In his *Rosicrucian Novel*, Dr. Arnold Krumm-Heller, "Huiracocha" (Colonel Physician of the Mexican Army and Professor of Medicine at the University of Berlin), stated that every atom is a trio of matter, energy, and consciousness.

We, the gnostics, know that subatomic particles possess consciousness. We emphatically affirm that the electrical and gravitational characteristics of any given particle represent its mental qualities.

The substance of the mind exists in all of the kingdoms of nature, including the mineral, plant and animal kingdoms.

Indeed, the only difference between a beast and an intellectual animal (mistakenly called a human being) lies in the fact that the latter has transformed his mind into intellect.

Life and consciousness also exist in certain forms within the elemental particles of nature.

These particles receive information beyond time and space. This reminds us of the extrasensory perceptions of certain very psychic individuals, with whom many experiments have been made in the laboratories of parapsychology.

When an electron and a positron (a positive electron) are annihilated in order to liberate energy, two gamma rays (or gamma photons) are produced. These rays are found to be intimately related. When one of them suffers a transformation, the other inevitably receives its influence; this occurs without having an ordinary physical link between the two.

Let the similitude of this phenomenon be observed with those who study parapsychology.

The Chinese Lee and Yang scientifically demonstrated (by means of experiments with atomic particles) that in our region of the universe, space is not symmetrical, and that smaller particles of matter tend to spin themselves towards an advantageous direction. These men of science do not yet know how the former phenomenon can be related with the essential symmetry of living matter.

Optical science is now approaching the fourth dimension. Thus, the day is not far away in which tetra-dimensional space will become visible through very powerful lenses.

In his books of medicine, Paracelsus talked about gnomes, undines, nereids, genii, salamanders, sylphs, etc. Naturally, imbecile ignoramuses laugh about all of these things.

Within the mineral atoms, we the gnostics find those gnomes of whom Paracelsus (the medieval physician) spoke. Thus, in the same way that the good Aureolus Paracelsus, in his epoch, utilized the elementals of plants in order to cure the sick, we too know how to do it, even if the ignoramuses of science laugh at us.

The consciousness of the elementals is dressed with supra-sensible protoplasmic bodies.

When universal life concentrates itself within the mineral kingdom, then the protoplasmic bodies or lunar bodies sprout by spontaneous generation. These types of bodies are susceptible to many changes and transformations.

When the gnomes from the mineral kingdom enter into the plant kingdom, they suffer transformations within their protoplasmic bodies.

When the elementals of plants enter into animal evolution, they suffer new transformations within their protoplasmic bodies.

When the evolving wave of life passes from the animal into the human being, that is, when the elementals of animals enter into human wombs for the first time, then new changes and metamorphoses are verified within their protoplasmic bodies.

The internal bodies, studied by the pseudo-esoteric and pseudo-occultist schools, are common property for all of the beasts of nature. These are the lunar bodies or protoplasmic bodies.

The laws of evolution and devolution are enclosed within the lunar protoplasmic bodies.

Chapter 10
The Pluralized "I"

The organism of the tri-cere-brated biped (mistakenly called a human being) is a precious machine with five marvelous psy-cho-physiological centers.

The order of these centers is as follows: intellectual, emotional, motor, instinctual, and sexual.

Each of these five centers penetrates the entire organism; nonetheless, if one self-observes profoundly, one becomes aware that each one of the centers has a central, basic point situated at a specific area of our organic machine.

The center of gravity of the intellect is found in the brain.

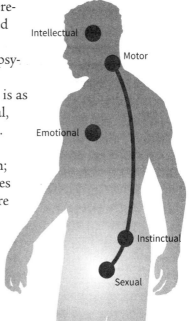

THE THREE BRAINS OR FIVE CENTERS

The center of gravity of emotions is situated in the solar plexus.

The center of gravity of movement is situated in the superior part of the dorsal spine.

The center of gravity of instinct is found in the inferior part of the dorsal spine.

The center of gravity of sex clearly has its roots in the sexual organs.

Each one of the centers of the "machine" has absolutely defined specific functions.

An in-depth study of the five centers allows us to comprehend that there are different speeds amongst them. This has already been proven.

Students of pseudo-occultism and pseudo-esotericism believe that the center of thought is extraordinarily fast; how-

ever, they are lamentably mistaken, because the motor and
instinctual centers are 30,000 times faster.

We have been told that the emotional center is still faster
than the motor and instinctual centers. Great sages affirm
that the emotional center is indeed 30,000 times faster than
the motor and instinctual centers.

The specific functions of each center indicate, point to,
certain dualisms in each center, as the dualism of the mind
with its incessant battle of antitheses, dividing thoughts;
the dualism of emotions, splitting them into pleasant and
unpleasant emotions; the dualism of instinctual sensations,
splitting them into pleasure and pain; the dualism of sexuality, splitting them into attraction and repulsion of sex, etc.
Without a doubt, each one of the five centers is, at the same
time, positive and negative.

All of the five cylinders of the human machine are fundamental for life, but without a doubt, the sexual center, the
fifth center, is indeed the most important and the fastest of
all. The very roots of our existence are found within it.

The sexual center (because of its fine energy) is extraordinarily subtle and fast. The majority of its manifestations take
place on a molecular level, where its impulses are transmitted
thousands of times faster than those of the mind.

The idea of "love at first sight" (if indeed it occurs in
certain cases) is based on the concrete fact that at a given
moment, the sexual function can instantaneously know if a
sexual affinity with a certain person of the opposite sex can or
cannot exist.

Indeed, the search for our sexual complement occurs in
each function of our human organism. The sense of attraction, indifference, and repulsion between a man and a woman
is the outcome of a highly complicated calculation of the
existing factors of reciprocity of each of its functions and of
the average or total function of all of those factors together.
Fortunately, such a complex and difficult calculation can
never be performed by the intellectual center, but only by the
sexual center. This center can attain a correct result in a second or even less.

❦ There are infinite possibilities within the sexual center (when it is developed) that can either convert us into angels or devils.

The fifth center possesses a certain electronic, solar fire that, when wisely awakened, can transform us radically.

In ancient times (due to a certain mistake performed by some sacred individuals), humanity developed the negative side of the sexual center, its tenebrous Luciferic aspect.

When the electronic sexual fire is directed downwards into the atomic infernos of the human being, it becomes the abominable Kundabuffer organ, the tail of Satan. Fortunately, after its development, the Luciferic organ vanished from humanity; nevertheless, its fatal consequences still remain.

It is urgent to know that the disastrous consequences of the abominable Kundabuffer organ remained deposited within the five cylinders of the human machine.

It is indispensable to know that the evil consequences of the abominable Kundabuffer organ constitute the lunar ego, the pluralized "I."

Lamentably, the five psycho-physiological centers of the intellectual beast (mistakenly called a human being) are absolutely controlled by that legion of devil-"I's" that every person carries within.

It is painful to know that the soul, the buddhata,[19] the Essence that we carry inside, is bottled up within the lunar ego.

The incorrect function of the five psycho-physiologic centers of the human machine is due to the pernicious activities of the pluralized "I"; these are the evil consequences of the abominable Kundabuffer organ. — EGO

It is urgent to dissolve the pluralized "I" in order to liberate the Essence, the buddhata, the embryo of soul, the psychic material.

Those who have never (in any of their lives) preoccupied themselves with the dissolution of their pluralized "I," those who have never by any means wanted to terminate the evil consequences of the abominable Kundabuffer organ, will have

19 From buddhadatu, "buddha nature," the potential for attaining enlightenment.

to enter into the infernal worlds when their cycle of lives concludes at their journey's end.

The entrance of the failures into the submerged mineral kingdom is indispensable for the disintegration of the pluralized "I" (within which, unfortunately, the Essence, the soul, is bottled up).

The lunar ego (that conjunction of distinct and diverse entities that travel in an independent way through the supra-sensible worlds) is hidden within the lunar bodies.

The terrible and painful devolution of the pluralized "I" (with their lunar protoplasmic bodies) in the infernal worlds is a fall (backwards descent) towards the original primitive chaos.

Devolution descends down the animal, plant, and mineral steps. On the last rung of the ladder, the fossilized lunar egos are reduced to cosmic dust. This is the Second Death.

The absolute destruction of the pluralized "I" and its lunar vehicles is indispensable for the liberation of the Essence.

This lunar race, this perverse Adamic race, is entering into the infernal devolution through successive cataclysms.

Wars, hurricanes, sicknesses, fires, inundations, and earthquakes will terminate this lunar race.

Chapter 11

The Consciousness

In our former chapter, we talked about the abominable Kundabuffer organ or tail of Satan. We clearly stated that it is an electronic, sexual, Luciferic fire that descends from the coccygeal bone (situated at the base of our dorsal spine.) This electronic, sexual, Luciferic fire is projected downward into the atomic infernos of the human being.

We stated that due to a lamentable mistake made by certain sacred individuals in times of yore, humanity developed the Kundabuffer organ, which later, fortunately, vanished from humanity.

Now, the electronic sexual fire (that was mistakenly projected towards the atomic infernos) looks like a serpent that is coiled up three and a half times within a certain magnetic center (situated in the coccyx).

THE COILED SERPENT IS THE DORMANT DIVINE MOTHER KUNDALINI.

It is clear that in its positive aspect, the electronic solar fire can guide us to "final liberation"; however, not a single human being is free from the negative flames or from the Kundabuffer fire.

Esoteric investigations have demonstrated that this infernal fire exists within the lower atomic depths of the intellectual beast (who is mistakenly called a human being).

If those splendid and marvelous worlds that cluster in infinite space are simple granulations of that positive solar Fohat, then we can affirm (without fear of being mistaken) that those demonic "I's" (that we carry within) are mere crystallizations of the negative and blind Fohatic force of the Kundabuffer organ.

The consciousness, the Essence, the buddhata, that embryo of soul which every creature carries within, is always the innocent victim of all those granulations of the negative sexual Fohat.

It is lamentable that our consciousness is bottled up within those multiple demonic "I's," which in their conjunction constitutes the lunar ego, the myself, the oneself.

There is no true individual within the wretched intellectual beast. Each idea, each sentiment, each movement, each sensation, each desire, etc., are simply psychological manifestations of the distinct, different "I's," which are never connected amongst themselves nor coordinated in any way. Any given "I" will mechanically follow another "I," and some of them may even have the luxury of appearing to work together, but not in any systematic order.

These satanic "I's" (horrible crystallizations of the negative sexual fire) are frightfully subconscious and bestial in their depths.

Each one of these devil-"I's" has stolen our consciousness, our life, our Essence, or psychological material.

In any given moment, each one of these satanic "I's" represents only a meager part of our psychological function; nonetheless, that "I" believes itself to be the lord, the unique one, the whole.

The "I" that today swears eternal love to a beloved is displaced tomorrow by another "I" that cares nothing for that oath. Thus, as usual, the individual eventually withdraws and leaves the unhappy beloved one awfully disheartened.

The "I" that today swears fidelity before the gnostic altar is later displaced by another "I" that has nothing to do with such an oath. Thus, such an individual withdraws from our Gnostic movement and leaves all of our brethren astonished.

(Human)

The intellectual beast is an unconscious machine without responsibility whatsoever. He does not have true individuality.

Within each "I" (of the legion of Satanic "I's"), the consciousness sleeps profoundly. The consciousness dreams within each "I."

People are hypnotized by that blind Fohatic force of the Kundabuffer organ.

There are four states of consciousness: dream, vigil consciousness, self-cognizance, and objective consciousness.

Imagine a house with four floors: the intellectual beast lives on the two inferior floors. By no means is it an exaggeration to affirm that the two superior floors in the house of consciousness are absolutely unknown to the wretched intellectual beast.

The first state of consciousness is normal, ordinary sleep. The pluralized "I" (enveloped by its lunar protoplasmic bodies) abandons the physical body and ambulates within the molecular world.

The second state (mistakenly classified as a state of vigil consciousness) is in its depth a simple continuation of our dreams. Indeed, this state is much more dangerous than the first state. People of this present humanity are dreamers, one hundred percent; as someone once unmistakably said, "Life is but a dream." The intellectual beast labors and drives cars while in a state of slumber; he is born in a dream state and dies while in a dream state.

The four Gospels of Jesus Christ insist upon the necessity of awakening; however, the intellectual beast believes that he is awakened. When someone accepts that he is asleep, it is an unmistakable sign that he wants to awaken.

The world has "seven dimensions"; however, the intellectual animal only perceives three because his consciousness is asleep.

The intellectual animal has a frightful, tri-dimensional, psychological idiosyncrasy; this is why his deficient spatial sense only perceives length, width, and height.

The development of the spatial sense is only possible once the consciousness is awakened.

The clear perception of the superior dimensions of space is only possible with the "awakening of the consciousness."

A line is the print that a dot leaves while moving through space. A plane is the print that a line leaves while moving through space. A solid is the print that a plane leaves while moving through space. A hypersolid is the print that a solid leaves while moving through space; it is the fourth dimension of any given body.

Hypersolids, hypervolume, and hyperspace are only perceptible with the awakening of the consciousness.

We have been told that the fourth dimension is time (in its exclusively temporal aspect).

We have been informed that the fifth dimension is eternity. Without a doubt, the sixth dimension is beyond time and eternity.

In dimensional subject matters, there is an absolute zero. The zero dimension is pure spirit; this is a seventh dimension.

The intellectual beast is bottled up in Euclidean geometry because he has never awakened his consciousness. The consciousness that slumbers is content with Euclid's tri-dimensional geometry.

One-dimensional creatures possess only sensations of pleasure and pain, likes and dislikes, such as the snail, for example.

Bi-dimensional creatures such as dogs, cats and horses, etc., possess sensations and representations.

The tri-dimensional biped (mistakenly called a human being) possesses sensations, representations, and concepts.

The spatial sense can never be developed without the awakening of the consciousness.

The spatial sense includes, in an absolute manner, the five senses and many other senses that physiologists absolutely ignore.

This present humanity has their consciousness asleep and they are entering into the underworld in this state; yet, they are totally convinced that they are doing very well.

Chapter 12

Reincarnation – Return

Among the angels of death there are distinct degrees of splendor and hierarchy; however, all of them rely upon the supreme commands of the third aspect of Prakriti, mother space, the blessed goddess mother death, Hekate, Proserpina, Coatlicue, Kali, etc.

Despite their spectral, skeletal figure (with a scythe held in the right hand and dressed in funeral attire) these ministers of death indeed have a terribly divine appearance.

According to the law of destiny, the angels of death cut the thread of life on a precise day and hour.

Within the sepulchral tomb, the physical body and the personality come to an end. However, the personality slowly disintegrates and does not always remain within the tomb, since it usually wanders around the cemetery or pantheon.

Pseudo-occultist literature has abundantly spoken about the vital body or Lingam Sarira (which is the foundation of organic life). The existence of the physical body would be impossible without the vital body. However, the vital body is not the personality.

At the rate at which the cadaver disintegrates, so too does the vital body. Yet, the personality ambulates within the pantheon and its disintegration is slower than that of the vital body.

Those who affirm that the personality reincarnates are unfortunately lying, because the personality is a child of its own time. The personality is born in its own time and dies in its own time. There is no tomorrow for the personality of the dead.

That which continues beyond death is the ego (dressed with lunar bodies). That which never dies is the Essence, the buddhata, the soul, that unfortunately is bottled up within the ego.

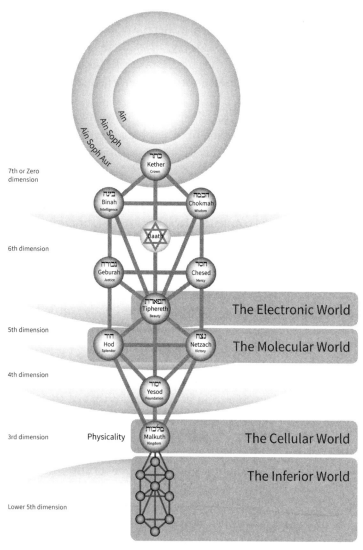

7th or Zero
dimension

6th dimension

5th dimension

4th dimension

3rd dimension   Physicality

Lower 5th dimension

כתר
Kether
Crown

בינה
Binah
Intelligence

חכמה
Chokmah
Wisdom

Daath

גבורה
Geburah
Justice

חסד
Chesed
Mercy

תפארת
Tiphereth
Beauty

הוד
Hod
Splendor

נצח
Netzach
Victory

יסוד
Yesod
Foundation

מלכות
Malkuth
Kingdom

Ain

Ain Soph

Ain Soph Aur

The Electronic World

The Molecular World

The Cellular World

The Inferior World

THE ELECTRONIC, MOLECULAR, CELLULAR AND INFERIOR WORLDS ON THE TREE OF LIFE

The retrospective vision (of the life that has just ended) is made with the sole purpose of taking an inventory of that existence. This way, we know what we have and what we lack.

After the inventory is taken (of the existence that has just ended), the judgment before the tribunals of karma is precise.

In ancient times, almost all of the souls were temporarily released from within their ego. In this way, they were able to experience a so-called "vacation" within the molecular and electronic worlds. Nevertheless, after such a vacation they reincorporated themselves within this valley of tears (much like a genie who reenters the same bottle).

In this day and age of anguish and perversity, souls hardly have such vacations within the superior worlds. Now the disincarnated enter into the infernal worlds or return immediately to this valley of tears in order to finish (as quickly as possible) their cycle of successive lives.

The pseudo-occultist literature mistakenly affirms that millions of lives are designated to every human soul until it achieves perfection; however, this concept is false. According to the law of number, measurement, and weight, only a certain number of existences are assigned to every human soul. Indeed, only one hundred and eight lives are assigned to every human soul. These are the one hundred and eight beads of the Buddha's necklace.

Brahmans symbolize the cycle of successive lives with the ritual of the sacred cow. They perform one hundred and eight liturgical rounds around the cow while holding a collar of one hundred and eight beads, and chant the magical mantra **Om Mani Padme Hum**.

The souls who conclude their cycle of existences (without having reached the angelic state) enter into the infernal worlds.

In these times (after the Final Judgment of 1950), almost all of the souls have completed their cycle of existences or are very near to completion.

Disincarnated souls are now entering into the infernal worlds in surges because times have come to an end for this Aryan root race.

Pseudo-occultist literature has abundantly written about the law of reincarnation; however, this law is only for sacred individuals.

Reincarnation implies a reincarnating individuality, and if individuality does not exist, then reincarnation is not applied.

Pseudo-occultist literature asserts the concept that the intellectual animal has already achieved individuality; however, this concept is as false as the one that affirms that humans (from this present humanity) already have authentic solar astral, mental, and causal vehicles within their possession.

The ego is a conjunction of different and diverse entities unknown to one another. That is not individuality, therefore it is an absurdity to affirm that those entities reincarnate.

It is better to affirm that the pluralized "I" regresses, reincorporates, or returns to this valley of tears.

The ego continues through our descendants. The agony of a man is identical to the ecstasy of his conception. Death and conception are found intimately joined; they form a unique whole. The path of life is made by the hoof prints of the horse of death.

Death and conception are one. Death and judgment are one. Judgment and conception are one. Death, judgment, and conception are one.

At the moment of conception, the psychological design (of the one who agonizes while dying) enters along with the zoosperm into the egg.

Just as a wave transmitted by a television station carries an invisible image of an actor who acts, likewise the disintegration of the elements (from the old body) originates a vibration that invisibly passes through time and space. Such a vibration carries the design of the man who agonizes while dying. Thus, just as the broadcasted image is recaptured by an appropriate device and becomes visible (many hundreds and thousands of kilometers away from the place where it was actually emitted) likewise, the fecundated egg is the receptive organ for the psychological design of the agonizing man.

After death, the different entities that constitute the ego come and go through the molecular region; however, not all

of these entities return into a new human womb. Some of
these entities enter into the underworld. Others enter into
inferior wombs of the irrational animal kingdom. Others
enter into the plant kingdom and some (finally dressed with
their lunar bodies) continue on through their descendants.

On a certain occasion, Pythagoras scolded a disciple who
wanted to kick a howling dog. He said, "Do not hurt that dog,
because in his painful howling I have recognized a friend of
mine who died some time ago." This is the wise law of metempsychosis that is so detested by the fanatics of the dogma of
evolution.

Souls also enter into the infernal worlds in fractions.
Thus, many people who presently live within the physical
world already have parts of themselves within the infernal
worlds.

Thus, in the abyss Dante found fractions of souls who
were condemned to the Second Death inside sepulchers (the
sepulcher is the symbol that corresponds to these souls).
Dante asked his master, "May those who lie within these sepulchers be seen? Already all the lids are raised, and none over
them keeps watch."

Virgil the poet from Mantua answered, "They shall be
closed all, when they here from Josaphat returned shall come,
and bring their bodies, which above they now have left."

Saint Josaphat is the Buddha, and the valley of Josaphat is
this world of samsara.

The Final Judgment has already taken place. The egos in
their totality are entering into the infernal worlds. Thus, this
is how the symbolic sepulchers of Dante are closed.

The final objective of the infernal worlds is to destroy the
ego and the lunar bodies in order for the soul to become liberated through the door of the Second Death. The suffering of
the failed souls in the infernal worlds is symbolically written
by Dante in his *Divine Comedy*.

The most perverse black magicians live within the infernal
worlds; it will take trillions of years before they can reach the
Second Death. Ordinary people can reach the Second Death
in 800 to 1000 years, more or less. The souls pay a karmic

invoice within the infernal worlds every 100 years. In the infernal worlds, time is extremely long and terribly boring. It is time of millenarian rocks.

The Second Death is necessary so that the failed souls can return into the primeval original chaos. Here, they have to reinitiate their journey, passing through mineral, plant, and animal evolutions until finally reaching the human state anew.

Chapter 13
The Law of Recurrence

By judiciously analyzing the theory of reincarnation that has been stated by many different pseudo-esoteric and pseudo-occultist thinkers of this day and age, we have arrived at the conclusion that all of these authors are totally confused.

The doctrine of reincarnation comes from the cult of Krishna, which is an ancient Vedic religion. Unfortunately, this sublime doctrine was extremely adulterated by many reformers.

In the cult of Krishna, it has been wisely stated that only the gods, demigods, heroes, titans, divine kings, masters, and guides of humanity reincarnate.[20] Nevertheless, the diverse pseudo-esoteric and pseudo-occultist schools have propagated this concept in a very mistaken way; these schools mistakenly preach onto the multitudes that every human being reincarnates.

Alongside the doctrine of reincarnation, there also is the idea of the transmigration of souls,[21] which includes the reincorporation of human souls into animal creatures. Obviously, terrible human pride considered the reincorporation of human souls into animal creatures as an alteration or distortion of the wise doctrine of reincarnation. Thus, inevitably, by dint of pride, the theory of the transmigration of souls was rejected.

In the four gospels, Jesus Christ emphasizes the difficulty of entering into the kingdom. The great master never said that all human beings would enter into the kingdom. Here enters the law of natural selection:

"For many are called, but few are chosen." –Matthew 22:14

The entire human species, with the exception of a few, enter into the infernal worlds, where they are terminated

---

20 In *The Bhagavad-gita*. See *The Mystery of the Golden Blossom* Ch 32 by Samael Aun Weor.

21 As taught by Pythagoras, Plato, and Socrates.

through the Second Death. This event is always repeated in all of the planets of infinite space.

We have already stated that only with the Second Death can the lost souls be liberated from the infernal worlds.

The law of eternal return always brings the failed souls (who lived within the underworld and who passed through the Second Death) to a new cosmic manifestation.

The law of eternal return provides the foundation for the doctrine of the transmigration of souls; millions of failed souls (from past cycles of manifestation) are now elementals from the mineral or plant kingdoms and also animal creatures who long to re-conquer the human state that they lost in times of yore.

The wise idea of the eternal return of all things is invariably united to Pythagorean wisdom and to the sacred Hindustani cosmogony.

The entire doctrine about the life of Brahma, mahamanvantaras and pralayas, kalpas, the breath of Brahma, etc., is intimately related to the doctrine of Pythagoras and to the law of recurrence or eternal return.

An in-depth analysis of Buddhism takes us to the conclusion that Buddha taught the law of eternal return or recurrence in his doctrine of successive lives.

Simplicius, cited by Ouspenski, wrote,

> "The Pythagoreans said that the same things are repeated again and again.

> "In this connection it is interesting to note the words of Eudemus, Aristotle's disciple (in the 3rd book of Physics). He says: "Some people accept and some people deny that time repeats itself. Repetition is understood in different senses. One kind of repetition may be in the natural order of things, like repetition of summers and winters and other seasons, when a new one comes after another has disappeared; to this order of things belong the movements of the heavenly bodies and the phenomena produced by them, such as solstices and equinoxes, which are produced by the movement of the Sun."

> "But if we are to believe the Pythagoreans, there is another kind of repetition in quantity, in which the same things exist a number of times. That means that I shall talk to you and sit exactly like this and I shall have in my hand same stick, and everything

will be the same as it is now. This makes it possible to suppose that there exists no difference in time, because if movements (of heavenly bodies) and many other things are the same, what occurred before and what will occur afterwards are also the same. This applies also to their number, which is always the same. Everything is the same and therefore time is the same."

To the law of recurrence (magnificently exposed by Eudemus in the former paragraphs), the only thing we have to add is the spiral that, according to Pythagoras, is the curve of life.

Time is round, and everything is repeated, at times in higher spirals, at times in lower spirals.

The incessant repetition of the same dramas, the same scenes, the same events in each one of the one hundred and eight lives (that the cosmic law always assigns to every human soul) is interesting and yet simultaneously painful.

Each life is a repetition of the previous life plus its good or bad, pleasant or unpleasant karmic consequences.

When a man dies, the anguishing moments of his agonizing death, his last moments and realizations, his last sensations and his last fears are all found intimately related with the enjoyments of love that originate his new birth.

A new life starts exactly under the same conditions as that of the previous one; clearly, it cannot start in any other way.

According with the law of recurrence, when we are reborn again within this valley of tears, the past is converted into the future.

The intellectual animal (mistakenly called a human being) cannot change his circumstances. He is a victim of circumstance. Everything that happens to him is as mechanical as one season flowing into another. However, he has the illusion of doing things; yet, in reality he does not have the power to do anything. Through him, all things happen.

Only the Being is capable of doing. Only the Being can originate new circumstances. Only the Being can change the order of things. But alas, the intellectual animal has not incarnated the Being.

Within this valley of bitterness there are human-machines with absolute repetition. They are one hundred percent mechanical. These are people who repeat even the most insignificant details from their previous lives.

Constantly reincorporating themselves within this valley of Saint Josaphat, there are certain people whose repetition varies. At times, they revive their previous lives in higher spirals and at times in lower spirals.

On our very intriguing planet there are also certain types of people who have an increasing tendency towards degeneration. They resolutely march upon the descending spiral path; these are the drunkards, suicides, homosexuals, prostitutes, drug addicts, thieves, assassins, etc. In each life, these types of people repeat, over and over again (in a descending manner), the same crimes. Thus, finally, they enter into the infernal worlds.

On the other hand, in apparently stark contrast to the previously mentioned descending life (yet, in a position equally abominable) we find upper class people, such as the great celebrities who worship the great harlot; millionaires, multi-millionaires, and perverse scientists who invent destructive weapons. Likewise, we find the tenebrous henchmen of the dialectic materialism who take from humanity their eternal values. Sports fanatics and the great boxing contenders are there as well. Vain record breakers and comedians (who love to play with their monster of one thousand faces) exist there too. Famous movie stars who justify all of their adulteries with innumerable matrimonies and divorces also abide there. Here too can we find the degenerated artists of this new age: painters, rock and roll bands, dancers and singers (of rap, pop, Latin, etc.) Likewise we find the founders of harmful sects, the writers of pornographic literature, etc. All types of skeptical people are found here as well, etc.

All types of celebrities are hypnotized by triumph; this is precisely their great danger. They ignore that they are going down on a descending spiral. Thus, they enter into the infernal worlds inebriated by triumph.

Triumphant types of people know exactly what they have to do each time they return to this worldly scenario. Thus, this is how they repeat their same adventures.

So, the law of recurrence is the cause for the devolution of all of these types of people in the infernal worlds. Within the abyss they have to repeat (in a devolving manner) all of the animal, plant, and mineral processes (which, in times of yore, they had already passed through, yet in an evolving manner).

The final disintegration in the underworld is necessary and indispensable in order to liberate the lost souls. After having passed through their frightful millenarian journey within the underworld, these souls return to a new manifestation that has to begin on the lowest level, which is the mineral kingdom.

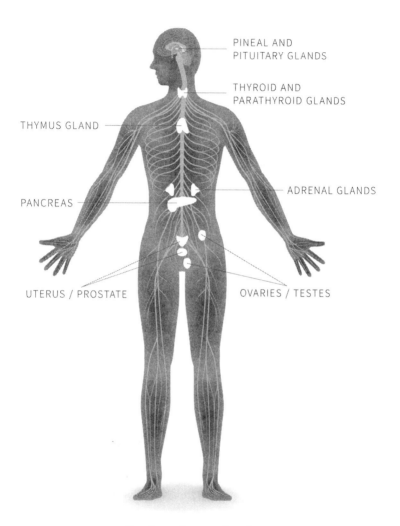

PINEAL AND
PITUITARY GLANDS

THYROID AND
PARATHYROID GLANDS

THYMUS GLAND

ADRENAL GLANDS

PANCREAS

UTERUS / PROSTATE

OVARIES / TESTES

THREE NERVOUS SYSTEMS AND SEVEN GLANDS

Chapter 14
The Human Machine

If we vividly imagine in a clear and precise manner the resplendent and elongated body of the solar system, we will see all of its beautiful coverings and intertwined threads that were formed by the marvelous traces of the planets. Then, from such a receptive state, the living image of the human organism (with its skeletal, lymphatic, arterial, nervous, etc., systems) will come into our minds. Without a doubt the constitution of the human organism is also constituted and reunited in a similar manner.

In space, when looking upon the solar system of Ors from afar (which is the solar system in which we live, move, and have our existence), it looks like a human being who walks throughout the inalterable infinite.

The microcosmic human being is, in his turn, a solar system in miniature, a marvelous machine with various distributed nets of energy that are in distinct degrees of tension.

The structure of the human organism is constituted by seven or eight systems that are held together by a formidable skeletal assemblage that (thanks to its connected tissue) is reunited into a solid whole.

Medical science has verified that all of these systems (from the human organism) are properly united and harmonized by the heart, which is the sun of this physical organism. The existence of the microcosmic human being depends upon its vivifying heart.

Each organic system embraces the entire human body. Through its internal secretion, one endocrine gland reigns with sovereignty over each system. Indeed, these marvelous glands are living micro-laboratories that are situated on specific places (such as regulators and transformers).

In summary, we can emphatically affirm that the highest mission of these glandular micro-laboratories is to transform the vital energies produced by the human machine.

It has been stated that the human organism obtains its nourishment from the air that we breathe, from the food that we eat, and from the solar light.

These glandular micro-laboratories have to transform the vital energies from the above mentioned nourishments. Indeed, this is an amazing and marvelous labor.

Each endocrine gland has to transform the vital energy acquired through these three types of nourishments into the degree of tension required by its own system and function.

The human organism possesses seven superior glands and three nervous systems. The law of seven and the law of three intensely work within the human machine.

The central nervous system produces those very seldom conscious functions that occasionally manifest themselves through the intellectual animal.

The sympathetic nervous system marvelously stimulates the unconscious and instinctual functions.

The parasympathetic or vagus restrains the instinctual functions and acts as a complement of the latter.

Thus, we are totally accurate when affirming (without fear of being mistaken) that these three nervous systems represent the law of three, the three primary forces within the human machine. Likewise, the seven endocrine glands and their secretions represent the law of seven with all of their musical scales.

Indeed, there is a system that controls the release of active nervous impulses; there is another that controls the release of passive nervous impulses, and also a third that controls the release of the mediator nervous impulses emanating from our thoughts, our reasoning, and our consciousness.

The nerves, agents of the law of three, control the endocrine glands that (as we have already stated) represent the law of seven.

The glands are controlled by the nerves, but in turn, these are also controlled. This is similar to the specific functions of the planets that move around the Sun; the planets control and yet are controlled.

We mentioned and we repeat again that the human machine has five centers: first, the intellectual center; second, the emotional center; third, the motor center; fourth, the instinctual center, and fifth, the sexual center.

We have explained many times that the five cylinders of the human machine are unfortunately controlled by the pluralized "I," by that legion of "I's" that lives within these psychological centers.

The human machine (as any other machine) moves under the impulses of the subtle forces of nature.

The secret agents that move the human machines are first the cosmic radiations and secondly the pluralized "I."

The cosmic radiation is formed by two great component groups that work within the great laboratory of nature in the same way that they do within the human machine.

The first group is formed by rays of great hardness and elevated penetration. These rays come from sidereal space; they have energies which oscillate at about five billion electro-volts. When penetrating our planet, these rays collide with the particles of the high atmosphere, thus originating impacts that segregate into nourishing beams of light and starry rays.

The hardness of this cosmic radiation is formed by protons, neutrons, and mesons. The latter are already classified as positive, negative, and neutral according to the law of three.

The second group or bland radiation is formed by secondary rays that are produced within the terrestrial atmosphere. According to investigations performed by scientists, these types of rays are impacts that are the outcome of hard radiation that has collided against the atoms in the air (which also originate beams of light and starry rays). Some of these are formed by 500,000 particles, which within their development tend to extend through very broad areas.

It is stated that the energy of bland radiation's component corpuscles oscillates between one million and one hundred million electro-volts.

The influence of any given adverse planetary conjunction (any ominous quadrature of planets or any given tension produced by the exaggerated approach of two planets) is enough in order for millions of human machines to throw themselves into war. Obviously, such a war would be justified by many reasons, mottos, flags that must be defended, motives for which it would be imperative to fight, etc.

Thus, the gravest foolishness of the intellectual animals is to believe that they are doing things, when indeed, they cannot do anything. They are simple human marionettes moved by unknown forces.

Cosmic radiation originates infinite changes within the subjective psyche of the intellectual animal, within his psychological idiosyncrasy. This is how certain "I's" emerge and others immerse. This is how some diabolic "I's" emerge to the surface while others get lost within the forty-nine regions of the subconsciousness.

This is how bewilderment and surprise take place: the one who swore eternal love unexpectedly walks away; the one who swore fidelity to gnosis soon betrays it; the one who never drank alcohol is now drinking it; the one who wanted to perform a certain business suddenly loses all interest, etc.

Human machines have no sense of moral responsibility whatsoever; they are simple marionettes who think, feel, and act in accordance to the type of "I" that controls the capital centers of the human machine in a given moment. In fact, if one type of "I" is displaced, then the human marionette modifies his mental and sentimental processes; thus, the outcome is different and may even be in the form of completely opposite actions.

Sometimes certain diabolic "I's" (which do not belong to a certain person but which belong to other people's psyche) come and accommodate themselves within any of the five cylinders of the human machine. This is how the honest citizen becomes a thief and the one who never dared to kill, not even a little bird, is suddenly converted into a cruel assassin, etc.

The "I," which all human beings carry within themselves, is a plurality, and its true name is legion. The sequence of these diabolic "I's," (their continuance and terrible struggle for supremacy) depends upon many external and internal influences and finally... upon cosmic radiations.

The heat of the Sun and the good or bad weather immediately gives way to the emergence of certain "I's" that take over the human machine. Some of these "I's" can be stronger than others.

Rains, contrarieties, and vain, swift happiness originate new and annoying "I's." Nevertheless, the wretched human marionette does not even have the smallest notion of these changes, because his consciousness is asleep, his sense of being is always within the last manifested "I."

Among themselves, certain stronger "I's" dominate other weak "I's"—however, their strength comes from the energy of the cylinders of the human machine. All of the "I's" are the outcome of the external and internal influences. True individuality does not exist within the intellectual animal. Present humans are merely machines.

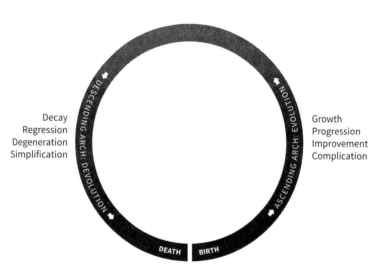

Decay
Regression
Degeneration
Simplification

Growth
Progression
Improvement
Complication

DESCENDING ARCH: DEVOLUTION

ASCENDING ARCH: EVOLUTION

DEATH

BIRTH

EVOLUTION AND DEVOLUTION

Chapter 15
Evolution and Devolution

According to the dictionary, the ordinary definition of the word evolution is "a process of progressive development" that is governed by certain precise, yet unknown laws.

For the epicurean swine or henchmen of dialectical materialism, the concept of evolution, first of all, rejects the idea of an intelligent plan and a creator Logos. The foolish fanatics of that farce written by Karl Marx (which is called dialectical materialism) stupidly believe that evolution is an independent and mechanical process without God or law.

For the students of the different pseudo-esoteric and pseudo-occult schools, the concept of evolution, first of all, includes the idea of an intelligent plan and a creator Logos.

Thus, the word evolution contains in itself a dogmatic significance; precisely, this is its characteristic feature.

The present materialistic scientific bases of evolution are: first, the nebular theories related with the origin of the universe, with all their innumerable alterations, modifications, additions, restrictions, and so on. Indeed, all of these do not even minutely alter this originally mistaken theory of conception related with the mechanical constructive processes. Second, the capricious theory of Darwin related to the origin of the species with all its corrections and subsequent changes.

There is a lot to comment upon regarding nebular conceptions. In this day and age, very ingenious theories about the origin of the universe have been invented. Nevertheless, all of them are purely fantastic speculations without any corroboration; they are merely games of the mind, foolishness.

The evolution and transformation of the species (in a strictly Darwinist sense) is based upon artificially selected "facts." In order to prove that theory, they rely on comparative anatomy, on morphology, on embryology, on paleontology, etc. However, in each decade they deny the "facts" from the previous decade and substitute old "facts" for new "facts." Nevertheless, that theory remains untouchable.

Indeed, the appearance of new species (as a result of the law of evolution) is no more than a simple hypothesis, since it has never been verified. Nobody has ever witnessed the appearance of a new species.

When creating the theory of evolution, modern thought forgot about the destructive, devolving processes of nature. The reason lies in the intellectual vision's much too limited field in these times. Due to this, pompous theories are elaborated upon; all of them are very beautiful but all have an insufficient number of "facts." Within these theories, none of the processes are certainly and entirely known; these theories only observe part of the process of evolution. Erudites state that this process consists as a type of evolving change.

In this day and age, the human mind is already so degenerated that it has become incapable of even comprehending the inverse degenerative process on a greater scale.

Present erudites' minds are so trapped (bottled up within the dogma of evolution) that their minds only know how to think or function according to their own bottled up condition. This is why they attribute unto the other phenomena (that is: devolution, destruction, decadence, and degeneration) the qualification of evolution, development, and progress.

People and cultures in this era who seem to be from the "Stone Age" are neither from the beginning nor from the end of the world. These "Stone Age" people are only the declination and degeneration of very wealthy, ancient civilizations. This is demonstrated by the remains of prehistoric cultures, also by the data of comparative philology which shows the astonishing psychological wealth of archaic languages and the irrefutable ancient documents of art and literature.

In this oh-so-boasted-about modern civilization, not all of the isolated villages are savage. It is not a sign of savagery to reject this present "civilized" barbarism. However, this does not mean that there are no isolated villages in a state of complete savagery. The truly savage or semi-savage villages found by modern explorers are, without a doubt, degenerated descendants of extraordinarily cultured people who existed before the Stone Age.

None of the truly primitive villages found by explorers have shown any sign of evolution; on the contrary, in all of the cases without exception, the unmistakable signs of degeneration and devolution have been observed.

All of the savage or semi-savage villages have or preserve legends and traditions from a golden age or from an heroic epoch. Indeed, these legends and traditions talk about their own past or their own ancient civilizations.

This very fact demonstrates with meridian clarity the indisputable superiority of their Paleolithic drawings, in other words, the most ancient drawings found within the profound caves of the Earth. These are related to the Neolithic drawings, meaning the most recent ones.

The gnostic brother C. Iturralde V. sent us an interesting letter from his country Bolivia; he said:

"Here there is something very intriguing and peculiar in relation to a certain legend. This legend is not just a fantastic tale made up by some minds; instead, it is something that has an objective reality. In this village there was a certain Lilliputian tribe with human bodies that scarcely reached some 15 centimeters and others that were 25 centimeters in stature; they lived in a kind of village or community which had houses along with utensils, pots, etc., and they were built by them.

"When I was a child I heard about such beings living near the city where I lived, in Lipez exactly, which is a plateau surrounded by mountains (the Andes) and an enormous surface facing the east. Now, I know that close to Potosi (about 120 kilometers away) there is a village whose buildings are about 30 centimeters in height. Within the homes utensils can be found which correspond to extremely small people. People say that this village is surrounded by very odd pointed hills which extend two to three meters in height; yet for this village those hills appear to be mountains. The most elevated mountains (measuring many hundreds of meters in height) rise above it."

It has been said that the indigenous of that area do not allow anyone to approach this oddity.

This is a devolving Lemurian race. This is a Lilliputian and Jinn race of Cimmerian myths, authentic Nibelungs. Scientists of today are beginning to study indelible prints of these human-ants that came from their (the Lilliputian) galleries and that have even been found on rupestrian paintings.

The so-called primitive European races of the Stone Age (such as the Cro-Magnon that lived in the caverns of the Earth) were formerly very beautiful, but the degenerative, descending cyclical impulse acted terribly on those races of Atlantean origin. Finally, the Paleolithic man left his position to his successor, disappearing almost completely from the scene.

Inside any evolving process there is a degenerative, devolving process. The law of evolution and its twin sister the law of devolution work in a synchronized and harmonious way in all of creation.

The laws of evolution and devolution constitute the mechanical axle of nature.

We, the gnostics, do not deny the law of evolution; this law exists. However, it is wrong to assign mistaken and false factors and principles onto this law.

The realization of the Innermost Self of the human being is not the outcome of any mechanization. The law of evolution and the law of devolution are mechanical laws.

The realization of the Innermost Self of the human being is the outcome of tremendous, self-cognitive super-efforts made by oneself and within oneself, here and now.

To deny the law of evolution would be an absurdity. Nonetheless, to attribute to this law factors that it does not have is stupidity.

There is evolution in any creative process, for instance, in the seed that dies so that the stalk must sprout, in the creature that is gestated within the maternal womb and is born. There is evolution in the plants that bloom.

Yet, there is devolution in any destructive process; for example, the tree that withers and that eventually becomes a pile of wood; the plant that grows old and dies. There is devolution in the elder who agonizes and finally inhales his last breath.

Everything that exists in creation evolves until a certain point perfectly defined by nature. Thereafter, it devolves until returning to the original point of departure.

Therefore, no single living being can Self-realize or attain liberation through the mechanical law of evolution.

Chapter 16
The Revolution of the Consciousness

The Bhagavad-Gita, the sacred book of Lord Krishna, literally states the following:

"Of many thousand mortals, one, perchance, strives for perfection; and of those few that strive, and rise high to perfection—one only—here and there knoweth Me perfectly, as I am, the very Rightness."
—7:3

Jesus the great Kabir said:

"Strive to enter in at the strait gate: for many, I say unto you, will seek to enter in, and shall not be able. When once the master of the house is risen up, and hath shut to the door, and ye begin to stand without, and to knock at the door, saying, 'Lord, Lord, open unto us'; and he shall answer and say unto you, 'I know you not whence ye are: Then shall ye begin to say, 'We have eaten and drunk in thy presence, and thou hast taught in our streets'. But he shall say, 'I tell you, I know you not whence ye are; depart from me, all ye workers of iniquity. There shall be weeping and gnashing of teeth, when ye shall see Abraham, and Isaac, and Jacob, and all the prophets, in the kingdom of God, and you [yourselves] thrust out.'" —Luke 13:24-28

Within the four gospels (which are indeed four texts written in alchemical and kabbalistic codes) Jesus the great Kabir emphasizes the tremendous difficulty of entering into the kingdom.

The *Dhammapada,* the sacred book of Buddhism, states:

"Few among men are they who cross to the further shore. The other folk only run up and down the bank on this side." —6:85

Any scholar of science can verify by themselves the scientific process of natural selection.

"Because strait is the gate, and narrow is the way, which leadeth unto light, and few there be that find it." —Matthew 7:14

The Florentine Dante, disciple of Virgil, the poet of Mantua, starts the recitation of his *Divine Comedy* in the following way:

"In the midway of this our mortal life, I found me in a gloomy wood, astray, gone from the path direct: and even to tell it were no

easy task, how savage wild that forest, how robust and rough its
growth, which to remember only, my dismay renews, in bitterness
not far from death. Yet, to discourse of what there good befell, all
else will I relate discovered there. How first I entered it I scarce can
say, such sleepy dullness in that instant weighed my senses down,
when the true path I left.”

Dante Alighieri, that powerfully illuminated one who
wrote *The Divine Comedy,* also committed the mistake of having gone astray from the upright path; thus, he fell into the
gloomy forest of mundaneness.

It is very difficult to find the path, yet what is even more
difficult is to stay firmly on the path and never abandon it.

Whosoever wants to ascend must first of all descend; this
is the law. Initiation is death and birth at the same time.

When Dante wanted to ascend to the summit of the
august mountain of initiation, his guru made him descend
into the infernal worlds; this is the law.

Within the underworld, the Florentine poet saw and heard
the suffering souls of the ancient condemned ones. There
he also found the sincere but mistaken ones who, within the
Luciferic flames of their own passions, are naively awaiting
the day and hour in order to occupy their place among the
blessed ones.

Dante would not have found the terrible mysteries of the
abyss without those symbolic women named Lucia (divine
grace), Beatrice (spiritual soul), and Rachel (mercy).

Within the underworld, Dante found many sages and
many men full of prestige and knowledge. He also found
many centaurs (half human, half beast).

Within the underworld live very famous centaurs, such as
the great Chiron who nursed Achilles; Pholus prone to wrath
is found there too, and the cruel Attila (who was the scourge
of God on Earth) and many others who in this day and age in
certain countries are venerated as national heroes.

The path that leads to the realization of the Innermost
Self, of the Being, begins within the very atomic infernos of
the wretched intellectual animal (mistakenly called a human
being); thereafter, it continues in the molecular purgatory

of the initiate, and concludes in the electronic regions of the Empyrean.

Every neophyte must learn how to distinguish between a downfall and a descent. The conscious descent of Dante into the infernal worlds is not a downfall.

Only on the path (based on tremendous, intimate super-efforts within ourselves) is it possible to develop all the marvelous, hidden potentialities of the human being. The development of these possibilities has never been a law.

Undoubtedly, we can and must emphatically affirm that the law for the unhappy intellectual beast (before being swallowed up by the mineral kingdom) is that he has to miserably exist within the vicious circle of the mechanical laws of nature.

Thus, even if the weak and the cowards become frightened, it is urgent to state that the path that guides the brave to the realization of the Innermost Self is frightfully revolutionary and terribly dangerous.

We need to rise up in arms against nature, against the cosmos, against mundaneness, against ourselves, against everything, against everybody, it does not matter what the cost might be.

This is the path of the revolution of the consciousness; this is the difficult path; this is the path greatly detested by the perverse of this lunar race.

This path is the opposite of ordinary, daily life. It is based on other principles, and it is submitted to other laws; precisely on this lays its power and significance.

Ordinary daily life, the routines of daily life (even in their most amiable and delectable aspects) lead human beings towards the infernal worlds and the Second Death. It cannot lead them to any other place.

What is normal and natural is that this race of Adam will serve as nourishment for the entrails of this planetary organism on which we live. It would be odd, strange, and difficult for someone to be saved and enter into the Kingdom.

Now, beloved reader, you will comprehend the frightening tragedy in which we live. Fortunately, this is why, the Omni-merciful, the infinitude that sustains all, the very, very sacred Absolute Sun, periodically sends avatars,[22] saviors, to this valley of tears.

These sacred individuals, these messengers, these saviors, are living incarnations of the Omni-merciful. Nevertheless, this lunar race, this perverse race of Adam, mortally hates such helpers.

In *The Bhagavad-Gita,* the blessed Lord said:

"Albeit I am Unborn, undying, indestructible and the Lord of all living creatures, nonetheless by dominating my Prakriti I incarnate on floating Nature-forms through my own Maya.

"When Righteousness declines, O Bharata! when wickedness is strong, I incarnate, from age to age, and incarnate in a visible shape, and move a man with men, succoring the good, thrusting the evil back, and setting Religion on her seat again.

"Who knows the truth touching my reincarnation on earth and my divine work, when he quits, the flesh puts on its load no more, falls no more down to earthly birth; to Me he comes, Oh Arjuna!" —4:6-9

The blessed Krishna, the blessed Buddha, the blessed Lama, the blessed Mohammed, the loving, essential Ashiata Shiemash, Moses, Quetzalcoatl (and many others) were all avatars.

The doctrine of all avatars has its roots in the three basic factors of the revolution of the consciousness: to be born, to die, and to sacrifice the self for humanity.

Jesus the great Kabir magisterially synthesized the doctrine of the revolution of the consciousness when saying:

"The Son of man must suffer many things, and be rejected of the elders and chief priests and scribes, and be slain, and be raised the third day." —Luke 9:22

But, he also added:

"Verily I say unto you, there be some standing here, which shall not taste of death, till they see the Son of man coming in his kingdom." —Matthew 16:28

---

22   Sanskrit अवतार, "incarnation"

Chapter 17
The Moon

It is absolutely false to state that the Moon is the off-spring of the Earth. The Greek legend of Selene (the Moon) is very suggestive and goes beyond purely geological explanations.

Selene is the lunar race, this perverse race of Adam. It was born of Theia (the Earth) and of Hyperion (the Sun) as a giver of life, who was loved by Pan (the world of nature).

The Greek legend states that the beautiful and enchanted Selene was enamored with Endymion, this lunar race, which was put to sleep by Zeus in an unfinished dream.

The Greek legend of Selene refers to the lunar race and has no relation to that capricious theory from the nineteenth century that affirms that the Moon is from a cosmic cataclysm, a detached fragment from the still unformed Earth.

Based on very ancient archaic documents and on esoteric investigations performed within the Akashic Records of nature, the great martyr of the nineteenth century H. P. Blavatsky affirmed that the Moon is anterior to Earth, it is the mother of the Earth.[23] The Moon is a dead world.

During the past mahamanvantara the Moon was a densely populated world, filled with sun, life; yet now, it is a cadaver.

The lunar anima mundi[24] was absorbed within the Abstract Absolute Space during the great Pralaya, the "cosmic night."

When the dawn of the new mahamanvantara, the "cosmic day," was initiated, the lunar anima mundi took on a new form again on the planet Earth.

When this subject matter related with lunar and terrestrial events is seen from a cosmic angle, then we can affirm that H.P.B. was not mistaken when she stated that the Moon is the

---

23   *The Secret Doctrine* vol 1 (1888)
24   Greek for "world soul": "...this world is indeed a living being endowed with a soul and intelligence ... a single visible living entity containing all other living entities, which by their nature are all related." —Plato, Timaeus.

EARTH

MOON

PERIGEE

APOGEE

mother of the Earth, the antecessor of our globe. The Moon is where our parents or Pitris came from.

Now, in relation to our satellite, the Earth has a responsibility that appears to be unique within the solar system. Our afflicted planet seems to hold ten times more weight than the Sun. The total mass formed by all of the planets of our solar system is just an eight hundredth part of the mass of the Sun. However, the lunar mass is nothing more than the eightieth part of the Earth.

Nonetheless, the lunar mass in itself is not the only thing that afflicts our planet. The space-distance (from the Earth to the Moon) that the Earth utilizes in order to hold its Moon also afflicts our planet. Only the Ancient of Days, old Saturn with its resplendent rings, holds a big moon at such a distance, and that moon is comparative to a feather.

If we compare the Earth with a clock, then we would say that the Moon is its pendulum, and if we compare it with a ship, then we would say that the Moon is its ballast.

Wherever the motive-power energy is applied to any given mechanism, any type of weight is indispensable in order to soften and accentuate its animating force and to also impede its whole from being precipitated into space.

Medics know very well that the organism of this wretched intellectual animal is constituted by a defined number of elements. Thus, they know that the dense weight of iodine needs to be below in order to balance the active principle of hydrogen which is located above.

Since the Moon regulates and administers solar energy, it acts as a mechanical commander for the Earth.

Without the Moon as a powerful equilibrator of weights, the rotation of the Earth and the magnetic solar attraction would cause all the liquids from the terrestrial surface of the Earth to inevitably be tossed into outer space.

The effect of the Moon on the tides is something that nobody can deny. Facts are facts, and by facing the facts we surrender to them.

The Moon controls the whole mechanism of nature. The Moon acts upon the incorporeal and inorganic liquids and also upon the liquids that are incorporated into organic matter. The Moon controls the growth of plants; it exercises influence upon the sexual fluids. The Moon regulates the menstrual flux of women. The Moon governs the conception of all creatures, etc.

Indeed, the Moon is like the weight of the pendulum of a clock. The mechanism of the clock is the organic life on planet Earth. The whole mechanism enters into movement thanks to the oscillation of the weight (the Moon).

Everything that happens in this valley of tears is due to the lunar influence. All of the multiple processes of organic life are lunar.

All of the processes of people's thinking, feeling, and acting are lunar. All the vices and evilness of crowds are lunar. Wars, hatred, adulteries, fornications, envy, ambition, avarice, all degenerations and abominations of this great harlot (humanity), whose number is 666, are lunar.

The Moon, as a tenebrous vampire, sucks the sensible pellicle of organic life that covers the planet on which we live.

The wretched intellectual biped (mistakenly called a human being) fatally carries the Moon within himself: he carries it in his ego and in his protoplasmic lunar bodies.

The entire mechanization of the Earth is governed by the Moon, and disgracefully, the rational animal is nothing more than a machine.

Only through the revolution of the consciousness is it possible to become absolutely liberated from this lunar mechanization.

The Moon is that great apocalyptic harlot that every intellectual beast carries within.

This perverse race of Adam is one hundred percent lunar. This lunar race mortality hates the solar race, the sons of the Sun, the prophets, the masters of wisdom.

Lunar multitudes crucified Christ, poisoned Buddha, incarcerated and calumniated Cagliostro, gave venom to Milarepa, burned Joan of Arc, betrayed the omni-cosmic and very sacred avatar Ashiata Shiemash and destroyed his work, etc.

The great war between the solar and lunar races in the submerged Atlantis was marvelously chanted by the Asians in their *Mahabharata*. Traditions state that such a war endured for many thousands of years. This war, made up of a series of wars, lasted for centuries, and started about 800,000 years ago. According to *The Secret Doctrine*, this is the date on which the first of the three Atlantean catastrophes occurred. The second catastrophe occurred 200,000 years ago. These wars ended with the third and last catastrophe related to Poseidonis Island in front of Gades, which happened about 11,000 years ago. People have a more or less befuddled memory of this latter catastrophe and its deluge.

The Garden of Hesperides, which was the most powerful initiatic center of the good law of Atlantis, was frightfully hated by the lunar race.

The Atlantean evil magic from the Black Islands was exceedingly frightful. The Moon is the black and smoking mirror. Black magic is lunar.

The left-hand adepts,[25] the black magicians, normally live in the sub-lunar regions of the submerged mineral kingdom within the infernal worlds.

Schools, sects, and orders of a lunar type mortally hate white tantra.

Very ancient kabbalistic traditions state that Adam had two wives: Lilith and Nahemah. Both wives represent lunar infrasexuality.

Lilith is the mother of abortions, pederasty, homosexuality, masturbation, hatred of sex, and every type of vice that performs great violence to nature.

Nahemah symbolizes adultery, sexual abuse, passionate fornication, and lust.

Infrasexuality is the foundation of perverse lunar magic. Infrasexuality reigns with sovereignty in the sublunar regions of the submerged mineral kingdom.

Within the sublunar regions, Dante found the lustful Empress Semiramis, who in vice of luxury was so shameless that she made pleasure lawful by public decree.

> *"This is Semiramis, of whom 'tis writ,*
> *That she succeeded Ninus her espous'd;*
> *And held the land, which now the Soldan rules."*
> —Divine Comedy, Inferno 5

Within the sublunar regions, Dante also found the woman who in amorous fury slew herself, and then broke her faith to Sichaeus' ashes. He also found the beautiful Helen and Cleopatra, the lustful queen.

Within the infernal worlds, under the faint light of the new Moon, Dante found the infamous Brunetto Latini and many other degenerated homosexual henchmen of Lilith.

---

25 See "left hand" in the glossary.

Adam and Eve Baptismal Font, St James's Church, London

Chapter 18
Limbo

Beloved gnostic brothers and sisters, on this Christmas night of 1967, I want you to know that all of the known and unknown caves form a broad and uninterrupted web that embraces the planet Earth in its entirety. These caves constitute the Orco of the classic Greeks, the Limbo of Christian esotericists; in short, the other world in which we live after death.

Dante Alighieri found Limbo in the first circle of the infernal worlds or inferior worlds. Indeed, we can emphatically affirm that Limbo is the region of the dead, the molecular world.

Blasphemies and complaints from condemned souls are never heard within Limbo, only sighs. These sighs are the outcome of grief without torment. Sighs that are uttered by a multitude of men, women, and children, whose entrance into the kingdom was not possible.

It is urgent that you, beloved gnostic brothers and sisters, know that the souls who are in Limbo did not sin, and if they had sinned, they repented. Some of these souls, while still physically alive, had acquired many merits and virtues, beauty, and innocence. However, these elements were not enough in order to attain entrance into the kingdom. They lacked the main requirement: the work with the spermatic waters of existence. They did not know the Arcanum A.Z.F., the Sahaja Maithuna or sexual magic. If somebody had talked to them about it, they only rejected it, believing that they could enter into the kingdom without the waters of baptism.[26]

It is relevant to clarify, once and for all, beloved brothers and sisters, that baptism clearly and specifically symbolizes the sexual work with the ens seminis[27] within which the whole ens virtutis[28] of the fire is found in a potential state.

---

26 See glossary.
27 (Latin) Literally, "the entity of semen." A term used by Paracelsus.
28 (Latin) "Power entity." A term of Paracelsus.

The baptismal font symbolizes sex, within which the spermatic waters of the first instant are contained. The philosophical stone of ancient, medieval alchemists, upon which we must edify our interior temple, is sex.

Peter, the great master of sex, said:

> "*Behold, I lay in Sion a chief corner stone, elect, precious: and he that believeth on it shall not be confounded.*
>
> "*Unto you therefore which believe he is precious: but unto them which be disobedient, the stone which the builders disallowed, the same is made the head of the corner, and a stone of stumbling, and a rock of offence.*" —1 Peter 1:6-8

Whosoever wants to ascend must first of all descend; this is the law. Remember that sex is "a stone of stumbling, and a rock of offence."

It is urgent to descend into the ninth sphere (sex) in order to work with the water and the fire, origin of worlds, beasts, human beings, and gods; every authentic white initiation begins there.

Since ancient times, the descent into the ninth sphere was the highest trial to prove the supreme dignity of the hierophant. Jesus, Hermes, Buddha, Mohammed, Moses, the Holy Lama, etc., had to pass through this difficult ordeal.

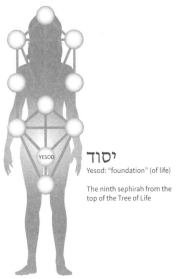

יסוד

Yesod: "foundation" (of life)

The ninth sephirah from the top of the Tree of Life

THE NINTH SPHERE: YESOD

It is urgent to build the solar bodies in the flaming forge of Vulcan. One is prohibited to assist the Lord's banquet with lunar bodies (beggar's clothing).

Mars descends into the flaming forge of Vulcan, into the ninth sphere, in order to retemper his flaming sword and to conquer the heart of Venus. Hermes descends in order to clean the stables of Augeas with the sacred fire. Perseus descends in order to cut off the head of Medusa.

Within Limbo, Dante found many innocent children, patriarchs, and illustrious men who never descended into the ninth sphere. Thus, for no other evil, they are condemned; their affliction is to live in constant desire without any hope.

Many people with the highest of values live in Limbo, and their only crime is that they have not built their solar bodies.

Dante also found in Limbo supremely famous poets such as Homer, Naso, and Flaccus the satirist.

Thus, while floating in Limbo, Dante arrived at the foot of a magnificent castle, which was surrounded seven times by lofty walls; around the castle there was a pleasant stream that defended it. Thus, he passed through seven gates until he came upon a meadow with fresh lively verdure, where he found austere sages of great authority; unfortunately, they were all dressed with lunar bodies.

Within Limbo, Dante found Electra accompanied by many, among whom he recognized Hector and Anchises' pious son (Aeneas). Within Limbo, Dante found Camilla and Penthesilea and the good old King Latinus seated by his child Lavinia.

Within Limbo, Dante found Brutus, he who chased Tarquin out of Rome; Lucretia, and Marcia, with Julia and Cornelia and also, sole apart retired, the Soldan fierce.

Within Limbo, Dante also found Socrates and Democritus, who pretended that the world was originated by chance; he also found Diogenes, with Heraclitus, and Empedocles, and Anaxagoras, and Thales sage, Zeno, all of them very wise; nonetheless, they were all dressed with beggar's clothing (with lunar bodies).

Within Limbo, Dante found Dioscorides, the observer of quality; as well as the moralist Seneca, the geometrist Euclid, and Ptolemy, and many other wise men from this lunar race.

Within Limbo live many just people who worked for humanity and who dissolved the "I," yet they committed the mistake of not building their solar bodies.

One is astonished when one sees Mahatma Gandhi dressed with lunar bodies and living within Limbo.

On a certain occasion, after having verified that the sacred fire had never ascended throughout the dorsal spine of Mahatma Gandhi, it was not inconvenient for me to address him and tell him the following, "You are without realization."

He answered, "I did not have time for that."

My final answer was, "That excuse is not just."

Indeed, Mahatma Gandhi could have built solar bodies in the flaming forge of Vulcan (sex) because he had a magnificent wife. However, he committed the mistake of abstinence; he believed that he could reach Self-realization by renouncing sex. He was a sincere but mistaken soul.

I also found Yogananda within a temple of Limbo; he was dressed with lunar bodies. He honestly believed himself to be Self-realized. I let him see his mistake when I told him, "You are not Self-realized." Full of great amazement, he then tried to start a discussion with me; thus, the intervention of the superior master of the temple was necessary in order for him to comprehend his situation.

I will never regret the fact of having warned the great yogi, the noble Yogananda, that if he ever wants to enter into the kingdom, he has to reincorporate himself again into this physical world and get married; thus, by working in the ninth sphere, he can build his solar bodies.

Within Limbo there live thousands of holy hermits, sublime yogis, and noble mystics who felt disgusted by sex and who innocently believed that they could enter into the kingdom with lunar bodies.

Limbo is the region of innocents, of those mystics, saints, penitents, who did not know the great arcanum, the Maithuna. If they did know about it, they rejected it, because they very honestly believed that based only on sexual abstinence, pranayamas, penitences, yogic exercises, etc., they would attain Self-realization; this is why Peter stated that sex is a stone of stumbling and a rock of offence.

There are thousands of pseudo-esoteric and pseudo-occult schools within Limbo. These schools impart sublime

HERMES / MERCURY

knowledge onto their affiliated souls. Their knowledge does not harm anyone; on the contrary, it benefits everybody. Nonetheless, their knowledge unfortunately does not aid in their realization of the Innermost Self, because these schools do not teach the Gospel of Peter, the Sahaja Maithuna.

Thus, only Mercury, the messenger of the gods, the arch-magus with his caduceus of Mercury — a symbol of the dorsal spine within which the two serpents named Ida and Pingala are entwined — can, by means of Maithuna, evoke to a new life those unhappy souls who have precipitated into Limbo.

Many have departed from within Limbo: the soul of our first father and Abel his child, Noah the righteous man, Moses the lawgiver, the patriarch Abraham, King David, Israel with his father and with his sons, and with Rachel. All of these souls had to reincorporate into the physical world in order to work in the ninth sphere, to build their solar bodies. This is how they achieved the Second Birth. Now they are angels of an indescribable splendor.

One is full of amazement when conversing with the Angel Israel; all of the sublime verses of the Old Testament harmoniously resound within his solar aura.

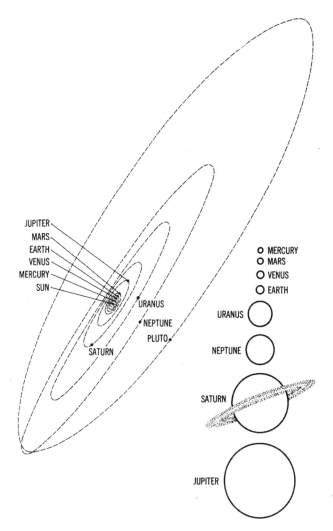

JUPITER
MARS
EARTH
VENUS
MERCURY
SUN

URANUS

NEPTUNE

PLUTO

SATURN

○ MERCURY
○ MARS
○ VENUS
○ EARTH

URANUS

NEPTUNE

SATURN

JUPITER

OUR SOLAR SYSTEM, AND THE RELATIVE SIZES OF THE PLANETS

Chapter 19
Mercury

Mercury (the messenger of the gods) is at a distance of 42 times the diameter of his progenitor, the Sun.

If we make a chart with minor and major conjunctions, we would then anticipate (with absolute certainty) that the planetary influence would increase or decrease; thus, we will see that Mercury and Venus repeat their maximum effect every eight years.

The concentrical orbits of the planets are, without a doubt, intimately related with the Law of Bode. If we take the following geometrical development: 0, 3, 6, 12, 24, 48, 96, 192, and if we add 4 to each number, then we achieve a series of numbers which, more or less, represent the distance between the planetary orbits and the Sun.

The sizes of the planets vary among them. They marvelously grow from the smallest "Mercury" (which is the planet nearest to the king star, the Sun, or which is nearest to the center of the system) to the largest, "thundering Jupiter," which is located at half of the distance between the center and the periphery. After Jupiter, the planets decrease in size again until reaching the most distant known planet; this is the terrible Pluto, which is a little bit bigger than Mercury.

While more distant, the apparent velocities of the planets are slower; these diminish from about 50 kilometers a second for Mercury, until 5 kilometers a second for the mystical and wise Neptune.

It is clear that this is a characteristic of the decrease of the Sun's emitted impulses. The Sun's impulses decrease when penetrating more and more profoundly into the distance.

The fast movement of the planet Mercury has a decisive influence upon the thyroid gland.

The orbit of Mercury is so eccentric and its period so ephemeral that any of its cycles seriously studied will actually be excessively erratic.

As an astrological planet, Mercury is even more mysterious than Venus itself, and it is identical to the Mazdeist Mithra. Mercury is Buddha, the genie or god who is situated between the Sun and the Moon. He is the perpetual companion of the Sun of wisdom.

In Greek mythology, Mercury displayed wings in order to express how he assisted the Sun on its sidereal course. Mercury was called Nuncio and Wolf of the Sun: Solaris Luminis Particeps. "He was the chief and the evoker of the souls, the Kabir and Hierophant."

Virgil describes Mercury holding the caduceus or hammer of two serpents in order to evoke to a new life those unhappy souls who were precipitated into the Orco of classic Greeks, the Christian Limbo, tum virgam capit, hac animas ille evocat orco,[29] with the purpose of having them enter into the celestial militia.

Mercury, the aurean planet, is the one the hierophants prohibited to name. In Greek mythology, Mercury is symbolized by the famous hare-hunting dogs, or guardian dogs of the celestial cattle that drink from the very pure fountains of esoteric wisdom. This is why Mercury is also known as "Hermes-Anubis," the good inspirator, or Agathodaemon.

He flies over the Earth like the bird of Argos, thus the Earth mistakes him for the Sun itself. Respectively, they both represent the Hindu Sarama and Sarameya.

Traditions state that the emperor Juliano prayed every night to the hidden sun through the intercession of Mercury, for as the very wise Vossius stated:

> "All theologians asseverate that Mercury and the Sun are one... This is why Mercury was considered to be the most eloquent and wise of the gods, a fact which is not strange since Mercury is found so close to the wisdom and to the Word (or Logos) and was mistaken for both...."

Within the now-submerged Atlantis, under the domes and roofs of the Temple of Hercules, within the divine crypt of the mysterious Hermes, the planet Mercury gloriously shined upon the sacred altar.

---

29 "Then he takes his wand; with this he calls pale ghosts from Orcus." — Virgil, *Aeneid* 4.242

Mercury, the astrological Hermes, is the god of wisdom known in Egypt, Syria, and Phoenicia as Thoth, Tat, AD-AD, Adam Kadmon, and Enoch.

In the Temple of Hercules, inside that mysterious mansion covered by gray clouds, the neophyte was only allowed to see the planet Mercury as a supreme spirit, floating upon the Genesiatic waters of the first instant.

The well-known "initiatic lake" was never missing from within that crypt of Mercury where (for every representation of mystery) the waters appeared sinisterly black like bitumen.

Before the sight of Atlantean neophytes, such a fatal lake appeared to be framed between four typical hills (such as the ones that are usually represented in certain nobiliary paintings). This sexual symbol reminds us of one of the tales from *The Thousand and One Nights* with the title "The Prince from the Four Black Islands." The prince of that tale truly existed in Atlantis, in the mysterious Olisis. He was the son of an initiate-king from the Garden of Hesperides, which was the initiatic center of the good law. That prince could not be crowned king because when he was submitted to initiatic ordeals, he could not successfully resist the cruel sexual temptations of Katebet (she of the gloomy destinies).

Adam and Eve came out of paradise for having eaten the forbidden fruit. However, the apples of gold or the apples of Freya and the liquor of Soma or Biblical Manna, constitute the fundamental food for the astral.

Let us remember that the sexual hierogram of "IO" corresponds to the host of Elohim,[30] the fathers or Pitris of humanity.

The ens seminis is the Mercury of secret philosophy within which the whole ens virtutis of the sacred fire is found.

The Nordic swastika contains within itself the secret clue of sexual transmutation. This is why this rune is the electric mill of physics.

The swastika is an alchemical, cosmogonical, and anthropological sign, under seven different interpretative clues. The swastika is the symbol of transcendental electricity, the alpha

---

30 Hebrew: "gods and goddesses." See glossary.

and the omega of the universal sexual force, from the spirit down to the matter. Therefore, whosoever achieves the comprehension of its mystical significance is free from the great Maya or illusion.

The three letters A. Z. F. are the three initials of the great arcanum; whosoever knows the great arcanum can transmute the black waters of Mercury of the secret philosophy in order to liberate energy within the lunar human quaternary.[31]

Only with violence and rebelliousness can the kingdom of heaven be conquered.

In ancient times, there were five most celebrated temples of mysteries that remind us of the Temple of Hercules in Atlantis. The first of these temples was indeed named after Hercules; the second was the Temple of the Gallic Mars; the third was the Temple of Minerva Meliense; the fourth was the Temple of Diana of Ephesus, and the fifth was the Temple of Isis of the Nile.

Every temple of mysteries has three successive altars. The first is the altar of poverty, of the beginner. The second is the altar of the supreme art of alchemy, of the companion. The third is the altar of death, upon which any resurrected master has triumphed.

The Sahaja Maithuna (sexual magic) is the science of Peter; this holy apostle from the mysteries of Jesus has the keys of the kingdom.

The original name of Peter is Patar, and the three consonants P T R are carved with a chisel and hammer upon the living stone that serves as a door to the kingdom. The letter P reminds us of the Pitris or parents of humanity. The letter T reminds us of the man and the woman sexually united. The mystical letter R reminds us of the Egyptian Ra, the sacred fire.

The sexual stone, the philosophical stone of medieval alchemists, is the magical beryllium of all countries, the Aesculapian Ostrite; it is the stone with which Machaon healed Philoctetes. Let us remember the howling, oscillating,

---

31   The lowest four bodies: physical, vital, emotional, mental.

runic, and uttering stones of the Teraphim, as well as the stones of lightning, and of the Orphic Galactite, etc.

Only Mercury of secret philosophy, the messenger of the gods, can—by means of the Sahaja Maithuna (sexual magic)—summon the innocent souls out of Limbo.

FEMALE

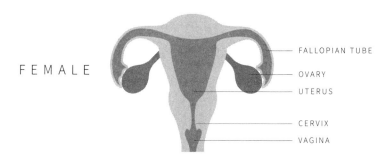

FALLOPIAN TUBE

OVARY

UTERUS

CERVIX

VAGINA

MALE

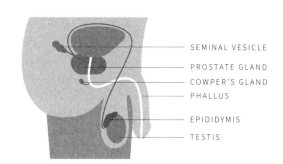

SEMINAL VESICLE

PROSTATE GLAND

COWPER'S GLAND

PHALLUS

EPIDIDYMIS

TESTIS

REPRODUCTIVE ANATOMY

Chapter 20
The Sexual Glands

The gonads of the woman are the ovaries, breasts, and the uterus. The gonads of the man are the testicles, the phallus, and the prostate gland.

These are the generative, reproductive, or sexual endocrine glands, within which is found salvation or condemnation for human beings.

An in-depth study of the sexual glands shows us that these glands are governed by Uranus, the planet of Aquarius. The sexual glands have a dual function, because they not only have external secretion, but also internal secretion.

Scientists know very well that the ovaries produce not only ova, they also generate a marvelous endocrine substance,[32] a very rich elixir that vitalizes the woman and makes her feminine.

As an external secretion, the testicles have the ens seminis (the Mercury of secret philosophy) that carries the spermatozoids collected by the prostate gland. The intimate hormonal incretion of the cortex of the testicles is the marvelous force that gives energy to the male and what makes him essentially masculine in the most complete sense of the word.[33]

The great nineteenth century female initiate Helen Petrovna Blavatsky stated in her book *The Secret Doctrine* that in the beginning, life was reproduced and perpetuated by means of sprouts or buds, or by means of fissures or gaps.

The collective host of Elohim (symbolized by the sexual hierogram "IO") was reincarnated within the first three root races in order to populate the world. They populated the world without the necessity of sexual intercourse, because in those ancient times humanity was first androgynous and later hermaphrodite.

The division into opposite sexes and reproduction by sexual cooperation transformed the human biped into a beast.

32 Estrogen
33 Testosterone

The transcendental electricity, the universal creative force, is the alpha and the omega, the beginning and the end of all things; through the sexual force we can convert ourselves into angels or into devils, into gods or into beasts.

In the name of truth, we declare that we will never commit the mistake of recommending sexual abstinence.

The realization of the Innermost Self cannot be achieved based on sexual abstinence. The only thing that lunar people will achieve with sexual abstinence is to charge themselves with terribly malignant Poisoninioskirian vibrations.

The Poisoninioskirian vibrations produce a high degree of fanaticism and expert cynicism in people. These types of people were abundant among the great Inquisitors, for example, Tomas de Torquemada.

During many years of observation and experience, we have proven that the tenebrous Poisoninioskirian vibrations have the power of awakening the abominable Kundabuffer organ.

Obligatory sexual abstinence is only for the members of the esoteric fraternity. Obligatory sexual abstinence is only for geniuses like Jesus, Hermes, Buddha, Zoroaster, and for all the Twice-born initiates in general, the children of the Sun, the selected ones, the solar race.

In depth Self-realization is only possible in normal men and women. It is understood that a normal man is a male who has normal masculine sexual gonads. It is understood that a normal woman is a female who has normal feminine sexual gonads.

Not a single degenerated seed can germinate. This is why the realization of the Innermost Self is impossible for either homosexuals or lesbians.

An excessive number of pregnancies indicates too much fornication. The karmic outcome of these pregnancies is a sickness known as osteomalacia or deformities caused by the softening of bones. This is very common in the densely populated countries of Europe and Asia.

Several pregnancies deplete the reserves of calcium; thus, naturally, the bones begin to give way.

There is a vulgar saying that states, "Each pregnancy costs a tooth." Many women suffer disturbances in their teeth during pregnancy.

The cooperation among the endocrine glands is marvelous. Some of the endocrine glands act as accelerators of the sexual glands, and others diminish such an action.

It has been completely proven that the thymus gland restrains the sexual appetite. Scientists have discovered that the thyroid and pituitary glands exert certain very intimate functions related with sexual expression.

The prostate gland, where the seminal fluid (the Mercury of secret philosophy) is stored, is situated at the base of the bladder (around its neck).

A very exceptional importance was always given to the prostate gland by ancient medic-magicians. Since archaic times, the hierophants or kabirs of the sacred initiatic colleges considered the prostate as one of the most important organs for the exercise of high magic.

The prostate gland exercises a decisive influence upon the vital fluids that circulate through the nervous system.

Through observation and experience, many medics have proven that males become irritable neurasthenics, marked with suicidal tendencies, when their prostate gland is inflamed. Therefore, if their prostate is treated, many of these individuals could be restored and would be able to return to their normal activities.

The hypertrophy of the prostate gland is very common amongst elders. This is due to the hyper-secretion of the masculine hormone. Fundamentally, this hyper-secretion is due to an over-excitation of the testicles through the gonadotropic hormone secreted by the pituitary gland.

Sexual abuse originates prostatic sicknesses.

It is known that the ovaries emit an ovum every twenty-eight days in accordance with the lunar cycle.

According to the lunar cycle that governs conception, every twenty-eight days the ovaries emit a feminine egg that is collected inside one of the fallopian tubes and is wisely conducted into the uterus, where it has to encounter the masculine germ or zoosperm, if another life is to begin.

The impelling force performed between the masculine and feminine germs is astonishing when they want to encounter each other.

The rich nourishment for the newly born child is formed within the maternal breasts. The maternal milk cannot be replaced by any other food.

Menstruation periods define the epochs of feminine sexual activity. During these cycles of passionate impulses, the egg is maturing; it is prepared and ejected towards the uterus for its fecundation. At the same time, certain astonishing, marvelous, functional changes are effectuated within the female's external and internal sexual organs; these changes also occur within the micro-laboratories called "mammary glands."

The uterus is the sacred maternal cloister, the feminine sexual organ, within which the fetus is developed. The uterus is the vestibule of the world.

Uterine inflammation produces irritability, sadness, and neurasthenia.

Biology has discovered that there is a very intimate alliance between the posterior pituitary and the uterus. If some drops of the post-pituitary extract are injected into circulation, then an intense contraction of the uterus will inevitably happen.

Scholars of science still do not assert that they comprehend the reason for the miracle (during parturition) of the opportune intervention of the post-pituitary endocrine substance, which reaches the uterine cells in order to produce (at the precise moment) the rhythmic contractions which are so necessary in order to expel the child.

The sexual force is the creative energy of the Third Logos, without which nobody would be able to achieve the realization of the Innermost Self.

To disclose the most profound themes of sexual mysteries within the field of medical science is equivalent to the unleashing of winds enclosed within the skin bag that Aeolus gave unto Ulysses.

Chapter 21
The Caduceus of Mercury

The vertebral or rachis column is harmoniously formed by the perfect superposition of thirty-three vertebrae, which form a precious sheath for the spinal medulla. With absolute precision, the spinal medulla is situated in the posterior and in the middle of the trunk, and five parts or regions are exposed with complete clarity: cervical, dorsal, lumbar, sacral, and coccygeal.

Among the total vertebrae (pyramids or canyons, as stated in esoteric science) seven are cervical, twelve are dorsal, five are lumbar, five are sacral, and four are coccygeal.

Doctors of medicine know very well that the cervical, dorsal, and lumbar vertebrae remain independent from one another; yet, the sacral and coccygeal are united with an astonishing eurhythm in order to respectively form the sacrum and the coccyx.

A careful study of the vertebral column allows us to comprehend that all of the vertebrae have a series of common characteristics, but they also present other characteristics particular to each of their regions.

In itself, a vertebra is constituted of an osseous mass of a more or less cylindrical body that occupies its anterior part. From that anterior

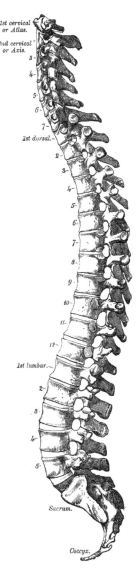

THE SPINAL COLUMN

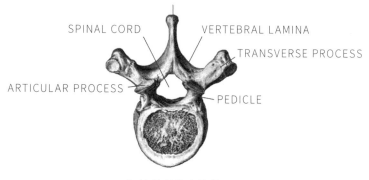

STRUCTURE OF A VERTEBRA

part, two anteroposterior columns are detached in the lateral parts of its posterior face; these are called pedicles, which wisely connect the body with a series of protrusions called transverse process, articular process, spinous process, and vertebral lamina.

Between the latter and the vertebral body, a broad orifice remains that, in union with the rest of the vertebrae, forms an approximately cylindrical conduct or vertebral conduct very well known by scholars of science; within this tube the spinal medulla is situated in a marvelous and extraordinary way.

The vertebral body is more or less cylindrical; in its lateral and anterior faces it has its surface excavated in a vertical way, while the posterior face is slightly excavated in a transverse manner, thus constituting the rachis tube.

The base of the cylinder or superior and inferior faces of the body are horizontal and a little concave, since the periphery is clearly more protruded than in the center; in the latter, they present multiple and marvelous orifices while the periphery is extraordinarily composed of a compact tissue.

> "According to the Yogis [from Hindustan], there are two nerve currents in the spinal column, called Pingalâ and Idâ, and a hollow canal called Sushumnâ running through the spinal cord. At the lower end of the hollow canal is what the Yogis call the 'Lotus of the Kundalini.' They describe it as triangular in form in which,

in the symbolical language of the Yogis, there is a [solar, electronic, sexual] power called the Kundalini, coiled up [within that lotus or coccygeal magnetic center]." —Vivekananda, Raja Yoga

When this electronic solar fire is awakened in a truly positive way, it opens the membranous bag (within which the solar fire is enclosed) and penetrates through the inferior orifice of the spinal medulla. That membranous bag is hermetically sealed in ordinary people, yet the seminal vapors open up that orifice so that the solar fire can penetrate through it.

The successive layers of the spirit open up one after the other as the electronic solar fire is elevated degree by degree through the Sushumna canal. This is how the initiate acquires all of the different visions and marvelous powers of the saints.

When the electronic solar fire reaches the brain, then one is completely detached from the physical body and from the external sensorial perceptions.

"We know that the spinal cord is composed in a peculiar manner. If we take the figure [of the holy] eight horizontally (∞) there are two parts which are connected in the middle. Suppose [beloved reader] you add eight after eight, piled one on top of the other, that [all of these horizontal eights] will represent the spinal cord." —Vivekananda, Raja Yoga

Ancient wisdom teaches that there is a pair of sympathetic nervous cords that in the form of a holy eight are entwined around the spinal medulla.

Many pseudo-esoteric and pseudo-occultist authors mistakenly suppose that those cords depart from the coccygeal region. However, Sivananda goes further is this matter in his book *Kundalini Yoga*: he affirms that these cords have their origin in the very sexual organs. The root of those cords must be found within the testicles of the male and the ovaries of the female.

In a man, the left side is Ida and the right side is Pingala. The profound canal that runs within the spinal medulla is Sushumna. Within a woman, the order of Ida and Pingala are inverted, thus Pingala is on the left side and Ida on the right side.

To its disciples, the secret doctrine teaches that Ida is of a lunar nature and that Pingala is of a solar nature.

Hindustani yogis affirm that Ida is found intimately related with the left nostril and that Pingala is related with the right nostril. As we already stated, in the woman the relation of these cords with the nostrils is inverted. However, the order of these factors does not alter the product.

The Gnostic Movement teaches its disciples that from their seminal system (during the esoteric practices of sexual transmutation) the lunar atoms ascend through the nervous canal of Ida and the solar atoms victoriously ascend through Pingala.

Ida and Pingala are the two witnesses of the Apocalypse (Revelation), "the two olive trees, and the two candlesticks that stand before the god of the Earth."[34]

In depth investigations allow us to comprehend that Ida and Pingala end by forming a gracious knot in that frontal region situated between the eyebrows. Thereafter, they continue through certain subtle conduits that depart from the root of the nose through some very fine osseous canals, where the endings of some nerves are stimulated (these nerves also receive stimulation during certain esoteric practices).

In the final synthesis, those canals connect Ida and Pingala with the esoteric heart or marvelous magnetic center situated in the region of the thalamus.

The esoteric heart is the capital center that controls the physical heart. The chakra of the tranquil heart is controlled by the capital chakra that is situated in the thalamus.

The esotericist sages of Laya Yoga[35] state that within the region of the thalamus that mysterious nervous canal called Amrita Nadi is found. This accomplishes the specific mission of connecting the esoteric heart with the famous Anahata chakra, the magnetic lotus of the physical heart.

By means of all of these mysterious sets of subtle canals, Ida and Pingala continue until reaching the heart; factually, this is how Ida and Pingala connect the sexual organs with the heart.

Subsequent investigations allow us to comprehend that the Amrita Nadi has amongst other functions one that is very

34 Revelation 11:3-4
35 Another name for Kundalini Yoga. Laya means "dissolution."

remarkable: that is to connect the esoteric heart of the thalamus with that lotus of one thousand petals situated in the pineal gland, in the superior part of the brain.

The dorsal spine is that reed similar to a measuring rod the book of Revelation refers to; this is the staff of Brahma, the rod of Aaron, the caduceus of Mercury with its two entwined serpents.

The spinal medulla ends with a type of swelling. This is the rachis bulbar; this is not attached to the brain, but instead floats over a certain kind of liquid; thus if the head receives a whack, the force of that impact is safeguarded by the liquid and the rachis bulbar does not receive any damage.

The salvation of the human being resides exclusively in the medulla and in the semen.[36] Thus, everything that does not go through this way is a lamentable waste of time.

---

36 Literally, "seed," which obviously in our bodies has two components: one in the male and one in the female. Thus, in esotericism, semen is defined as the sexual energy in the body, whether male or female. See glossary.

KANDARYA MAHADEVA TEMPLE, KHAJURAHO, INDIA

Chapter 22
White Tantra

Some esotericists with tendencies to Asian esotericism
who traveled in the East investigated the Asian continent and
arrived at the conclusion that in Tibet as well as in India, tantra[37] is the only truly practical school.

There are many ashrams[38] in the sacred land of the
Vedas.[39] They practice and study yoga within these ashrams;
however, the most serious ashrams are exclusively those where
the tantric teaching is abundant.

In the Hindustani markets, studious travelers can find
marvelous tantric books like *Kama Kalpa* and *Kama Sutra*.
These books are illustrated with splendid photographs related
to certain sacred sculptures and bas-reliefs of their temples. A
careful examination of those photographs allows us to collect
very interesting information about tantric Maithuna (sexual
yoga).

The tantric type of Hatha Yoga[40] is extraordinary and
leads the esotericist to the realization of the Innermost Self.
However, Hatha Yoga without tantra is like a garden without
water.

The Hindu esoteric school of Laya Yoga with its famous
Laya-Kriya[41] tantric sadhana is marvelous, by all means, and
leads the neophytes to the realization of the Innermost Self.

If Yogananda would have accepted matrimony, it is clear
that his guru would have given him the complete Kriya.

An in-depth tantra exists in Chinese (Ch'an) Buddhism
and also in Japanese Zen. It is lamentable that many

---

37 A tradition of esoteric teachings of Hinduism and Buddhism, some of
which are positive ("white" for purity), while most are impure ("grey" or
"black"), being corrupted by desire in many forms, especially lust. The
Sanskrit word Tantra means "thread, flow, continuum," and refers to
the vital energy of the body.
38 A place for spiritual instruction.
39 Ancient scriptures of Hinduism.
40 The commonly known yoga of stretching the physical body.
41 Kriya: physical action or exercises.

PADMASAMBHAVA AND YESHE TSOGYAL DEMONSTRATING THE PADMASANA OF WHITE TANTRA

Orientalists are content with the mere exterior cortex of Buddhism.

The medullar bone of esoteric Buddhism and of Taoism is tantra, Maithuna (sexual yoga).

The tantric practitioners from secret Tibet and sacred India practice the positive sexual yoga; this is to connect the lingam-yoni[42] without the ejaculation of the ens seminis.

The tantric gurus of Tibet and Hindustan are very strict. Before the male and female yogi couple has the right to practice the tantric sadhana[43] (which is a very special sexual position for sexual connection among tantric practitioners), they first must become experts in the exercises of Laya-Kriya.

Frankly, we cannot and must not deny that the *Kama Kalpa* teaches many tantric sadhanas; however, here we only cite the one in which the male is seated in Padmasana (in the style of a Buddha, simply with his legs crossed in the Asian

---

42 Lingam, "phallus." Yoni, "vagina."
43 "spiritual practice"

way) and practices sexual union with his female yogi [see illustration above]. Thus, the female yogini initiate has to sit on top of the legs of her male yogi, and skillfully cross her legs in such a way that the trunk of her male yogi is enveloped by them.

An interchange of caresses between the man and the woman is previously required in order to perform the sexual connection of the lingam-yoni during this tantric sadhana, thus the woman finally absorbs the phallus.

This tantric connubial practice demands an absolute quietude and mental silence in order to avoid the tenebrous intervention of the pluralized "I."

Strong electromagnetic currents exuberantly flow in those instants of supreme voluptuousness; thus the couple enters into ecstasy or samadhi.

A guru directs this esoteric work, making strong magnetic strokes on the coccyx of both man and woman with the purpose of awakening the electronic solar fire, the igneous serpent of our magical powers.[44]

This is a system that transmutes the sexual energy into Ojas[45] (Christic force). The couple must restrain the sexual impulse and avoid the ejaculation of the semen.

"The coitus interruptus," the restrained sexual impulse, makes the sexual energy of the Third Logos to inwardly and upwardly return throughout the canals of Ida and Pingala.

Maithuna originates within the coccyx, close to the Triveni of the microcosmic human being, an extraordinary contact between the solar and lunar atoms of the seminal system.

The advent of the fire is the outcome of the contact between the solar and lunar atoms of the seminal system.

The gnostic tantric sadhana is very simple. During the tantric act, man and woman practice in the normal or ordi-

44 "...each of the seven serpents has its specialized masters who watch over
     the student... When the student awakens the first serpent, he is attended
     by a specialist, and when the second serpent is awakened, he is helped
     by another and so on. These specialists take the serpent through the
     medullar canal...The specialists live in the astral world." —Samael Aun
     Weor, *The Perfect Matrimony*
45 Sanskrit ओजस्, literally "power or force of life"

nary sexual position; what is important is to withdraw from the sexual act before the spasm in order to avoid the ejaculation of their semen.

I.A.O. is the tantric mantra of excellence. The letter "I" reminds us of ignis, the fire. The letter "A" is the aqua, the water. The letter "O" signifies origum, the spirit. I. A. O. must be chanted during the practice of Maithuna.

It is very interesting that the sexual gonads are esoterically governed by Uranus, the planet of Aquarius. Uranus was a divine king from primeval Atlantis. Uranus reminds us of Ur-anas, the primordial fire and water. This is equivalent to the establishment of the first luni-solar cult of the androgynous "IO," in other words, the apparition of the astrological Chaldean; therefore, Uranus, the Asura-maya, the first Atlantean, is factually the first revealer of the sexual mysteries.

One has to descend into the ninth sphere (sex) in order to work with the primordial fire and water, origin of worlds, beasts, human beings, and gods. Every authentic white initiation begins there.

The advent of the fire is the most extraordinary cosmic event. The fire transforms us radically.

It is worth remembering the chaos of the ancient, sacred fire of Zoroaster, or the Atash-behran of the Parsis, the fire of Hermes, the fire of Helmes of ancient Germans (do not mistake Hermes with Helmes).

Let us remember the flashing lightning of Cybele, the torch of Apollo, the flame of the altar of Pan, the imperishable fire in the Temple of Apollo, and in the Temple of Vesta; the fiery flame in the helmet of Pluto, the shining sparks on the hats of the Dioscuri, on the head of the Gorgons, on the helmet of Pallas, and on the caduceus of Mercury.

Other representations of the advent of the fire are the Egyptian Ptah-Ra, the Greek Cataibates Zeus (who according to Pausanias descended from heaven to earth); likewise, the Pentecostal tongues of fire and the flaming bush of Moses (this is very similar to the burning tunal which brought about the founding of Mexico). Also the column of fire in the Exodus, the imperishable lamp of Abraham. Moreover, the eternal fire of the bottomless abyss or Pleroma, the fulgent vapors of the Oracle of Delphi, the sidereal light of the Rosicrucian-Gnostics, the Akash of the Hindustani adepts, the Astral Light of Eliphas Levi, the aura and fluid of magnetizers, the Od of Reichembach, the psychod and the ectenic force, the thury that is analogous to the highest hypnotic states of Rochas and Ochorowist, the rays of Blondot and many others, like the psychic force of Sergeant Cox, the atmospheric magnetism of some naturists, Galvanism, and in sum, electricity. These examples are nothing more than different names for the unlimited number of manifestations of that mysterious Proteus that has been named the Archaeus of the Greeks.

The ascent of the sacred fire degree by degree through the Sushumna canal is very slow and difficult. Any single ejaculation of semen is enough in order for the fire to descend one or more spinal vertebrae in accordance with the magnitude of the fault.

Jesus the great Kabir said:

"The disciple must not allow himself to fall, because the disciple who consents in falling, must fight very hard afterwards in order to recuperate what he has lost."

The Maithuna, sexual yoga, gnostic tantra, can only be practiced between a man and a woman who are legitimately constituted as spouses.

White tantra forbids its male adepts and affiliates to practice Maithuna with many women. White tantra forbids the gnostic sisters to practice Maithuna with different men. They must only practice sexual magic with their own spouse.

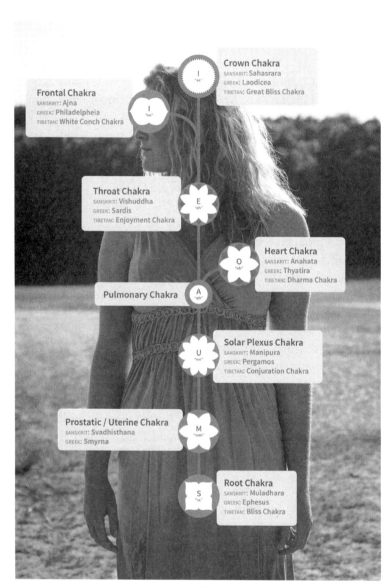

Crown Chakra
SANSKRIT: Sahasrara
GREEK: Laodicea
TIBETAN: Great Bliss Chakra

I
"ee"

Frontal Chakra
SANSKRIT: Ajna
GREEK: Philadelpheia
TIBETAN: White Conch Chakra

I
"i"

Throat Chakra
SANSKRIT: Vishuddha
GREEK: Sardis
TIBETAN: Enjoyment Chakra

E
"eh"

Heart Chakra
SANSKRIT: Anahata
GREEK: Thyatira
TIBETAN: Dharma Chakra

O
"oh"

Pulmonary Chakra

A
"ah"

Solar Plexus Chakra
SANSKRIT: Manipura
GREEK: Pergamos
TIBETAN: Conjuration Chakra

U
"ew"

Prostatic / Uterine Chakra
SANSKRIT: Svadhisthana
GREEK: Smyrna

M
"mm"

Root Chakra
SANSKRIT: Muladhara
GREEK: Ephesus
TIBETAN: Bliss Chakra

S
"ss"

CHAKRAS / CHURCHES

Chapter 23
The Chakras

Very interesting data and references in relation to chakras, churches, lotus flowers, or magnetic centers of the dorsal spine are abundant in esoteric literature.

A very careful analysis of this matter of the seven magnetic centers of the dorsal spine takes us to the logical conclusion that there are three in particular that are most important: Muladhara at the base of the dorsal spine, coccygeal bone; Sahasrara, the cervical lotus of one thousand petals; and Manipura, the umbilical lotus.

It is urgent to eliminate from our perceptions all subjective elements. It is indispensable to perceive in a spatial and self-cognizant manner everything that we see and imagine. It is indispensable to awaken the consciousness.

> "Everything that we [the human multitudes] see, or imagine, or dream, [has a real existence] we have to perceive in space. This is the ordinary space, called the Mahâkâsha, or elemental space. When a Yogi [a gnostic initiate, observes the dreams of each person who wanders in the streets with their consciousness asleep, when he] reads the thoughts of other men, or perceives supersensuous objects he sees them [and can verify for himself that in reality everything exists] in another sort of [superior] space called the Chittâkâsha, the mental space. When perception has become objectless, and the soul shines in its own nature, it is called the Chidâkâsha, or knowledge space. When the [electronic solar fire called] Kundalini is aroused [by means of Maithuna or sexual magic, when the igneous serpent of our magical powers has been shaken from its languourousness], and enters the canal of the Sushumna, all the perceptions are in the mental space. [It is indispensable to know that] when [the electronic solar fire] has reached that end of the canal which opens out into the brain, the objectless perception is in the knowledge space." —Vivekananda, Raja Yoga

Any human being can send an electric current through a wire; yet, nature does not need a certain type of wire in order to send its formidable currents.

> "...all the sensations and motions of the body are being sent into the brain, and sent out of it, through these wires of nerve fibres.

The columns of sensory and motor fibres in the spinal cord are the Ida and Pingala of the [Hindustani] Yogis." —Vivekananda, Raja Yoga

These fibers are the two witnesses of Revelation, the marvelous canals through which the afferent and efferent currents splendidly circulate.

The spirit can send its messages, its news, its information, without any type of conductor thread.

Gnostics asseverate that they can send any mental current through that profound Sushumna canal without any nervous fiber playing the part of a conductor thread.

The longing for every gnostic is to become the owner and lord of that marvelous Sushumna canal. In fact, to gain control of such a canal signifies that one holds the scepter of power.

It is a relatively easy task to send someone a mental message or a telepathic message when the vibratory current of thought is sent through the Sushumna canal.

"This Sushumna is in ordinary persons [run of the mill individuals, or wretched intellectual animals] closed up at the lower extremity; no action [not a single action] comes through it. The [gnostic] Yogi proposes a practice by which [the Sushumna canal] can be opened, and the nerve currents made to travel through." —Vivekananda, Raja Yoga

The seminal vapors have the power of opening up the Sushumna canal. The Sushumna canal is opened by means of Maithuna.

In fact, to directly receive the messages of the spirit through the Sushumna canal means to be free from any material slavery.

To transmute the sexual energy into Ojas (Christic force) is only possible through the formidable magical powers of the chakra Muladhara in the coccyx.

" It is only the chaste man or woman who can make the Ojas rise and store it in the brain; that is why chastity has always been considered the highest virtue." —Vivekananda, Raja Yoga

It has been stated:

"Now this Ojas is stored up in the brain, and the more Ojas is in a man's head, the more powerful he is, the more intellectual, the more spiritually strong." —Vivekananda, Raja Yoga

Any fornicator can utilize beautiful words and express beautiful thoughts without causing the least bit of an impression in those who listen to him. However, the chaste person, even when he lacks beautiful language, can enchant an auditorium with his words, because all of his movements and mannerisms, words, and looks carry the power of Ojas.

It is impossible to acquire complete control over the waters of life without the marvelous magical powers of the prostatic or uterine chakra, Svadhisthana.

Not a single magician can dominate the fire of the volcanoes of the Earth without the formidable igneous powers of the umbilical chakra, Manipura.

Without the extraordinary powers of the Anahata chakra, the magnetic center of the heart, the gnostics could not project themselves in their astral bodies at will, or place their physical bodies in jinn state in order to soar through the air or walk on the waters or pass through a mountain from one side to the other (through the subterranean world) without receiving any harm.

Indeed, the synthetic conceptualism of the great initiates would not exist and the development of clairaudience (or the magic ear of the wise) would be impossible without the mysterious powers of the Word contained within Vishuddha, the laryngeal chakra.

Without the formidable esoteric powers of Ajna (famous frontal chakra), no one can develop that marvelous faculty called clairvoyance, which allows us to read the thoughts of our fellowmen as easily as when we read an open book.

Not a single initiate can conquer the powers of polyvoyance and intuition without the crown of saints, the famous lotus of one thousand petals situated in the pineal gland, within the superior part of the brain.

We know by direct experience that the electronic solar fire has the power of opening those lotus flowers, those magnetic chakras of the dorsal spine.

The Hindustani school of Laya Yoga affirms that the spinal medulla is a prolongation of the brain. We do not have any objections to the former statement because it is right.

However, another thing is the mistaken explanation that school gives in relation to the chakras or magnetic centers of the dorsal spine. They erroneously consider the chakras to be an absolute exclusivity of the brain.

The cited Asian school erroneously states that these psychic centers reside exclusively within the brain and that by physiological sympathy they give the impression of being situated within certain parts of the body.

Allow us to asseverate along with H.P.B. that, indeed, esoteric anatomy teaches that the seven spinal chakras are in the already mentioned places, and that these spinal chakras are controlled by the seven capital chakras of the brain.

We accept that the magnetic center of the physical heart is controlled by the esoteric heart situated in the region of the cerebral thalamus. Thus, any spinal chakra has its correspondent capital chakra in the brain.

Indeed, it is an absurdity that the cited Asian school considers the spinal chakras as mere illusory reflections of the psychic cerebral centers based on the above mentioned statements.

The seven capital chakras intensely vibrate in any brain that is charged with Ojas (Christic force).

The Sanskrit term Ojas means "transmuted sexual energy," a type of Christic force (read chapter 22).

The semen is transmuted by means of Maithuna into subtle vapors, and these in turn convert themselves into energies that bipolarize in order to rise through Ida and Pingala up to the brain.

To be converted into Ojas (Christic force) the semen must become "cerebrated." In order to be charged with Ojas (Christic force), the brain must become "seminized."

Maithuna, sexual yoga, allows us to lead the electronic solar fire towards the cerebral region called Kamakala. Here are found the five centers that in their conjunction constitute the Sahasrara, the lotus of one thousand petals situated in the pineal gland, the king of the chakras.

The first of Sahasrara's five lotuses is the lotus of twelve petals; the second is the trikona or triangle of fire [a-ka-tha];

the third is Nada-Bindu; the fourth is Manipitha, and the fifth is Hamsa.[46]

The triangle is wisely situated over the Manipitha with Nada below and Bindu above. Hamsa is the habitat of the soul, and it is placed above all of the former ones.

The five flowers of Sahasrara gloriously shine with the Kundalini.

---

46 These terms are from Padukapanchakastotram Stotra

DANTE AND VIRGIL IN THE NINTH CIRCLE

Chapter 24
The Magisterium of Fire

Beloved souls who sincerely study this message of this cosmic festival of Christmas 1967, the time has come to profoundly comprehend what the magisterium of fire truly is.

It is urgent to descend into the ninth sphere, into the somber well that is the very depth of the whole universe, in order to work with the fire and the water, the origin of worlds, beasts, human beings, and gods. Every authentic white initiation begins there.

But let those melodious maidens from ancient times (by whose aid Amphion lay down the foundation of Thebes) assist me with this chapter, so that with truth, my style will not detract from the nature of this matter.

You who descend into the obscure well (sex), you who are going to work in the magisterium of fire, you who want to hold the scepter of kings, the rod of Aaron, the staff of Brahma, in your dexterous hand, remember at every moment the Dantesque warning:

"Look how thou walkest. Take good heed thy soles do tread not on the heads of thy poor brethren." -Dante, Inferno 32

That frozen lake whose frozen surface seems as if it were made out of a liquid, flexible, malleable glass: this is the intimate, secret aspect of the semen within the sexual glands of the lost souls.

Within the ninth sphere of hell, Dante found those weeping and livid shadows submerged within the ice, all the way up to that mysterious area where the sexual organs are found.

Such a depressing fate appears in lunar people; their faces held downward, their mouths exhaling the cold, and their terrene eyes expressing the pain of their hearts with frozen tears.

Only the fire can melt the frozen pools, those pools where the lost ones live.

The secret fire of alchemists is the Kundalini; it is the serpentine or annular power working within the body of the ascetic.

Indeed, this is an electrical, igneous, occult, or Fohatic power. It is the great, pristine, marvelous, and astonishing force that underlies every organic or inorganic matter.

Undoubtedly, this is an electronic, spiritual type of force, a creative power that, when awakened to action, can easily heal or kill, create, or destroy. Now you will comprehend the reason for the Dantesque warning to all those who dare to descend into the ninth sphere (sex).

In reference to this living and terribly divine fire, the Rosicrucian Gnostics state:

> "The potentialities in nature are aroused by the action of the secret fire, assisted by the elementary fire. The secret fire is invisible, and is contained within all things. It is the most potential and powerful fire, with which the external visible fire cannot be compared. It is the fire with which Moses burned the golden calf, and that which Jeremiah hid away, and which seventy years after was found by the knowing ones, but which, by that time had become a thick water. (2 Maccab. I. and II.)

> "Without the possession of this magic fire, no alchemical process can be accomplished, and therefore it is recommended in the "Secret Symbols of the Rosicrucians," that the student of Alchemy should above all seek for the fire." —Franz Hartmann

The authentic and genuine Rosicrucian school does not exist in the physical world. In the name of truth, I have to state that I have the high honor of being a member of the Rosicrucian Temple of Kummenes in the internal worlds.

The four alchemical rules are:

1. **"Dominate the animal nature."** Remember that without Thelema (willpower) the weak and cowardly intellectual beasts fail in the great work.

2. **"First know, then act."** Remember that real knowledge is only acquired through profound meditation.

3. **"Use no vulgar processes. Use only one vessel, one fire, one instrument."** Remember that this signifies that Maithuna (sexual yoga) must be practiced only between a man and a woman who are legitimately constituted as spouses. Those who practice Maithuna to perform adultery will enter into the submerged devolution within the infernal worlds.

4. **"Keep the fire constantly burning."** Remember, good disciple, that whosoever ejaculates the seminal liquor loses the sacred fire.

"Woe unto the Samson of the Kabbalah if he permits himself to be put asleep by Delilah! The Hercules of science who exchanges his royal scepter for the distaff of Omphale will soon experience the vengeance of Dejanira, and nothing will be left for him but the pyre of Mount Oeta, in order to escape the devouring folds of the coat of Nessus."

The symbolic coat of arms of Aracena, Spain, made up by Don Benito himself or by his Templar antecessors, is a magisterial, heraldic compendium that encloses in itself the whole magisterium of fire.

COAT OF ARMS OF ARACENA, SPAIN

Actually, this magisterial compendium (coat of arms) is formed by three sections which are separated by what seems to be a Templar Tau. The Tau (T) is formed by a horizontal throne of clouds that can be climbed up by the vertical pole that forms that Tau; in turn, the vertical pole is formed by one symbolic sword and one symbolic club which are united by five rungs or strides that are made up of a number of princes' crowns, mundane crowns, passionate crowns, vain crowns. The crowns must be trampled upon by the aspirant in order to climb up to that heavenly throne. Above that throne, amidst the clouds, only a hermetically sealed door can be seen. Undoubtedly, this is a porta-coeli (heavenly door); a mysterious hand armed with a key goes towards the door. The key symbolizes the clue keeper of the great secret of initiation into the mysteries of the kingdom, which is behind that mystic door.

The section of the left shows a marvelous embattled tower similar to the section of the Cardenalist coat of arms of Bishop Moya. A splendid torrent of living water (ens seminis) resplendently flows from that tower.

The section of the right shows the delectable Elysian Fields with the Goddess Eve (Vesta, Hestia, or the Earth herself) crowned with flowers and fruits under a paradisiacal tree.

Across this marvelous coat of arms gloriously shines a Latin phrase that says, "Ac itur ad astra," meaning, "This is the way that leads to heaven."

The entire coat of arms is the symbol of the sexual Tau with its horizontal pole formed by the clouds of mystery. The clouds hide the narrow path that lead to the truth, and its vertical pole is the difficult ladder that rests on the flaming sword and on the scepter or club, symbol of dominion over our passions.

The five prince-like crowns that are placed in a manner of rungs (which we must trample upon in order to climb this ladder) reminds us that in the ascension through all the esoteric degrees of the five initiations of fire, we must trample upon any ostentation, any human ambition, until by climbing the ladder, we reach the closed door (porta-coeli) whose magical key can only be given to us by a master.

On the left and right of the vertical pole of the sexual Tau stand the Castle of the Saved Jewel (speaking chivalrously) from which the splendid torrent of living water (ens seminis) resplendently flows to fecundate the world — "ego sut resurrectio er vita"[47] — and the Elysian Fields where Ceres the mother Earth appears crowned with flowers and fruits.

The symbolic coat of arms of Aracena is absolutely sexual. The clue of any power is found in the connection of the phallus and the uterus.

The electronic solar fire has seven degrees of power. There are seven serpents: two groups of three, plus the coronation of the seventh tongue of fire that unites us with the One, with the Law, with the Father.

To raise the five fundamental serpents by means of Maithuna (sexual yoga) is basic, because the two superior serpents are always raised.

---

47   From Latin "dixit ei Iesus ego sum resurrectio et vita" which means "Yeshua said to her, "I am the resurrection and the life." —John 11:25

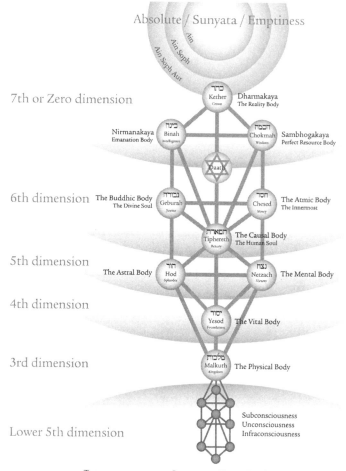

THE TWELVE BODIES OF THE BEING ON THE TREE OF LIFE (KABBALAH)

When we carefully observe any solar human, we can then verify that each one of the seven serpents is raised in the medullar canal of his respective vehicles.

The first serpent corresponds to the physical body. The second serpent corresponds to the vital body or Hindustani Lingam Sarira. The third serpent victoriously rises through the Sushumna canal of the authentic and genuine astral body. The fourth serpent victoriously rises in the authentic solar mental body. The fifth serpent rises through the medullar canal of the true solar body of conscious will.

A Masonic ladder, from Freemasons' Hall, the United Grand Lodge of England

Chapter 25
Pranayama

A judicious study of the marvelous esoteric work *The Voice of the Silence* by Helena Petrovna Blavatsky takes us to the logical conclusion that there are seven tremendous initiatic gates.

By all means it is clear that to reach the fifth gate is fundamental, because for the warrior the two superior gates are always open.

In various Masonic degrees, they make reference to that symbolic, esoteric ladder that unites the Earth with heaven. This is the same ladder that the incarnated Angel Israel (whose profane name was Jacob) saw in his dreams.

Many mistakenly believe that the coccygeal chakra (with its four marvelous petals) is the first rung of the holy ladder.

Many suppose that the prostatic (uterine) chakra (splendid lotus of six petals) is the second rung of the mystical ladder.

There are many who hold the opinion that the umbilical chakra (luminous jewel of ten petals, located in the center of the lumbar region) is the third rung.

Many pseudo-esotericists and pseudo-occultists want to see the fourth rung in the cardias with its famous twelve petals.

Opinions exist about many things; this is why they believe that the laryngeal chakra (with its sixteen precious petals) is the sixth rung.

Many are convinced in an erroneous way that the sixth center, situated in the head between the two eyebrows and with its two extraordinary and resplendent petals, is the sixth rung of the mystical ladder.

In sum, we never fail to see pseudo-esotericists and pseudo-occultists who still believe that the lotus of one thousand petals, the seat of Shiva in the pineal gland, superior part of the brain, is the seventh rung of Jacob's ladder.

In synthesis, it is right to state that Sahasrara, the precious lotus of one thousand petals, is located in the vertex of the head; it is also right to asseverate that this is the seat of the Holy Spirit; thus, indeed, the Holy Spirit is only waiting for his luminous and extraordinary union with Shakti (or igneous sexual force) that, as a serpent of fire, is dormant and coiled up three and a half times within the lowest of the seven centers. The objective of yoga is to acquire liberation with this splendid union.

However, another thing is to analyze, to experiment, and to comprehend the marvelous analytical studies of the Laboratorium-Oratorium of the Third Logos.

We have already stated—yet we repeat again—that the sacred fire has seven degrees of power. There are seven serpents: two groups of three, plus the sublime coronation of the seventh tongue of fire that unites us with the One, with the Law, with the Father.

It is urgent to know that the seven serpents are the seven rungs of Jacob's ladder, the seven gates of *The Voice of the Silence.*

The two first serpents—the serpent of the physical body and the serpent of the vital body— only reach the magnetic field at the root of the nose after having

SEVEN SERPENTS PROTECT THE BUDDHA.

placed into activity the lotus of one thousand petals. However, the five remaining superior serpents always reach the cardias through the Amrita Nadi.

No one can pass through the seven initiatic gates in an instantaneous and simultaneous way; no initiate can jump to the seventh rung immediately. In all of this there are degrees and degrees.

Whosoever wants to lift the third serpent must first of all lift the second, and no one can lift the second serpent without having previously lifted the first.

It is an absurdity to try to lift the fourth sacred serpent without having previously lifted the third, and it is stubbornness to intend to lift the fifth serpent without previously having lifted the fourth.

Thousands of pseudo-esoteric and pseudo-occultist students commit the embarrassing error of believing that one can achieve the revolutionary development of the Kundalini by working with the "bellows system."[48]

In Limbo there live many yogis who, in spite of having practiced pranayama intensely during their entire lives, have not even achieved the awakening of their Kundalini.

With respiratory exercises, we can raise some igneous flames through the spinal medulla, but we will never achieve the ascension of each one of the noble serpents of fire with such practices.

Undoubtedly, it is very recommendable to utilize those flames of sacred fire that are enclosed within the Muladhara chakra for the awakening of the consciousness. However, this does not signify the awakening of the Kundalini.

By all means, it is clear that the nostrils are connected to the sexual gonads through Ida and Pingala; this is why by means of respiratory exercises it is relatively easy to utilize certain sacred flames for the awakening of the consciousness.

The best initiates of Laya Yoga, Zen, and Ch'an intelligently combine meditation with pranayama when comprehending the urgent necessity of awakening the consciousness.

When a minute fraction of vital energy travels through the length of a nerve fiber and provokes reactions in certain centers, it is perceived as a dream or as imagination; however, when under the effects of pranayama (in combination with meditation) any minute fraction of sacred fire rises through the medullar canal; the reaction of such centers is formidable, immensely superior to that of a dream or imagination.

Any minute fraction of the reserve of Kundalini becomes formidable for the awakening of the consciousness; therefore, it is, by all means, marvelous to combine meditation with respiratory exercises.

---

48 A system of breathing exercises, known also as "pranayama."

Meditation combined with pranayama serves for the awakening of the consciousness. However, they will never serve for the awakening of the Kundalini.

Some mystics achieve the ascension of some sacred flames through the medullar canal by means of prayer and meditation; however, this does not signify the awakening of the Kundalini.

Any given fraction of the Kundalini can produce illumination during prayer and meditation; nonetheless, this does not signify the awakening of the Kundalini.

There are many formidable mantras for the awakening of the Kundalini; however these only take effect if they are chanted in the ninth sphere during the Maithuna (sexual magic).

At this moment, that formidable mantra that the Angel Aroch (angel of command) taught me comes into my memory:

KANDIL BANDIL Rrrrrrrrrrrrrrrr.

This mantric song is sung as follows:

Kan is sung with a resounding voice and Dil with a decreasing voice.

Ban is sung with a resounding voice and Dil with a decreasing voice.

The letter Rrrrrrrrrrrr is rolled; it should be vocalized as if imitating the sound of a high pitched motor, but with the sweetness of a child's voice.

This is one of the most powerful mantras of sexual magic; thus, every gnostic alchemist must chant it during Maithuna.

The canals of Ida and Pingala can and must be purified with pranayama. The sexual energies can be sublimated with pranayama.[49] Nevertheless, one cannot awaken the Kundalini with pranayama, because the Kundalini only enters into activity with the sexual contact of the positive and negative, masculine and feminine polarities, during the sexual act.

We find many things on this planet; this is why, for the limit of all absurdities, there are certain stubborn people who believe that because within every human being there are two

---

49 The author taught pranayama techniques in other books, such as *The Magic of the Runes*, *The Yellow Book*, *The Major Mysteries*, and *Kundalini Yoga*.

polarities one can (according to these stubborn people) awaken the Kundalini without the need of Maithuna. These dim-witted people should give unto women, as a gift, the formula to conceive children without the necessity of a sperm, without the necessity of sexual contact. These foolish people should give to men the clue of how to engender children without the necessity of a woman's ovum.

THE SERPENT IS NOURISHED AND DEVELOPED BY OUR USE OF SEXUAL ENERGY.

Chapter 26
Black Tantra

Within the perpetual snow of the millenarian Tibet, full of so many traditions, there are diverse black tantric schools. Whoever becomes affiliated with those tenebrous schools will be miserable.

"It were better for him that a millstone were hanged about his neck, and be cast into the sea." –Luke 17:2

The fundamental, basic objective of the black tantric schools is the development of the abominable Kundabuffer organ (the tail of Satan).

White sexual yoga teaches that the igneous serpent of our magical powers awakens with the contact of the seminal system's solar and lunar atoms in the Triveni, close to the coccyx, in order to initiate its inward and upward march through the medullar canal.

However, the black yogis from the Drukpa[50] clan never perform the contact of the solar and lunar atoms inside the organism; they always do it outside the organism.

These black yogis (asura-sambhava[51]) commit the crime of ejaculating the semen (zukra[52]) during the Maithuna. They do this in order to mix their semen with feminine raja.[53] Thus, this is how they achieve the contact of the solar and lunar atoms within the same woman's yoni.

Undoubtedly, the most difficult for these red hat Bons[54] and Drukpas is reabsorbing the seminal liquid after its ejaculation.

In this reabsorption process there is a certain terribly malignant psychic type of force.

Incorrectly applied, the Vajroli Mudra (in combination with their mental force) allows these red hat Bons and

---

50 See glossary.
51 असुर asura-sambhava, "demon-existence."
52 शुक्र zukra, "semen, seed, Venus, juice, essence, brightness"
53 रज raja, "menstrual excretion."
54 See glossary.

Drukpas to absorb their spilled seminal liquor through their urethra.

During ordinary sexual contact, the intellectual animal spills millions of solar atoms of very high voltage. These are immediately replaced by billions of Satanic atoms from the Secret Enemy,[55] and these are collected from within the atomic infernos of the human being by means of the process of contraction (orgasm) of the sexual organs after the coitus.

When the semen is not spilled, then the solar atoms return inward and upward through Ida and Pingala. Then the solar atoms extraordinarily multiply in quantity and quality.

However, the spilled semen (which the black tantrikas reabsorb through their urethra by extracting it from within the vagina) has in fact already converted itself into a frightful accumulator of Satanic atoms.

When these types of abnormal Satanic atoms intend to rise up to the Golgotha of the Father (the brain), they violently are cast down against the coccyx by the three Akashic breaths that work in Ida, Pingala, and Sushumna.

These types of malignant seminal atoms are precipitated through Ida and Pingala. They violently struggle in order to reach the brain; however, all of their efforts are useless because the three Akashic breaths cast them down against that region of the coccyx where a malignant atom has its habitat, and also the power to place the abominable Kundabuffer organ into activity.

Within any ordinary person, the igneous serpent of our magical powers remains enclosed within the coccygeal center; it is coiled up in a marvelous way, three and a half times.

We convert ourselves into angels when the serpent rises through the medullar canal. However, we convert ourselves into terribly malignant lunar demons when the serpent descends, when the serpent precipitates from the coccyx downwards into the atomic infernos of the human being.

The rising serpent is the Kundalini. The falling serpent is the abominable Kundabuffer organ

---

55   A term from M. See glossary.

When the serpent is rising throughout the medullar canal, it is the bronze serpent that healed the Israelites in the wilderness.[56] Yet, the falling serpent is the tempting serpent of Eden, the terrible serpent Python with seven heads that was writhing in the mud of the earth and that Apollo furiously hurt with his darts.

The abominable Kundabuffer organ confers onto the black tantric magicians terribly malignant psychic powers (siddhis).

The abominable Kundabuffer organ can never open the seven apocalyptic churches of the book of Revelation (which are the seven vital centers of the dorsal spine), because it can never succeed in rising through the medullar canal.

However, the abominable Kundabuffer organ can place the antitheses of the seven churches into activity. The antitheses are seven malignant centers or seven tenebrous chakras of the lower abdomen.

Muslims affirm that the inferno has seven gates, and that they are in the lower abdomen. The abominable Kundabuffer organ has the power of opening those seven gates.

To develop the abominable Kundabuffer organ and to place into activity the seven infernal chakras of the lower abdomen is in fact equivalent to converting ourselves into that filthy beast with seven heads and ten horns upon which is seated the great harlot (humanity), whose number is 666.

Those who commit the crime of developing the abominable Kundabuffer organ divorce themselves from their immortal spiritual triad "Atman-Buddhi-Manas" and sink forever into the infernal worlds.

Kundalini is a compound word: kunda reminds us of the abominable Kundabuffer organ, and lini is indeed an Atlantean word which signifies "termination." Therefore, the Pentecostal fire rising through the medullar canal signifies that the abominable Kundabuffer organ comes to an end.

The fire of the Holy Spirit ascending throughout the medullar canal opens the church of Ephesus (coccygeal chakra), opens the church of Smyrna (prostatic or uterine

---

56 Numbers 21

chakra), opens the church of Pergamos (umbilical chakra), opens the church of Thyatira (chakra of the heart), opens the church of Sardis (laryngeal chakra), opens the church of Philadelphia (frontal chakra), opens the church of Laodicea (lotus of one thousand petals), and the abominable Kundabuffer organ comes to an end.

In fact, the damned serpent, the Luciferic fire, the tail of Satan, opens the seven antithetic infernal churches of the lower abdomen.

The ascending fire confers onto the Innermost, the spirit, powers over Prithvi, the element earth, in the church of Ephesus. It confers powers over Apas, the water, in the church of Smyrna. It confers power over Tejas, the fire, in the church of Pergamos. It confers power over Vayu, the air, in the church of Thyatira. It confers power over Akash, the ether, in the church of Sardis. It confers power over the light with the eye of Shiva in the church of Philadelphia, and it confers the union with the Innermost in the church of Laodicea.

Even when the abominable Kundabuffer organ, the descending fire, gives the black yogi certain siddhis (magical powers intimately related with the seven infernal chakras from the lower abdomen) it also converts him into an inhabitant of the subterranean world, into a slave of the elements.

In the Western world, the left-hand adepts have established many schools of black tantra. Such tenebrous organizations display sublime titles.

We know the case of a certain great initiate who founded a school of white tantra before disincarnating; unfortunately, he committed the mistake of leaving his son (an inexperienced young man) as general director. Thus, this naïve youngster (without any true esoteric experience) soon allowed himself to be cheated by certain black tantric adepts and concluded by publicly teaching black tantra.

The outcome of all of this was frightful, because some members of this brotherhood, also inexperienced, accepted the black tantric teachings and ended up converting themselves into terribly malignant demons.

Sex is "a stone of stumbling, and a rock of falling"; sex is "a chief cornerstone, elect, precious."[57]

We must never forget the words of Peter, the master of Maithuna. Peter warned us against the false prophets and false masters who, in disguise and with sublime and ineffable false appearances, introduce many destructive heresies, much black tantra, and pernicious practices.

Beloved gnostic brothers and sisters, follow the straight path, the path of perfect chastity, the path of absolute sanctity, and great sacrifice for our fellowmen.

---

57 1 Peter 2:6-8

VIII. CLAVIS.

EIGHTH KEY OF BASIL VALENTINE

Chapter 27
Gray Tantra

If we carefully observe the symbolic caduceus of Mercury, we will discover with mystical astonishment that the two serpents entwined around its holy pole form the holy eight.

Ida and Pingala entwined around the dorsal spine are indeed the perfect eight. Joyful be the one who comprehends the profound mysteries of the holy eight.

The number eight placed horizontally is the sign of the infinite ∞. The eight has the image of a clepsydra. The succession of time in different cycles can be indicated with the eight; each cycle (or circle of the number eight) is without a doubt the continuation of the other.

The spiral of life exists within the holy eight. The evolving and devolving processes are always performed in a spiral form.

CLEPSYDRA

"The fire of Phlegethon and the water of Acheron cross within the ninth sphere, forming the symbol of the infinite." —Hilarion IX

The double current with which one must work in the great work (in order to attain the realization of the Innermost Self) is wisely represented in the mysterious Eighth Key of Basil Valentine. This is a variation of the caduceus, and naturally it symbolizes the Mercury (☿) of secret philosophy; the marvelous properties of sulfur (♄) and the productive fecundity of salt (O) are united extraordinarily within this Mercury. Thus, this is how the mystical connubial of two luminaries is performed in three worlds.

The world and the superworld are marvelously entwined with the holy eight. The underworld and the world are entwined with the holy eight.

The superior circle of the holy eight is a living representation of the human brain. The inferior circle is hidden within mystery, in order to symbolize the cup of Hermes within which the Mercury of secret philosophy, the ens seminis is contained.

It has been wisely stated onto us that the heart-temple is precisely situated at the point where the fire of Phlegethon and the water of Acheron cross, forming the sign of the infinite.

The struggle is terrible; brain against sex, sex against brain, and the most terrible is that of heart against heart. You know this.

The sign of the infinite, within which the brain, heart, and sex of the genie of the Earth is represented, is discovered by every esotericist within the interior of the planetary globe in the ninth circle.

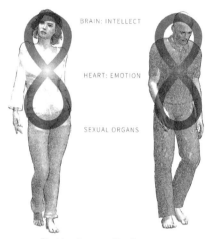

THE HOLY EIGHT AND OUR PSYCHOLOGY

The bodies of all creatures that live upon the Earth, from the most insignificant microbe to the human being, are found organized upon this archetypical base of the holy eight.

The eight Kabirs [Cabiri, Kabeiroi], those powerful, Semitic, ineffable, and terribly divine gods (who were later worshiped by the Greeks and Romans, and whose principal sanctuary was found always in Samothrace) are intimately related with the holy eight, with the sacred symbol of the infinite.

The eight Kabirs are the children of Ephestus or Vulcan and an adorable daughter of Proteus. They were born from the sacred fire (that manifests itself within the terrible profundities of the Earth) by the forging action of Proteus upon that universal substance that naturally has the property of taking any form.

These eight Kabirs are the fundamental intelligences of this nature. They are the extraordinary regents of the great mysteries of life and death.

According to a very ancient esoteric tradition, one of those eight Kabirs was assassinated by one of his own brothers; however, later on he was resuscitated with the help of Hermes. This reminds us of the symbolic death and resurrection of Hiram, Osiris, and Jesus that must be comprehended in depth by the M. M.

The holy eight is therefore the base and the living foundation of the great work. If someone violates the scientific rules and principles contained within the symbol of the infinite, they will totally fail in the great work.

Whosoever wants to successfully work in the magisterium of fire must never spill the cup of Hermes (must not spill the semen) because they will fail in the great work.

The double current of fire and water must be exactly crossed in the ninth sphere in order to form the symbol of the infinite.

If the alchemist loses the water, meaning if the alchemist commits the error of ejaculating the semen, then the crossing of the two currents is impossible.

In the hard battle of brain against sex and sex against brain, the brain loses the battle most of the time.

The intimate battles of the heart usually lead the alchemists towards final failure.

A Greek fable tells us the tale of Sisyphus the Colossus, who by carrying a big boulder on his back intends once again to reach the summit of the mountain. However, his attempts always fail because just when he is about to place the stone at the right point of

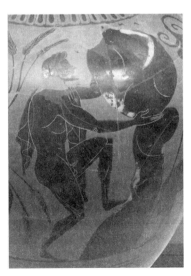

SISYPHUS ON A GREEK VASE

his desired goal, the stone always falls into the depths of the precipice.

Whosoever spills the cup of Hermes once in a while, whosoever at times does not spill the semen, and then later comes to spill it, violates the law of the holy Kabirs and converts himself into a gray tantric adept.

In this world of Samsara, we have evasions and false justifications for many things. Thus, this is how gray tantra also has its followers and its doctrine.

Any esotericist traveler who proposes to perform an in depth investigation among the secret schools of the Asian continent will verify for himself the crude and painful reality of gray tantra.

Tantra is found throughout Asia and is very abundant in the diverse schools of Theravada (Hinayana), Mahayana, Ch'an, Zen, Tantric Buddhism, etc.

The intellectual animals always find evasions and false justifications for all of their weaknesses. Therefore, it does not surprise us that even within these self-exalted and dignified schools of Zen, Tantric Buddhism, and others, much ballast of gray tantra is found.

It is lamentable that many disoriented instructors from those Asian schools offer valuable sexual yoga techniques and practices without ever comprehending the fundamental aspect of tantra, that being the urgent necessity of never committing the crime of spilling the semen during your whole life.

To prolong the coitus with the sole objective of enjoying animalistic pleasure and without any regard for seminal ejaculation is undoubtedly gray tantra that can easily degenerate into black tantra.

Fortunately, there is a lot of white tantra in Taoism, in Hindu and Tibetan tantra, in pure Zen, and in the original Ch'an.

In old Europe there were some sects of Persian origin (such as the famous Manicheans) who practiced white tantra or coitus interruptus; they called it Karezza, which is a word with Persian origins.

The medieval knights also practiced white sexual magic in the Donoi.

The alchemists who work with all the principles and laws of the holy eight Self-realize in depth, and they convert themselves into hierophants.

Every authentic esotericist knows very well that the symbol of the infinite is equal to the pentalpha, the famous star of five points.

Every esotericist knows very well that the eight Kabirs are found intimately related with the eight winds. Boreas, the wind of the north, was considered a raptor of youngsters. Noto or Austro, the wind of the south, dragged the tempests and the clouds. Cephiro, the wind of the west of the world, was venerated as the god of spring. Euro or Vulturno, at times dry, at times humid, was always venerated in winter.

Ancient sages never forgot Caecias the Greek, the famous, the northeastern wind. The ancient hierophants also never forgot Apelites, the southeasten wind. Neither had they forgotten Lips, the southwestern wind, nor Schiron, the northwestern wind.

The work with the philosophical stone, the eight steps of yoga,[58] are exclusively for those who respect the principles and laws of the holy eight, and never those of the henchmen of black or gray tantra.

---

58 Raja Yoga is also called Ashtanga, "eight-limbed," and has eight aspects:
1. Yama or Eternal Vows: Ahimsa (non-violence), Satya (truth), Asteya (non-stealing), Brahmacharya (sexual continence; ie. no orgasm) and Aparigraha (non-avariciousness);
2. Niyama or Observances: Saucha (purity), Santosha (contentment), Tapas (austerities), Svadhyaya (study) and Ishvarapranidhana (surrender to God);
3. Asana (firm, comfortable meditative posture);
4. Pranayama (the regulation of the vital force);
5. Pratyahara (abstraction of the senses and mind from objects);
6. Dharana (concentration);
7. Dhyana (meditation); and
8. Samadhi (superconscious state or trance)

KUNDALINI AND KUNDABUFFER

Moses raised the serpent "on a pole," a cross, symbol of the
crossing of male and female. Those who reject the cross of
sex are bitten by the fiery serpents, the kundabuffer.
See Numbers 21 in the Bible.

Chapter 28
Sexual Abstention

Esoteric investigations performed in my astral body have allowed me to verify that those people who renounce sex (without having previously worked in the magisterium of fire, without having achieved the Second Birth) charge themselves with terribly malignant Poisoninioskirian vibrations.

It is urgent to know, it is necessary to comprehend, that after having totally saturated the lunar bodies these unusual types of pernicious vibrations have the power of awakening the abominable Kundabuffer organ.

Any abstinent person already poisoned by these types of Poisoninioskirian vibrations characterizes himself by a fatal dualism of expert cynicism and a high degree of fanaticism.

Within the infernal worlds live many mistaken ascetics, many abstinent people who have renounced sex without previously having built the solar bodies in the ninth sphere, without having previously reached the Second Birth.

The path that leads into the abyss is paved with good intentions. The Averno is filled with mistaken but sincere people.

Within this painful planet on which we live, there are many asleep pseudo-esoteric and pseudo-occultist people who dream that they have awakened; meanwhile, they do not comprehend that they are trapped in the paws of the dream of their consciousness, and that many shadows of vengeance are lurking in their interior.

Those wretched people, who boast of being illuminated, have renounced sex without having previously worked in the ninth sphere, without having attained the Second Birth that the master Jesus spoke about to Nicodemus.[59]

The outcome of such absurd sexual abstention is always fatality. Those abstemious people always have their consciousness asleep, because if they had their consciousness awakened, they could prove by direct experience the tremendous activity

---

59 John 3

of the malignant Poisoninioskirian vibrations within their lunar bodies. This is how they would finally see, with unutterable terror, the frightful development of the abominable Kundabuffer organ within their submerged animal nature.

Those mistaken but sincere people do not want to comprehend that whosoever wants to ascend must first of all descend.

Mystical pride is a characteristic of the interior Pharisee. These are people who boast of being initiates, saints, and wise, who renounce sex without having previously built the solar bodies, without having previously worked in the ninth sphere, without previously reaching the Second Birth; thus, they wind up developing the abominable Kundabuffer organ.

It is difficult to take these mistaken but sincere people away from their error, since they feel themselves to be super-transcended; they boast about being gods without ever having placed a foot on the first rung of the holy ladder.

Certain types of infrasexuals of Lilith damn the Third Logos, they mortally hate sex; thus they do not have any problem with applying their wicked qualifications unto sex.

Infrasexual people get enraged against the gnostics because we give special preference to sex.

Every infrasexual person boasts about being wise, thus as usual, they view the sexually normal people in a very despicable way and qualify them as inferior or mistaken people, etc.

The great arcanum that is so hated by infrasexual people is found very well hidden between the two Masonic columns J and B.[60]

MASONIC DRAWING OF JACHIN AND BOAZ

---

60   "And he set up the pillars in the porch of the temple: and he set up the right pillar, and called the name thereof Jachin: and he set up the left pillar, and called the name thereof Boaz." - 1 Kings 7:21

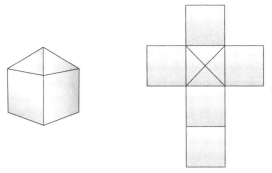

The study of the sacred novenary always concludes with the pointed cubic stone, which in itself unites (on its nine marvelous sides) the entire perfection of the cube and the equilibrated elevation of the pyramid with a quadrangular base.

By intelligently opening the sacred philosophical stone and by extending its marvelous and splendid faces, then with mystical astonishment, we obtain twice the sacred symbol of the holy cross. The union of the two crosses is the perfect expression of the magisterium of fire. The first cross is formed with the five square sides that are constituted by the four faces plus the bottom face of the stone, and the second cross by the four triangles of its pyramidal vertex.

Every true initiate knows very well that the first quadrilateral cross symbolizes nature with its four elements that are developed as crystallizations of Akash, Mulaprakriti, or universal ens seminis.

It has been wisely stated to us that the second cross (formed by the four ternaries or splendid esoteric triangles which emanate from a center or original point) is the esoteric cross, a living expression of the Triune Logos that is crucified in matter.

Upon this living stone of the temple situated between the columns of Adam Kadmon, plus ultra is found, the clue of the realization of the Innermost Self.

The philosophical stone is sex. It is the cubic stone of Yesod. Therefore, it is dumb to want to convert ourselves into a column of the temple of the living God without previously having chiseled the brute stone.

In other words, no one can attain mastery, adepthood, without having previously worked in the ninth sphere.

The pointed cubic stone has nine faces, nine vertexes, and sixteen edges.

The pointed cubic stone is telling us that every elevation requires a previous humiliation. Firstly, it is essential to descend into the infernal worlds, into the ninth circle under the surface of the Earth, in order to have the right to ascend into heaven.

It is impossible to enter into the kingdom if the laws of the cubic stone of Yesod are violated.

Those who renounce sex without having previously attained the Second Birth violate the laws of the holy stone.

The innocent souls who live on the other shore of the evil river, those sublime mystics, those venerable sages, those patriarchs who live in Limbo for the crime of having renounced sex (without having previously built the solar bodies), avoided the Poisoninioskirian vibrations behind the protective shield of their sanctity.

It is stupid to renounce sex without having previously achieved the Second Birth. It is absurd to violate the laws of the holy stone.

The innocent souls of Limbo need to reincorporate in order to work in the ninth sphere and attain the Second Birth; only then can they enter into the kingdom.

Chapter 29
Solar Laws and Lunar Laws

In these times of world crisis, scientific inquietudes are formidable.

Already Morrison and Cocconi, eminent North American physicists, think that in some parts of the Milky Way there may be scientific societies of extraterrestrial human beings who are immensely superior to us. These physicists believe it is possible that these extraterrestrials want to communicate with us. They have even discovered that such cosmic societies emit waves toward our direction at a frequency of 1,420 Mc/Sec.

The theory of the plurality of inhabited worlds has already been comprehended by the scholars of science.

One argument (among others) that favors this theory states that certain stars have weak angular velocities (such as the Sun).

Every scholar of science has verified through observation and experience that a small angular movement of any sun, indicates, denotes, or reveals the existence of a planetary system.

Scientists are already starting to comprehend that planets located in a similar position to that of the Earth (in relation to our Sun) could be found among all of those millions of worlds within our galaxy. To discard the possibility that some of those planets have civilizations immensely more developed than ours is an absurdity.

These scholars state that this possibility can and must be very carefully examined.

Certain news stated that Drake, a famous scientist, had the intention of seriously studying the very interesting zone of Ceti and Eridano. These two stars are found at a distance of 11.4 light-years, and these are the closest after the one from Centauri.

From the formidable list of the closest stars (intelligently elaborated upon by Morrison and Cocconi), it is clear that

Ceti and Eridano, as well as Indi, are indeed the most interesting, after discarding the double stars. It has been verified that the planets of double stars do not possess uniform climates for very long geologic periods because of their very marked perturbed orbits.

Gnostics state that there are many galactic societies. These galactic societies know about the critical moments in which we live, and they want and wish to help us.

Sirius, the sun of the suns of our Milky Way, is a double star. The twin brother of Sirius is a black world of a terrible and frightful density.

The vibratory influence of the double star Sirius is very strange. Its radiation is supra-solar and infra-lunar.

By simple logical deduction we can state that the double radiation of Sirius decisively influences all of the supra-heavens and all of the infra-infernos of the Milky Way.

It is true that Sirius is the great sun of the Milky Way; yet, also, it is no less true that its tenebrous twin brother has a density much more astonishing than one even conceivable within the interior darkness of the deadest moon.

The double star Sirius is composed of an immense radiant sun, twenty six times more brilliant than ours, with a circular trajectory of a period of fifty years around a white dwarf the size of Jupiter and five thousand times more dense than lead.

It has been said to us that the Milky Way gravitates around the double star Sirius. In a certain way, that double star seems to fill in the excessive gap between the cosmos of the solar system and the Milky Way.

The double star Sirius indicates an intense solar and lunar activity within our galaxy.

The double star Sirius influences us decisively here and now.

To become free of the lunar influence is something frightfully difficult, yet it is indispensable in order to achieve liberation.

On this planet in which we live, the lunar influence is double, because the Earth has two moons. Through telescopes, the second moon appears black and as the size of a lentil. Occultists have named the black moon Lilith. This second lunar satellite is a kind of eighth submerged sphere. It is a very malignant world.

On Earth, the sinister vibrations from the black moon originate many monstrosities, abominations, frightful crimes filled with repugnant savagery, inconceivable lust, homosexuality on a great scale, masturbation, pederasty, provoked abortions, etc.

Among the most abominable products of Lilith, it is opportune to cite the case of Count Dracula in Russia. This movie personage truly existed, and H. P. Blavatsky comments about him in one of her books. This great female master stated that in times of the Czars that count was the mayor of a certain Russian town. He mortally hated his wife, because vampires are homosexuals; they mortally hate the opposite sex. After his death, Count Dracula presented himself in the house of his abhorred widow in order to lash her violently. At midnight, certain Catholic priests uselessly tried to block Dracula's trot; at the bridge very close to the cemetery Count Dracula's chariot trampled the priests.

When Count Dracula's black and frightful crypt was opened, his living cadaver was found well preserved and submerged in human blood, since vampires nourish themselves with blood.

The great Master Helen P. Blavatsky states that the feet of the sinister cadaver were covered with mud; without a doubt this shows us that Dracula was escaping at midnight from his sepulcher.

Dracula's case concluded when the priests wounded his heart with a wooden stick.

There is an order of vampires in Palestine; they hide themselves behind the following title, "Order of the Immortal Guardians of the Holy Sepulcher."

Vampires are the outcome of homosexuality in combination with Tantra between persons of the same sex. It is an execrable monstrosity, a frightful abomination.

The double lunar influence of this planet on which we live is terribly mechanistic.

It is urgent to nourish ourselves with the apples of gold or apples of Freya and with the liquor of soma or Biblical Manna in order to build the solar bodies and to liberate ourselves from the lunar laws.

It has been stated unto us, as Brahman chronologies demonstrate, that our physical Sun rotates around a sun that is infinitely greater, or more luminous. That sun is very luminous; this is why it is invisible before our terrene eyes. Yet, it is mentioned in ancient theogonies with an indispensable mathematical rigor.

Yet, this equatorial or astral sun (which is the unknowable center, of which our physical sun is just a mere planet) is not the only one, but moreover, there are two other, more excelsior suns within the superior planes or hyper-dimensions of this cerulean space. The Tamil calendars (like the Tiruchanga and Panchanga) call these suns, respectively, the polar sun (or galactic center of our entire nebula with its one hundred million suns) and the central sun, the center of centers, which in turn entwine and unify as many nebulae (of millions and millions of suns) that could exist in the millions within the sky.

Before the eyes of a mystic, the astral or equatorial sun flamingly shines, assembled in the celestial group which we call the Pleiades or Seven Sisters from the constellation of Taurus.

Sirius, with its whole magnificence, is the gravitational center of this Milky Way; however, it has to gravitate around the polar sun.

Without the central sun, cosmic order would be impossible. Variety is unity. The central sun unifies, governs, and establishes unity within the infinite variety.

Chapter 30
The Astral Body

Within occultist literature, a great deal has been written regarding this very interesting theme of astral projection.

Here, it is very opportune to cite the undesirable hypnotic phenomena of the mentioned Laurent (July 10, 1894) in which the famous hypnotist Colonel Rochas experimented with hypnotism. He achieved with lamentable imprudence (like those who despise the classic *Ars Magna Brevis Experimentum Periculosum*) what can be summarized as hypnotic states separated from each other by many other lethargic states (people who are dedicated to this subject matter know all this very well).

Onto the three typical hypnotic states known as lethargy, catalepsy, and somnambulism, Colonel Rochas added many other more profound states, thirteen in all. These states were separated from each other by successive lethargic states in which the patient seems to sleep more and more in order to successively awaken into "new states" each time more distant from the state of vigil.

In state number five, a blue phantom appears on the left side of the hypnotized patient. Likewise, in state number six, on the patient's left side another phantom appears but red. Then, upon reaching state number seven, both phantoms unite and become one and when reaching state number eight interpenetrate into irregular white-violet bands.

In state number nine, the astral double, thus integrated, starts to enhance a relative liberty of movements, although without severing the silver cord that connects to the physical body, since the rupture of that cord would signify death.

In hypnotic state number eleven (according to the sayings of Colonel Rochas), the astral double tends to its emancipation, to become totally released from its physical ties, while some certain repugnant forms or diabolic "I's" viciously move in and out of the double, producing terrible convulsions within the patient.

Now that we have reached this section of this chapter, it is convenient to clarify that Colonel Rochas qualified the demonic "I's" of the patient as "repugnant larvae."

When the unhappy patient sees himself assaulted by such animalistic creatures (each time increasing in number), he feels the loss of his vital forces and anguishly asks to be awakened and thus liberated from that nightmare. This is state number twelve.

State number thirteen is definitive: the hypnotized patient is totally released from his physical ties; thus, he freely travels within the superior dimensions of space.

It is clearly comprehendible that all of these hypnotic experiments are criminal in their depth. The hypnotist in this case is similar to a pitiless vivisectionist that, with his bit of intelligence, boasts about being wise and tortures poor animals in order to discover the enigmas of nature. The only difference is that in the hypnotic experiment of our narration, the guinea pig is the unhappy hypnotized patient.

The universal Christian Gnostic Movement teaches practical and effective systems in order to separate the double from the physical body at will, and to consciously travel with the double without harmful and detrimental hypnotic trances.

The wise law of contrary analogies invites us to comprehend that if there are thirteen subjective and negative states during a hypnotic state for the projection of the double, likewise, there are another thirteen objective and positive states during a healthy and natural projection of the double.

It is urgent to comprehend that whosoever wants to learn how to consciously travel within the double, the first thing that he needs to do is to awaken his consciousness.

Astral projection is no longer a problem when the consciousness awakens. Sacred scriptures insist on the necessity of awakening, but people continue with their consciousness asleep.

The time has arrived in which we have to comprehend that the double (which was registered in some photographic films and which was analyzed by the Colonel Rochas) is not the true astral body.

The double has been, is, and shall always be of a molecular, lunar, and protoplasmatic nature.

The astral body is a body of an electronic, solar nature. The astral solar body has nothing vague, vaporous, or subjective. The astral solar body is a body of bones and flesh; it is made out of the flesh from paradise, not from the flesh that comes from Adam.

Ordinary human beings (except those very few rare cases) are always born with the famous lunar double and never with the solar astral body.

The wretched intellectual beast possesses the molecular body, body of desires, or lunar double. He does not have a solar astral body. He must build the solar astral body.

Intellectual animals live inside their physical body; yet, during normal sleep and also after death, they live outside of it. Thus, when outside of their physical bodies, they wander around dressed with their molecular double. Pseudo-esoteric and pseudo-occultist people have named the molecular body "astral body." Nonetheless, that molecular body is not the astral body.

The so-called "incorporeal travels" are always performed with the lunar double; after having released its physical ties, it can freely travel through the whole Milky Way without any danger.

Any monk can develop the superior emotional center, and if he is really self-determined, he can eliminate from his interior nature his lower desires and animal passions. Nevertheless, this is not how one builds the astral body.

This issue related with the building of the astral body has been, is, and shall always be an absolutely sexual problem.

There is an esoteric maxim that states: "As above, so below." We can also state: "As below, so above."

If sexual union of the phallus and the uterus is always necessary in order to engender a physical body, then it is also absolutely logical to state that the sexual act is indispensably necessary in order to engender the solar astral body.

Once in a while within this complicated and difficult labyrinth of pseudo-esotericism and pseudo-occultism, some

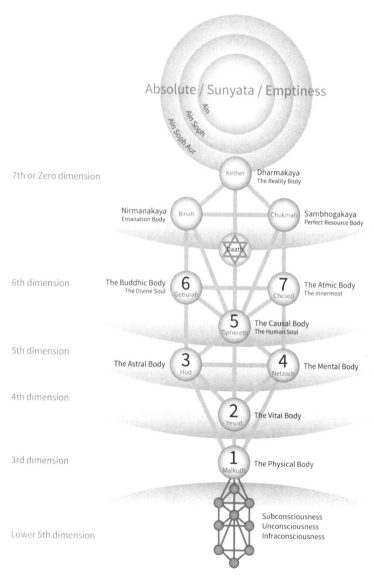

Absolute / Sunyata / Emptiness

Ain
Ain Soph
Ain Soph Aur

7th or Zero dimension — Kether — Dharmakaya
The Reality Body

Nirmanakaya — Binah — Chokmah — Sambhogakaya
Emanation Body — Perfect Resource Body

Daath

6th dimension — The Buddhic Body — **6** Geburah — **7** Chesed — The Atmic Body
The Divine Soul — The Innermost

5 Tiphereth — The Causal Body
The Human Soul

5th dimension — The Astral Body — **3** Hod — **4** Netzach — The Mental Body

4th dimension

2 Yesod — The Vital Body

3rd dimension — **1** Malkuth — The Physical Body

Lower 5th dimension — Subconsciousness
Unconsciousness
Infraconsciousness

THE SEVEN INITIATIONS OF MAJOR MYSTERIES AND THE SOLAR BODIES wandering degenerated infrasexual might appear who will possibly state that the astral body can be built without the necessity of the sexual act because we already have the two poles, masculine and feminine. Those imbecile ignoramuses do not want to comprehend that the time of the Lemurian hermaphrodites has already passed, and that creation without sexual cooperation, without the necessity of the sexual act between man and woman, can only be performed by an authentic hermaphrodite.

The Lemurian hermaphrodites had the phallus and the uterus and also all of the male and female organs totally developed; this is why they could create or reproduce themselves without the necessity of the sexual act. However, all of the pseudo-esoteric and pseudo-occultist people who hate sexual magic have never demonstrated unto us that they have the male and female sexual organs totally developed.

What is as abundant as evil weeds in this perverse, corrupted, and doomed Aryan civilization are the false hermaphrodites, meaning, the homosexuals of Lilith, the gays.

The sexual hydrogen is developed within the human organism according to the musical scale DO-RE-MI-FA-SOL-LA-SI.

The sexual hydrogen SI-12 is very abundant in the semen; this type of hydrogen crystallizes into new human bodies, and when it is wisely transmuted, it takes form within the astral body.

By restraining the sexual impulse in order to avoid the ejaculation of semen, the sexual hydrogen SI-12 receives a special shock that passes it into another second superior octave. This new octave is processed according to the seven notes of the scale DO-RE-MI-FA-SOL-LA-SI.

An esotericist must never ignore that the transformation of substances within the human organism is processed according to the law of the octaves.

The union of the sexual hydrogens SI-12 from a male and female and everything that accompanies these two unities allows us to pass the sexual hydrogen into a second, superior octave, whose outcome is the crystallization of the mentioned hydrogen into the marvelous form that is the astral body. That body of perfection is born of the same material, of the same substance, of the same matter from which the physical body is born. Indeed, this is what the transmutation of lead into gold is; in other words, the transmutation of the physical body into the astral body.

Any organism needs its nourishment, and the astral body is no exception. The nourishment of this body of gold is hydrogen 24.

Chapter 31
The Mental Body

In his great work entitled *Critique of Pure Reasoning,* the great German philosopher Emmanuel Kant demonstrated the possibility of a transcendental logic.

The formulae of a transcendental, superior logic that in itself has the power of opening the doors of mystery were delivered onto humanity written within the Hindustani sacred scriptures many centuries before Bacon and Aristotle.

Esoteric philosophy never believed in the infallibility and totalitarian omnipotence of Aristotle's logic.

It is necessary to comprehend, it is urgent to know, that superior logic existed before the deductive and inductive methods were formulated.

Transcendental logic is the logic of intuition, the logic of the infinite, and the logic of ecstasy.

Every esoteric investigator can find superior logic in the works of Plotinus, in that precious study that deals with intelligible beauty.

Petyr Ouspenski stated:

> "I have called this system of higher logic Tertium Organum because for us it is the third canon—third instrument—of thought after those of Aristotle and Bacon. The first was Organon, the second, Novum Organum. But the third existed earlier than the first."

It is clearly comprehendible that a human being who has this clue of the mind in his power can and must open, without any fear, the marvelous door of the world of cosmic causations.

Through many years of observation and experience, we have witnessed that authentic ecstasy is processed within mathematical laws and logic.

Firstly, let us remember the unity of the mystical experience, which is a very appropriate name. During the state of sacred rapture, all mystics concretely feel something in common, a similar sense and an unmistakable tie of identical character.

Secondly, let us consider the very interesting case of mystical language. By means of a judicious comparative study of religions, we have verified that mystics from different epochs speak the same esoteric language and use the same words. Without a doubt, this demonstrates to us the tremendous reality of mystical experiences.

Thirdly, let us mention the astonishing concordance of the data that in a very intimate way connects mystical experiences with the intrinsic conditions of the world.

From such conditions we can correctly identify the following: sensation of the unity of the whole, time, a very particular new sensation, the sensation of infinitude, pleasure or horror, the integral knowledge of the whole as one, and finally, the unforgettable experience of infinite life and infinite consciousness.

The reactionary, regressive, and retarded types of people who have their minds bottled up within formal logic and who have never bothered to study superior logic behave like true asses when they try to interpret an esoteric book.

Intellectual scoundrels reject mystical experience because they cannot bottle it up in their formal logic.

The gravest of all of this is that these know-it-alls of reactionary logic not only ignore all this, but moreover, they ignore that they ignore.

To qualify the data of mystical experiences is illogical indeed, and is the breaking point of ignorance.

Pure esotericism is based upon mystical experience, and the latter is submitted to mathematics of transfinite numbers and to the unmistakable laws of superior logic.

We studied the astral body in the former chapter. The complete manifestation of our superior emotional center takes place through the astral body.

In this present chapter, it is necessary to comprehend what the mental body is, what the mind is, what superior logic is.

The complete development of our superior mental center can be achieved only through a legitimately solar type of mental body.

Ordinary people only have lunar mental bodies. Such a protoplasmic body is of an animal nature.

The inferior manas or concrete mind about which Theosophy speaks so abundantly is only the lunar mind.

The fact that the intellectual animal has an animal mind is not a marvel, since the irrational beasts also have it. What happened is that the latter never gave an intellectual form to their minds; that is the only difference.

If we truly want to think with a Christ-mind, with superior logic, with the intelligence of a gnostic arhat, it is indispensable to build the mental body.

By restraining the sexual impulse (in order to avoid the ejaculation of semen), the sexual hydrogen SI-12 receives a second special shock, which in fact passes into a third superior octave that is then processed according to the seven notes of the musical scale, DO-RE-MI-FA-SOL-LA-SI.

The crystallization of the sexual hydrogen SI-12 (in the splendid form of the solar mental body) is performed in accordance with the wise law of musical octaves.

It is impossible to build the solar mental body without the seven notes of the third scale.

The yogi who has never practiced Maithuna can convert himself into a true athlete of mental concentration. Nevertheless, he will never build the solar mental body with pranayamas or mental exercises, because this is, has been, and always shall be a one hundred percent sexual problem.

The authentic and legitimate solar mental body is a body of paradise, a body of happiness filled with incalculable perfections.

People who suppose that the solar mental body is a vague, vaporous, and fluidic, etc., body are lamentably mistaken. The solar mental body is also an organism of bones and flesh, the flesh of paradise; it is flesh that does not come from Adam.

The solar mental body is born from the sexual act without the ejaculation of the ens seminis, and it also needs nourishment and development. The mental solar body is nourished with hydrogen 12.

The solar mental body has three hundred thousand clans or magnetic centers and all of them must vibrate within the same tone... and without even a hint of arrhythmia.

Those initiates who possess solar mental bodies always think with superior logic, with transcendental logic.

By taking the axioms of Aristotle as a model, we can intelligently express the principal axiom of superior logic in the following way, "A is as much A as it is not A. Everything is as much A as it is not A." Everything is everything.

The logical formula, "A is as much A as it is not A," corresponds to the formula of transfinite mathematics that states, "A magnitude can be bigger or smaller than itself."

After reading the above lines, intellectual scoundrels who are bottled up within formal logic will despise these formulae and will state that these are illogical and absurd.

People with lunar minds are incapable of comprehending the superior logic of solar men.

Now, beloved reader, you will comprehend why intellectual scoundrels become true asses when they try to interpret ancient theogonies.

The lunar mind is a true ass upon which we have to ride if what we truly want is to victoriously enter into the heavenly Jerusalem on Palm Sunday.

Chapter 32

The Causal Body

Through this chapter we are arriving at the causal world, at the marvelous world of conscious will, in the electronic region.

There below, in the molecular world, on the other shore across the evil river, there is a sad place not for martyrdoms but for sighs, with lamentations and loud moans, resounding through the air that forever whirls around through darkness.

There in that Limbo of the molecular world lives Virgil, the poet of Mantua, the master of Dante. There also live all of those pseudo-esoteric and pseudo-occult, naive, innocent souls who were not washed of their original sin, and who believed that they could Self-realize in depth without the need to work with the Maithuna in the ninth sphere. Those naive souls committed the mistake of not getting dressed with the three holy virtues (the three solar bodies: astral, mental, and causal).

In former chapters, we studied the astral and mental solar bodies; now we are going to study the body of conscious will, the causal body.

Gnostic students need to have a lot of faith and be very well cloaked with the three holy virtues, if indeed they do not want to continue in Limbo.

Asian fakirs fight in a frightful way within themselves in order to develop the force of willpower. The entire fakir's path consists of multiple, incredible, and difficult physical practices. Any fakir is very capable of adopting any difficult physical position while keeping his body steady for hours, months, and even years; or he can sit under a tree on top of an anthill or under the scorching rays of the tropical sun. Any fakir is very capable of sitting on a bare stone under the sun with his arms opened in the form of a cross, or amongst thorns and caltrops for entire months or years.

Indeed, fakirs develop the force of willpower in a severe way by means of all of these physical tortures. Nevertheless, they do not achieve the creation of the body of conscious will (causal body) because this is a one hundred percent sexual problem.

If the body of conscious will (causal body) could be built with the physical tortures of fakirs, then according to the law of correspondences and analogies and in obedience to the hermetic maxim that states, "As above so below," we would also have to state that the body of bones and flesh, the physical body, can also be built with such practices. Consequently, the sexual act of father and mother would be superseded. Therefore, to affirm such an absurdity would be the lamentable consequence of a mistaken idea.

The body of conscious will (causal body) can only be built within the flaming forge of Vulcan.

We can and must give onto the sexual hydrogen SI-12 (by means of Maithuna in the ninth sphere) a very special third shock in order to pass it into the fourth superior octave of DO-RE-MI-FA-SOL-LA-SI.

The crystallization of the sexual hydrogen SI-12 into the extraordinary form of the causal body (body of conscious will) is performed in accordance with the seven notes of the scale.

The solar astral body is born in the Third Initiation of Fire. The solar mental body is born in the Fourth Initiation of Fire. The causal body or body of conscious will is born in the Fifth Initiation of Fire.

To possess a causal body or body of conscious will is equivalent to converting oneself into a mahatma, into an adept of the White Lodge.

The First Initiation of Fire occurs when the serpent of the physical body makes contact with the atom of the Father at the magnetic field located in the root of the nose.

The Second Initiation of Fire occurs when the serpent of the vital body makes contact with the atom of the Father at the magnetic field located in the root of the nose.

The Third Initiation of Fire occurs when the serpent of the astral body reaches the third chamber of the heart, after having passed through the Amrita Nadi.

The advent of the Fourth Initiation of Fire occurs when the serpent of the mental body reaches the fourth secret chamber of the heart, after having passed from the brain into the cardias through the Amrita Nadi.

The Fifth Initiation is a marvelous cosmic event that occurs when the fifth serpent, the serpent of the causal body, reaches the fifth esoteric chamber of the cardias after having reached the brain.

The fifth cosmic festival is splendid; the newborn causal child is carried on the chariot of the centuries into the temple. For this glorious event, the altar is covered with Veronica's sacred shroud, upon which the divine rostrum crowned with thorns is resplendently shown.

Veronica's sacred shroud represents Christ-will, the body of conscious will.

The will of Christ can only perform the will of the Father, *"on earth as it is in heaven. Father, if it is possible, pass this chalice away from me, but not my will but Thine be done."*

Amidst the archaic ruins of the Age of Bronze, many heads crowned with crowns of thorns have been found, chiseled upon living rocks.

The figure of Ecce Homo has a crown not only to remind us of the historical event related with the martyrdom of our beloved Jesus Christ, but also to indicate the necessity of building the solar body of Christ-will.

It is urgent to know, it is necessary to comprehend, that the causal body is an ineffable organism that also needs food for its nourishment and development. The nourishment of the causal body or body of conscious will is hydrogen 6.

A lot has been written about the four bodies (physical, astral, mental, and causal). Some people have written to me and have asked, why we did not mention the Lingam Sarira (vital body)? My answer to these people is always the same: the vital body is only the superior part of the physical body, and therefore, in esotericism the vital body is considered one with the cellular body.

Inexpert clairvoyants confuse the lunar bodies with the solar bodies. They even commit the mistake of believing that the wretched intellectual beast (mistakenly called a human being) already has a perfect septenary constitution.

It is lamentable that inexpert clairvoyants confuse the buddhata (which is deposited within the lunar protoplasmic bodies) with the authentic and genuine causal body or solar body of conscious will.

The buddhata or Essence is only a fraction of the human soul within us. Therefore, to confuse the buddhata or Essence with the causal body is an absurdity.

On a certain occasion, at the table of a banquet, my real Being, the Innermost, took a seat with two other people; the first was my Buddhi, my Valkyrie, the other person was me, myself, the human soul dressed with the causal body.

My Lord took the floor and said, "I have two souls; the first is Buddhi, the spiritual soul, and it is feminine; the second is the human soul and it is masculine. The human soul is the soul who works. Thus, while the human soul works, the spiritual soul plays. This is my doctrine."

This lesson was taught onto me by my real Being Samael in the causal world or world of conscious will.

Chapter 33
The Second Birth

In our former chapter, we stated that the Being, the Innermost, the divine spirit of each living creature, has two souls: Buddhi and superior Manas.

The Being himself is Atman, the ineffable. If we commit the error of giving the Being the qualifications of superior "I," alter ego, subliminal "I," or divine ego, etc., we commit blasphemy, because that which is divine, the reality, can never fall into the heresy of separability.

Superior and inferior are two sections of the same thing. Superior "I" or inferior "I" are two sections of the same pluralized ego (Satan).

The Being is the Being, and the reason for the Being to be is to be the Being. The Being transcends the personality, the "I," and individuality.

Atman, the Being, rends himself asunder into Buddhi and Manas. Buddhi is our Valkyrie, our divine spouse (the Beatrice of Dante), the spiritual soul. Manas, the superior Manas (mistakenly called causal ego in Theosophy), is the human soul, the eternal spouse of Valkyrie.

Buddhi and Manas are indeed the two twin souls, the two fish of the zodiacal sign of Pisces within the profound waters of eternal mother space.

The opposites masculine-feminine are conciliated within the monad in order to form the immortal triad Atman-Buddhi-Manas.

The immortal triad of any lunar creature is not incarnated. That triad lives freely within the Milky Way; yet, it is connected to the physical body through the famous Antakarana, the thread of life (the silver cord).

The wretched intellectual animal (mistakenly called a human being) only possesses a fraction of the human soul within his protoplasmic lunar bodies. Unfortunately, that fraction, buddhata, or Essence is bottled up within the pluralized "I."

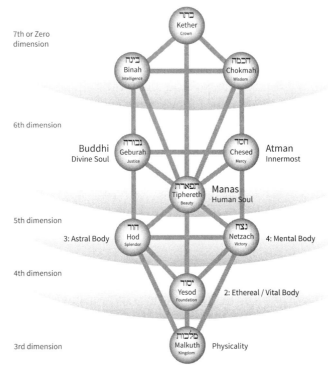

THE MONAD ON THE TREE OF LIFE

Thus, as Atman rends himself asunder into Buddhi and superior Manas, likewise the superior Manas rends himself asunder into the buddhata, into the Essence.

Indeed, the wretched intellectual animal could not incarnate in himself (within himself) his immortal triad because he only possesses internal protoplasmic lunar bodies. Obviously, in his condition he will not resist the tremendous electro-spiritual voltage of Atman-Buddhi-Manas and would die.

Whoever wants to incarnate in himself (within himself) the totality of his soul, his divine immortal triad, must first descend into the ninth sphere (sex) in order to create his electronic solar bodies.

Isabel lives within Atman. At this moment, the particle Is, the eternal and feminine principle and the Isiac mysteries come into my memory. Abel is the human soul, the noble spouse of the eternal, beloved, feminine soul.

In fact, to incarnate the divine immortal triad signifies the Second Birth, which means to come out of the ninth sphere.

The child who is born comes out from the womb. Whosoever is born within the superior worlds comes out of the ninth sphere (sex).

Whosoever reaches the Second Birth is admitted into the Temple of the Twice-born. Whosoever reaches the Second Birth has to renounce sex for all eternity. The sexual act is absolutely forbidden for the Twice-born. Whosoever violates this law will lose his solar bodies and will fall into the valley of bitterness.

Whosoever reaches the Second Birth (which Jesus taught to Nicodemus) enters in fact and by his own right into the Magis Regnum, Regnum Dei.

No one can enter into the Kingdom dressed in the rags of a beggar (lunar rags). I know the case of an adept lady who in ten years of intense work in the ninth sphere built her wedding gown, meaning, her solar bodies. Now, this adept lady is an inhabitant of the kingdom; she dwells among the Elohim.

It is difficult to establish the precise amount of time for the Second Birth, because this depends on the quality of work. Some people can attain the Second Birth in fifteen or twenty years of intense work in the ninth sphere; others can endure much more time.

Remember, gnostic brothers and sisters, that our motto is thelema (willpower). Realization of the Innermost Self is only for men and women with thelema.

Before any Twice-born, two paths are open: the path of the right, and the path of the left.

The path of the right is for those who work in the dissolution of the "I." The path of the left is for those who commit the error of not working with the dissolution of the "I."

The Twice-born who does not reduce his lunar ego to cosmic dust converts himself into an abortion of the cosmic mother. He becomes a marut, and there are thousands of types of maruts. Certain Asian sects and some Muslim tribes commit the lamentable error of rendering cult to all of those families of maruts.

Every marut, every hasnamuss, has in fact two personalities: one white and another black (one solar and another
lunar). The Innermost, the Being dressed with the electronic
solar bodies, is the white personality of the hasnamuss, and
the pluralized "I" dressed with the protoplasmic lunar bodies
is the hasnamuss' black personality. Therefore, these maruts
have a double center of gravity.

To comprehend each of our psychological defects in each
and every of the forty-nine regions of the subconsciousness is
vital. However, it is not enough for the elimination of all the
submerged entities that personify our errors.

The mind cannot radically change anything. The mind
itself can have the luxury of hiding its own errors, or justify-
ing them, or condemning them, or passing them from one
department of the mind into another. Nonetheless, the mind
is not capable of dissolving or eliminating them.

Extra help is necessary, a special aid; someone who can
take out, who can extract, who can remove the "I's" (those
submerged entities which personify our psychological errors)
and cast them into the infernal worlds.

Fortunately, each one of us has a particular cosmic mother, a Divine Mother. She is that mathematical point of mother
space. She is that mother point from where the Being, Atman,
emanated. She is, in fact, the very root of our monad, the particular mother of our monad.

That mathematical point, that mater point, is in itself
immeasurable. Its existence is more real than all that which is
measurable. Measurability is, without a doubt, an extremely
harsh indication of existence, because measurability is in itself
an extremely conditioned concept.

The monks of a Chinese Buddhist pagoda taught me a
very special way of praying; it is an asana or sacred posture in
order to pray to our inner buddha and, in fact, to the particular cosmic mother of the inner buddha.

Indication

First, kneel down. Second, sit on your heels in the Muslim
style. Third, extend your arms to form the horizontal beam

of a cross. Fourth, pray to your Divine Mother and bend your trunk forward, then backwards while keeping your arms extended and while remaining firmly seated on your heels.

After having comprehended this or that psychological defect in all and each one of the subconscious levels of the mind, we must pray for help to our particular Divine Mother; thus, we beg her to eliminate from the lunar bodies the "I," the entity that personifies the defect.

Without the help of our Divine Mother, it is impossible to eliminate the demonic "I's" that live within the lunar bodies.

Previous comprehension of any psychological defect is indispensable before our Divine Mother proceeds to eliminate the submerged entity that personifies it.

When the pluralized "I" has been absolutely eliminated, we depart from the atomic infernos and enter into the purgatorial molecular region.

We must fry or brown the seeds of the "I" within purgatory, because if these seeds are not burned, they will germinate again. Remember that the pluralized "I" can also resuscitate like the phoenix bird from within its own ashes.

The elimination of the protoplasmic lunar bodies is only possible when the pluralized "I" is dead and when the evil tendencies or seeds have been reduced (by means of fire) to cosmic dust.

> *"Render therefore unto Caesar the things which are Caesar's; and unto God the things that are God's."* —Matthew 22:21

The lunar bodies belong to nature; she lends them to us, and therefore we have to return them to her.

THE CRUCIFIXION OF PETER

Chapter 34

Peter, Judas, and John

It is written that there is a straight, narrow, and frightfully difficult path. However, to comprehend this better, we are going to divide the path into two sections, into two aspects, into two paths.

Peter, the master of Maithuna, Patar, dies crucified on an inverted cross, with his head towards the ground and his feet towards the heavens.

John, I.E.O.U.A.N., the Word itself, rests his head on the heart of the great Kabir Jesus, as if saying: love is nourished with love.

The manner in which the hierophant Peter dies crucified on an inverted cross is in order to indicate to us the work with the brute stone. It was necessary for Peter to die crucified with his head pointing towards the ground and his feet towards the heavens in order to show us the decent into the ninth sphere, into Dante's ninth circle of hell.

There is an intimate relation between the ninth sphere and the cubic stone. Let us remember that the study of the novenary always concludes with the pointed cubic stone. Let us remember, gnostic brothers and sisters, that the sacred stone has nine faces, and that the stone itself reunites the perfection of the cube and the equilibrated elevation of the pyramid with a quadrangular base.

It is urgent to know that the horizontal cteis[61] is crossed with the vertical phallus in order to form the cross. The cross itself is one hundred percent phallic. It is indispensable to know that when the pointed cubic stone is opened and its faces lie spread open, we inevitably obtain the symbol of the cross as a perfect expression of the magisterium of fire.

Hebraic kabbalah places the sephirah Yesod in the sexual organs. The cubic stone of Yesod is sex itself.

It is urgent, it is indispensable, to transport up to heaven the cup of election, the cup of Hermes; however, we must first

---

61 Greek symbol of the vagina. See glossary.

work with the hard stone and give onto it the perfect cubic shape by treading on the path of Peter.

It is written in the sacred scriptures that Peter asked Jesus, in reference to John:

> "Lord and what shall this man do? (The great Kabir) Jesus answered him: "If I will that he tarry till I come, what is that to thee? Follow thou me." —John 21:21, 22

Curled up, John (the Word) tarries in the depth of the Ark, lingering, waiting for the moment of his realization.

No one can work in the path of John without having tread upon the path of Peter.

The fundamental clue of the path of Peter is the Maithuna. In the path of John, the sexual act is absolutely forbidden.

There is an abyss between the path of Peter and the path of John. It is indispensable to establish a bridge over that precipice in order to unite the two paths. It is urgent to hang, to lynch, Judas on the bridge.

Judas is the pluralized "I," the myself that betrays the intimate Christ from moment to moment. In *The Divine Comedy*, Dante describes Judas' head within Lucifer's jaws, and his feet dangling.

Judas is the lunar legion of diabolic "I's" that every intellectual animal carries within himself; it is made out of the granulations of Luciferic fire or negative Fohat.

Lucifer is in the atomic infernos of the intellectual animal. It is that passionate, instinctual, sexual, and bestial fire that every person carries within.

Judas is the crystallization of Lucifer. It is Lucifer's word that takes form. This is why Dante places Judas inside the sinister jaws of Lucifer. The existence of Judas would be impossible without Lucifer. Just as the fish dies when it is out of the water, likewise Judas dies when out of the Luciferic fire.

The original sin is absolutely Luciferic, sexual, and passionate. The root of any psychological defect is one hundred percent Luciferic. The origin of all evil is in Lucifer. Judas is the word of Lucifer.

If you want to hang Judas on the bridge in order to unite the path of Peter and the path of John, then kill Judas first.

Remember, beloved reader, that Lucifer lives in the center of the Earth, in the ninth sphere, in the depth of the universe.

Lucifer is the staircase to ascend; Lucifer is the staircase to descend. Dante places in the mouth of Virgil the following phrase:

> "Expect that by such stairs as these, we must depart from evil so extreme." —Inferno, Canto 34

To gradually extinguish the Luciferic fire is equivalent to ascending the Luciferic staircase degree by degree.

> "Virgil (the poet crowned with laurels) and sublime Dante (as a child) clutched Lucifer's neck; he caught fast the shaggy sides when the wings were opened enough, and down from pile to pile he descended and stepped between the thick fell and the jagged ice. And when he reached the point (whereat the thigh upon the swelling of the haunches turns) with pain and much struggle, he turned his head around where his feet stood before, and grappled at the fell as one who mounts; that into hell he thought he turned again." —Inferno, Canto 34

One descends into the ninth sphere by the Luciferic ladder. One ascends or comes out from the ninth sphere by the Luciferic ladder.

Lucifer, that miserable worm that passes through the world, the passionate fire, the tempting serpent of Eden, the repugnant viper that granted onto Eve the bitter food, is our worst adversary.

Lucifer is the antithesis of Christ. It is that malignant reptile that slyly writhes through the green grass and perfumed flowers of spirituality.

It would be impossible to reduce Judas to cosmic dust without previously extinguishing the Luciferic fire.

We have to perform a double work within our own atomic infernos: first, to transmute the lead into gold, and second, to execute Judas by hanging.

When Dante performed this double alchemical and magical work, his guru told him:

> "'Arise,' my master cried, 'upon thy feet.
> The way is long, and much uncouth the road;
> And now within one hour and a half of noon

The sun returns.'

"It was no palace-hall
Lofty and luminous wherein we [master and disciple] stood,
But natural dungeon where ill - footing was
And scant supply of light." —Inferno, Canto 34

Any gnostic that has concluded the double work can verify this himself.

It is written that whosoever abandons the atomic infernos of nature immediately enters into the purgatorial region in order to fry or brown the seeds of the "I" (as the Hindustani yogis state). The evil tendencies of Judas remain within those malignant germs.

The complicated purgatorial work, that is, to incinerate satanic seeds, is terribly difficult, and bitterer than bile.

Judas has three Satanic aspects, because he betrays us in the world of desires, in the world of the mind, and in the field of willpower. This reminds us of the three traitors of Hiram Abiff. Also to my memory comes the image of Lucifer holding one traitor within each of his three jaws.

Dante stated that purgatory has seven regions. However, if we multiply seven by seven, then we will have the kabbalistic number forty-nine. These are the forty-nine regions of the subconsciousness, the forty-nine stables of Augeas.

It is a bitter and difficult task to eliminate the Luciferic fire in each and every one of the forty-nine regions of the subconsciousness. Whosoever performs this work has to weep tears of blood.

The esoteric ordeals in each and every one of the forty-nine subconscious regions are incessantly repeated, and the Twice-born intimately suffers within the frightful moral torments of the purgatorial state.

An in-depth analysis of this esoteric purgatorial work allows us to integrally comprehend that without the aid of our Divine Mother (within whom all of the powers of our sacred monad are contained), failure would be inevitable.

From the sphere of solar fire and the path of John, the great law excludes the souls who did not kill Judas within themselves and who did not purify themselves amidst the flames of intimate purgatory.

Hasnamussen are never admitted within the spheres of happiness.

The absolute access into the solar heavens is only possible after having burned even the seeds of the pluralized "I."

The Ark

Chapter 35

The Path of John

Since ancient times, the authentic and genuine esoteric work has always been symbolized by a chariot pulled by oxen transporting the Holy Ark. Therefore, to forget this basic symbol and to go astray from the path is frightening.

The chariot reminds us of the human being and his internal bodies. The oxen brings into our imagination the sacred cow with five legs, the sacred symbol of the Divine Mother. The sacred Ark encloses the mysteries of sex; the Ark itself is sex.

In other times, the humble psalmist always paved the way for the holy cup, the cup of Hermes, by dancing and jumping; and in that moment, he was nothing more than a king.

This also reminds us of the whirling dervishes of Mohammedan esotericism. The objective of all of these dances is to awaken the consciousness.

Within ancient schools of mysteries, sex yoga (Maithuna) was never taught to the neophytes who previously did not accomplish the basic requirement of awakening their consciousness.

Asleep, unconscious neophytes cannot have cognizant consciousness of the work that they are performing; thus sooner or later they abandon the great work.

Nevertheless, in these times of world crisis, we have to take the risk and publicly teach sex yoga no matter what the cost might be, because at the present time everything is lost. Therefore, at least we can rescue "the hat of the drowning one."

Present human beings are simple slugs from the mud who were born with the purpose of forming an angelical butterfly within them that could soar towards the justice of God without any impediments. Unfortunately, these defected insects, these miserable chrysalides, almost all remain without any development. Indeed, they only serve as nourishment for the entrails of this planet on which they live.

It is urgent to tread upon the path of Peter and to hang Judas on the bridge in order to have the right of treading upon the heavenly path, the path of the Word, the path of John.

If to practice sexual magic (Maithuna) is mandatory on the path of Peter, then on the path of John sex is absolutely forbidden.

The living, golden-feathered eagle of the spirit soars in the sky throughout the starry firmament, and hovers with open wings waiting to descend, in the habit of hunting exclusively in the purgatorial fields. Like lightning, this mysterious eagle of the spirit majestically lunges in order to snatch aloft the soul to the higher spheres of the universal fire. Ganymede, metamorphosed as an eagle, was snatched aloft to high Olympus in order to serve the gods as a cupbearer.

It is impossible to enter onto the heavenly path without having previously prepared oneself within the fields of the purgatorial region.

Whosoever enters into the interior purgatory receives the mark of the letter "P" seven times upon his forehead. Upon the sidereal forehead of the Twice-born, the guardian angel of purgatory inscribes such a letter seven times with the blunt point of his flaming sword.

The guardian angel of purgatory says, "Look, when entered, that thou wash these scars away." The washing of feet symbolizes the same. It is written that at the Last Supper, before rising onto Golgotha, Jesus the great Kabir washed the feet of his disciples. The scars of the seven "P's" upon the forehead are washed away little by little as the Luciferic fire and all of the seeds of Judas are eliminated.

The silver chariot (loaded with multiple stones made of the same lunar metal) must be delivered by the divine couple, Buddhi-Manas; the chariot must be delivered as a gift to the temple of the Divine Mother.

The sexual act is prohibited for the Twice-born not only in the physical world, but also in each and every one of the forty-nine regions of the subconsciousness.

Thus, just as a tree has many branches, likewise many transverse paths sprout from the direct path. Many of those paths take us to elemental paradises where we convert ourselves into genii or devas of nature. Other paths lead us into the entrails of the cosmos where we transform ourselves into planetary gods. Other paths submerge us into the joy of Nirvana, etc.

Those who abandon the direct path, those who enter onto the transverse paths, sooner or later have to reincarnate in order to return to the path of John, the heavenly path, the direct path.

Omniscience and omnipotence are very coveted qualities; they confer on us remarkable powers over all of nature. If we renounce these tremendous powers, then the destruction of certain seeds occurs that in one way or another (after every great pralaya) always brings us into new manifestations through successive mahamanvantaras.

It is urgent to know, it is indispensable to comprehend, that the universe is made up of an illusory nature. We need to die, to die, and to die within ourselves, and to renounce, renounce, and renounce, and to cease existing within all of the seven cosmos in order to have the right TO BE within the Absolute.

Wu

"no, not, nothing, non-existing"

Chapter 36
Story of the Chinese Master Kao Feng

The Chinese Master Kao Feng entered the priesthood at the age of fifteen and was ordained at the age of twenty in the monastery of Chin Tzu.

Kao Feng comprehended that all human beings are miserable, sleeping automatons. Therefore, he proposed to "awaken his consciousness" as soon as possible by means of the science of meditation.

> "First I worked under Master Tuan Chiao. He taught me to work on the Hua Tou, "Where was I before birth, and where will I be after death?" [I followed his instructions and practiced, but could not concentrate my mind because of the bifurcation in this very Hua Tou.]" —Garma C.C.Chang, The Practice of Zen (1959)

This Hua Tou divided his mind into many opinions and opposite concepts, and Kao Feng suffered unbelievably. He yearned with all of his heart and all of his soul to liberate himself from mental dualism.

It is impossible to experience reality as long as the Essence, the buddhata, the soul, continues bottled up within intellectual dualism.

Opposing opinions, the struggle between opposite concepts and antithetic ideas, correspond to the different illusory functions of the mind.

Thus, Kao Feng grievously wept tears of blood; he only aspired to free himself from the bottle of mental dualism, but he failed with the Hua Tou of Master Tuan Chiao.

The story goes on to tell of Kao Feng's terrible anguish and desperation. He sought Master Hsueh Yen who, feeling compassion for his pain, taught him the powerful mantra **Wu** 無. Master Hsueh Yen demanded daily reports from him about his work.

The mantra Wu is chanted with a double woo, woo... as if imitating a howling hurricane, amongst the boisterous waves of the furious sea.

During this exercise, the mind must be absolutely quiet and in a profound and frightful silence (both in the exterior as well as in the interior); not even the slightest desire, nor the most insignificant thought must agitate the profound lake of the mind.

> "Because his explanations [Master Hsueh Yen] were so systematic and understandable, [I became so dependent on him that through negligence and laziness] I did not make any effort in my own work." —Garma C.C.Chang, The Practice of Zen (1959)

However, Master Hsueh Yen, in spite of his accustomed sweetness, also knew how to be very severe when necessary.

> "One day, when I had just entered his room, he said to me, 'Who has dragged this corpse here for you?' He had hardly finished this sentence when he chased me out of his room.

> "Later I followed the example of Chin Shan and stayed in the meditation hall." —Garma C.C.Chang, The Practice of Zen (1959)

The exercises of inner meditation gradually provoke the "awakening of the consciousness," the awakening of the buddhata.

Before the internal supersensible representations, the neophyte begins to react in a very distinct, very different manner than usual. He begins saying, "I am dreaming. This is a dream." Later, happily he exclaims, "I am out of my physical body; my physical body is asleep, but I am out of my physical body, totally cognizant and awake."

> "One day in a dream I suddenly remembered the koan, "All things are reducible to one, but to what is the one reducible?" At that moment a "doubt-sensation" abruptly arose within me so that I did not know east from west or north from south. During the sixth day in this state [unhappy mental state], while I was chanting prayers [in the Lumisial of meditation, with infinite devotion] with the assembly, I lifted my head and [clairvoyantly] saw the last two sentences of the stanza composed by the Fifth Patriarch, Fa Yan:

> "'Oh, it is you, the fellow
> I have known all the time,
> Who goes and returns
> In the thirty thousand days of one hundred years!'

> "Immediately I broke up the sentence: 'Who has dragged this corpse here for you?' (For it had stuck in my mind since the day

Master Hsueh Yen had put it before me [it was impossible to forget].) I felt as if my spirit had been extinguished and my mind blown away and then revived again from death itself. It was like dropping the burden of a carrying pole weighing twenty pounds! I was then twenty-four years old, and so had achieved my original wish to realize Zen [the awakening of his consciousness] within three years.

"Afterwards I was asked, 'Can you master yourself in the bright daytime?' I answered, 'Yes, I can.' 'Can you master yourself when dreaming?' Again my answer was, 'Yes, I can.' 'Where, in dreamless sleep, is the Master?' To this question I had no answer or explanation [thus, new inner sufferings afflicted the depth of his soul]. The Master said to me, 'From now on I do not want you to study Buddhism or learn the Dharma, nor to study anything, either old or new. I just want you to eat when you are hungry and to sleep when you are tired. As soon as you wake from sleep, alert your mind and ask yourself, 'Who is the very Master of this awakening, and where does he rest his body and lead his life?'

"I then made up my mind [with total firmness] that I would understand this thing in one way or another even though it meant that I should appear to be an idiot for the rest of my life." —Garma C.C.Chang, The Practice of Zen (1959)

Kao Feng was certainly a man of thelema (willpower).

"Five years passed. One day, when I was questioning this matter while sleeping, my brother monk who slept beside me in the dormitory pushed his pillow so that it fell with a heavy thump to the floor. At that moment my doubts were suddenly broken up. I felt as if I had jumped out of a trap. All the pigling koans of the Masters and the Buddhas and all the different issues and events of both present and ancient times became transparently clear to me. Henceforth all things were settled; nothing under the sun remained but peace." —Garma C.C.Chang, The Practice of Zen (1959)

At that moment, Kao Feng became enlightened.

There are two types of enlightenment: the first is usually called "dead water" because it has attachments. The second is praised as the "great life" because it is enlightenment without attachments: the Illuminating Void.

The first type of enlightenment is awakened consciousness, Self-cognizance.

The second type of enlightenment (even when in the Fourth Way) is called objective knowledge, objective con-

192 THE NARROW WAY · Samael Aun Weor

sciousness; indeed, it transcends that which is called consciousness.

Therefore, the second type of enlightenment has nothing to do with the consciousness; it is the Being, and the reason for the Being to be is to be the same Being.

Kao Feng became, in fact, a Turiya,[63] because by means of in-depth meditation he achieved absolute independence from his mind.

The world is crystallized mind; this is why it is Maya (illusion). Therefore, this world, an illusory form of the mind, will at end of the great cosmic day be reduced to cosmic dust.

Indeed, my person, your person, people, things, and creatures of all kinds do not exist. They are merely illusory mental forms that must be reduced to cosmic dust.

The only reality is Brahma,[64] the spirit-infinite-space, within which the eternal feminine and the sacred monad are contained. All else is illusion.

In the end, we must become lost within something... millions of human beings become lost within the infernal worlds. But, the gnostics, we prefer to become lost within Brahma.

It is urgent to stop the mental contents (chitta) from acquiring diverse forms (vrittis) during profound inner meditation. When our mental waves have ceased and our intellectual lake has become calm, then the illusion produced by the waves of the opposites also ceases within us; thus, the experience of reality arrives.

When the spirit-infinite-space called Brahma assumes any shape in order to speak with his avatars, he is then Ishvara, the master of all masters; he is a very special purusha,[65] without mind, exempt of suffering, actions, results, and desires.

Unfortunately, the only thing that the Luciferic intellect does is torment us with the incessant battle of the opposites. Kao Feng liberated himself from the mind and became a Turiya.

---

63 The fourth and highest of the four states of consciousness. See glossary.
64 A Hindu symbol of the Absolute.
65 (Sanskrit) Supreme being.

Chapter 37
The Passion of Al-Hallaj

The omnicosmic and most holy Al-Hallaj was born in Madina al-Bayda, a little village in the ancient province of Fars, in southern Persia, in the year 224 A.H. / 857 C.E., and was the grandson of a devotee of the great Master Zoroaster.

Al-Hallaj was initiated into the great mysteries of Sufism. Arabian traditions tell us that when he was forty years old, he disagreed with the jurists and orthodox traditional, religious scholars; thus, he went to the streets to directly teach the multitudes the sublime principles of spiritual life.

It is written that Al-Hallaj, the great Sufi master, taught with his word and with his example. Indefatigably, he travelled throughout Iran, India, Turkey, etc., reaching even the very borders of ancient China.

The great Master Al-Hallaj was without a doubt a tremendous revolutionary. Jealous and envious politicians accused him of being a dangerous agitator. Religious scholars of the law accused him of being a heretic when he mixed the human with the divine. When divulging the esoteric mysteries amidst the people, the masters of Sufism themselves did not have any difficulty in accusing him of breaking the discipline of that which is arcane. Thus, as is natural in those cases, judges were willing to condemn him for many supposed crimes, for example: being a fraud, impostor, black magician, warlock, sorcerer, profaner of mysteries, people's agitator, ignorant preacher, enemy of the government, etc.

Al-Hallaj, the mystical Sufi, was imprisoned in an infamous jail for nine years, and afterwards vilely mutilated and executed on March 27, 922, in the year 309 of Hejira.

Sacred Islamic traditions tell us that when the terrible night came, the night in which he was taken from his dungeon in order to be executed at dawn, he stood and uttered the ritualistic prayer and prostrated himself two times.

Those who saw him said that when his prayer was concluded, he persistently repeated, "Deceitfulness, deceitfulness..." through the long and dark night, and after a long and profound silence, he exclaimed, "Truthfulness, truthfulness," and raised up again. He tied a veil on his head, covered himself with his blessed shroud, extended his sacred Christified hands, turned his divine countenance towards the Kaaba, entered into ecstasy, and spoke with his internal God.

At daylight, when he left the prison, the multitudes saw him happily dancing in a complete, joyful ecstasy under the weight of his irons.

The merciless executioners took him to the public square, where, after flagellating him five hundred times, they cut off his hands and feet.

Ancient traditions from the Arabian world state that after having been flagellated and mutilated, Al-Hallaj was crucified. Many people heard him talking in ecstasy to his Father who is in secret from his own Golgotha: "Oh God of mine! I am going to enter into the abode of my wishes; there I will contemplate thy marvels. Oh God of mine! If you manifest thy love even to him that wounds Thee, how then would Thou not give thy love to the one who is wounded because of Thee?"

After this prayer sprouted from the most holy heart of Al-Hallaj, the people who watched the torture saw Abu Bakr Al-Shibli, while advancing towards the scaffold of tortures, shout very strongly the following verse, "Did we not prohibit thee to receive guests, whether man or angel?"

Then Abu Bakr asked, "What is mysticism?"

Al-Hallaj answered, "Behold, his minor degree before thee."

Abu Bakr asked again, "And where is his supreme degree?"

Al-Hallaj answered, "Thou cannot have access unto it; nonetheless, tomorrow thou shall see what shall come. I testify it in the Divine Mystery within which it exists, albeit it is hidden for thee."

At the evening hour, the hour of prayer, came the order of the cruel sanguinary Caliph, authorizing the beheading of the victim; yet, his executioners said, "It is too late; let him be decapitated tomorrow."

Very early in the morning, the Caliph's command was fulfilled, and Al-Hallaj, still alive, was brought down from the cross and carried away in order to have his throat slit. Then, a certain witness heard Al-Hallaj uttering in a loud voice, "What the Ecstatic One wants is the Unique, and no-one else but Himself." Thereafter, filled with ecstasy he recited the following sacred verse, "Those who do not believe in the last hour are dragged with haste towards it; however, the believers wait for it with a reverential fear, since they know it is the Truth."

Thus, this is how with these solemn words the life of the omnicosmic and most holy Al-Hallaj concluded. Hence, his venerable, bleeding, blessed head fell under the edge of the sword as a sanguinary holocaust on the altar of supreme sacrifice for humanity.

The poisonous hatred of his executioners was so great that they did not even authorize his cadaver to be shrouded or have a burial service.

Ancient traditions of Islam tell us that the sacred ashes of the old Sufi Al-Hallaj were dispersed in the winds from the heights of the Manarah.

Ancient Arabic legends state that instead of a white blanket, this saint's cadaver was rolled up in a filthy rug formerly damped in petroleum.

When the holy body burned, consumed by the fire of the holocaust, the whole of nature shook filled with infinite terror.

The great hierophant Sufi Al-Hallaj, by means of chisel and hammer, transformed the brute stone and gave a perfect cubic shape onto it.

Before physically dying, the great, immolated Al-Hallaj was already absolutely dead psychologically.

The resplendent diamond soul of Mansur Al-Hallaj is treading upon the heavenly path heading towards the Absolute.

The great Sufi initiate Al-Hallaj was born, died, and sacrificed himself completely for humanity.

Now it is worthwhile to conclude this chapter with that ineffable prayer written with infinite love by the Mohammedan Christ Mansur Al-Hallaj entitled:

Oh Thou, Wholeness of My Wholeness...

*Lo and behold, here I am, here I am, oh
   my secret, oh my confidence!*

*Lo and behold, here I am, here I am, oh Thou my
   aspiration, oh Thou my consequence!*

*I call upon Thee... No, Thou art the one
   who calls me towards Thee!*

*How could I have talked to Thee, if Thou
   would not have talked to me?*

*Oh Thou, essence of the essence of my exis-
   tence, oh Thou, end result of my design,*

*Thou who makest me talk, oh Thou, my enun-
   ciations, Thou my blinks!*

Oh Thou, wholeness of my wholeness, oh my ear, oh my sight!

Oh my totality, my constitution, and my parts!

*Oh Thou, wholeness of my wholeness, whole-
   ness of everything, equivocal enigma,*

*I darken the wholeness of thy wholeness when
   wanting to express thy being!*

*Oh Thou, from whom my spirit was suspend-
   ed before now when dying of ecstasy,*

Ah... thy pledge continues being my misfortune!...

Oh supreme objective that I request and wait, oh my guest,

*Oh nourishment of my Spirit! Oh my life
   in this world and in the other!*

Let my heart be thy ransom! Oh my ear, oh my sight!

Why so much delay in my seclusion, so distant?

*Ah, albeit, thy presence, before my eyes, is hid-
   den within the invisible,*

*My heart by now contemplates Thee, from my
   remoteness, yes, from my exile!*

Final Salutations

Beloved Gnostic brothers and sisters,
We have finished this 1967/1968 Christmas Message.
Please, I beg you to study it in depth, to practice it, and to live
it.

Do not be like intellectual butterflies that flutter around
reading about everything and not knowing anything; today
they are in a little school, and tomorrow in another, and finally they die after having wasted their time miserably.

Study everything in depth; do not be superficial.
Remember that life in abundance, where thousands of fish
multiply, and where everything is happiness, is in deep waters
where the waters are clear and profound. However, the superficial puddles on the road, the vain puddles without profundity, soon dry up under the heat of the sun, and turn into mud
and rottenness.

Be profound, friends of mine; frequent always the rooms
of meditation (our beloved gnostic Lumisials).

Love your worst enemies with all of your heart and with
all of your soul. Kiss the whip of your executioner; bless those
who damn and persecute you; return good for evil.

Beloved brothers and sisters, I have the high honor of
inviting you to a constant epistolary interchange, but please
I beg you, I beseech you, do not send me any type of praise,
adulations, or cheers. It is urgent, it is indispensable, for you
to comprehend that I, as a person, am insignificant; I am
worth a little bit less than the ashes of a cigarette. Thus, I am
somebody who indeed does not have the least bit of importance. Therefore, with much sincerity, I tell you that any letter
containing praise, adulation, and cheers will be rejected.

Treat me heart to heart, from good to good, from love
to love. Remember that Hermetic maxim that states: I give
thee love within which the whole summum of wisdom is contained.

To my worst enemies, those who hate me, damn me, and
persecute me too much, those who criticize my books, I send

them through this Christmas Message a fraternal hug filled with true love.

I adore my enemies, I adore my critics, and wish for all of them, as is natural, a Merry Christmas and a Happy New Year.

Beloved gnostic brothers and sisters who study this 1967 Christmas Message, verily, verily, I say onto you that I feel joyful when I answer your letters, but you have to learn how to be patient because sometimes the answer is delayed due to the fact that it is not only your letter that I have to answer; remember that thousands of people write to me and I have to answer all of them.

Beloved, let the star of nativity shine within your hearts. With all of my heart and with all of my soul, I wish you a Merry Christmas and a prosperous New Year.

Inverential peace!

Samael Aun Weor

Glossary

Absolute: Abstract space; that which is without attributes or limitations. The Absolute has three aspects: the Ain, the Ain Soph, and the Ain Soph Aur.

"The Absolute is the Being of all Beings. The Absolute is that which Is, which always has Been, and which always will Be. The Absolute is expressed as Absolute Abstract Movement and Repose. The Absolute is the cause of Spirit and of Matter, but It is neither Spirit nor Matter. The Absolute is beyond the mind; the mind cannot understand It. Therefore, we have to intuitively understand Its nature." - Samael Aun Weor, *Tarot and Kabbalah*

"In the Absolute we go beyond karma and the gods, beyond the law. The mind and the individual consciousness are only good for mortifying our lives. In the Absolute we do not have an individual mind or individual consciousness; there, we are the unconditioned, free and absolutely happy Being. The Absolute is life free in its movement, without conditions, limitless, without the mortifying fear of the law, life beyond spirit and matter, beyond karma and suffering, beyond thought, word and action, beyond silence and sound, beyond forms." - Samael Aun Weor, *The Major Mysteries*

Alchemy: Al (as a connotation of the Arabic word Allah: al-, the + ilah, God) means "The God." Also Al (Hebrew) for "highest" or El "God." Chem or Khem is from kimia which means "to fuse or cast a metal." Also from Khem, the ancient name of Egypt. The synthesis is Al-Kimia: "to fuse with the highest" or "to fuse with God." Alchemy is one of the oldest sciences in the world, and is the method to transmute our inner impurity into purity. It is also known in the East as Tantra.

Aryan race: "(Sanskrit) arya [from the verbal root to rise, tend upward] Holy, hallowed, highly evolved or especially trained; a title of the Hindu rishis [initiates]. Originally a term of ethical as well as intellectual and spiritual excellence, belonging to those who had completely mastered the aryasatyani (holy truths) and who had entered upon the aryamarga (path leading to moksha or nirvana). It was originally applicable only to the initiates or adepts of the ancient Aryan peoples, but today Aryan has become the name of a race of the human family in its various branches. All ancient peoples had their own term for initiates or adepts, as for instance among the ancient Hebrews the generic name Israel, or Sons of Israel." - Theosophical Glossary

"From Sanskrit [=a]rya excellent, honorable; akin to the name of the country Iran, and perh. to Erin, Ireland, and the early name of this people, at least in Asia. 1. One of a primitive people supposed to have lived in pre-historic times, in Central Asia, east of the Caspian Sea, and north of the Hindoo Koosh and Paropamisan Mountains, and to have been the stock from which sprang the Hindoo, Persian, Greek, Latin, Celtic, Teutonic, Slavonic, and other races; one of that ethnological division of mankind called also Indo-European or Indo-Germanic." - Webster's Revised Unabridged Dictionary

While formerly it was believed that the ancient Aryans were European (white), most scientists now believe that the ancient people commonly referred to as Aryan were the original inhabitants of India, which Manu called Aryavarta, "Abode of the Aryans."

However, in universal Gnosticism, the word Aryan refers not to "white people" or to an ancient, dead civilization, but instead refers to to the vast majority of the population of this planet. In Gnosis, all modern races are "Aryan."

Astral: This term is derived from "pertaining to or proceeding from the stars," but in the esoteric knowledge it refers to the emotional aspect of the fifth dimension, which in Hebrew is symbolized by the sephirah Hod.

Astral Body: What is commonly called the astral body is not the true astral body, it is rather the lunar protoplasmatic body, also known as the kama rupa (Sanskrit, "body of desires") or "dream body" (Tibetan rmi-lam-gyi lus). The true astral body is solar (being superior to lunar nature) and must be created, as the Master Jesus indicated in the Gospel of John 3:5-6, "Except a man be born of water and of the Spirit, he cannot enter into the kingdom of God. That which is born of the flesh is flesh; and that which is born of the Spirit is spirit." The solar astral body is created as a result of the Third Initiation of Major Mysteries (Serpents of Fire), and is perfected in the Third Serpent of Light. In Tibetan Buddhism, the solar astral body is known as the illusory body (sgyu-lus). This body is related to the emotional center and to the sephirah Hod.

"Really, only those who have worked with the Maithuna (White Tantra) for many years can possess the astral body." - Samael Aun Weor, *The Elimination of Satan's Tail*

Atman: (Sanskrit, literally "self") An ancient and important word that is grossly misinterpreted in much of Hinduism and Buddhism. Many have misunderstood this word as referring to a permanently existing self or soul. Yet the true meaning is otherwise.

"Brahman, Self, Purusha, Chaitanya, Consciousness, God, Atman, Immortality, Freedom, Perfection, Bliss, Bhuma or the unconditioned are synonymous terms." - Swami Sivananva

Thus, Atman as "self" refers to a state of being "unconditioned," which is related to the Absolute, the Ain Soph, or the Shunyata (Emptiness). Thus, Atman refers to the Innermost, the Spirit, the Son of God, who longs to return to that which is beyond words.

"Atman, in Himself, is the ineffable Being, the one who is beyond time and eternity, without end of days. He does not die, neither reincarnates (the ego is what returns), but Atman is absolutely perfect." - Samael Aun Weor

In general use, the term Atman can also refer to the spirit or sephirah Chesed.

"The Being Himself is Atman, the Ineffable. If we commit the error of giving the Being the qualifications of superior "I," alter ego, subliminal "I," or divine ego, etc., we commit blasphemy, because That which is Divine, the Reality, can never fall into the heresy of separability. Superior and inferior are two sections of the same thing. Superior "I" or inferior "I" are two sections of the same pluralized ego (Satan). The Being is the Being, and the reason for the Being to be is to be the same Being. The Being transcends the personality, the "I," and individuality." - Samael Aun Weor

"Bliss is the essential nature of man. The central fact of man's being is his inherent divinity. Man's essential nature is divine, the awareness of which he has lost because of his animal propensities and the veil of ignorance. Man, in his ignorance, identifies himself with the body, mind, Prana and the senses. Transcending these, he becomes one with Brahman or the Absolute who is pure bliss. Brahman or the Absolute is the fullest reality, the completest consciousness. That beyond which there is nothing, that which is the innermost Self of all is Atman or Brahman. The Atman is the common Consciousness in all beings. A thief, a prostitute, a scavenger, a king, a rogue, a saint, a dog, a cat, a rat-all have the same common Atman. There is apparent, fictitious difference in bodies and minds only. There are differences in colours and opinions. But, the Atman is the same in all. If you are very rich, you can have a steamer, a train, an airship of your own for your own selfish interests. But, you cannot have an Atman of your own. The Atman is common to all. It is not an individual's sole registered property. The Atman is the one amidst the many. It is constant amidst the forms which come and go. It is the pure, absolute, essential Consciousness of all the conscious beings. The source of all life, the source of all knowledge is the Atman, thy innermost Self. This Atman or Supreme Soul is transcendent, inexpressible, uninferable, unthinkable, indescribable, the ever-peaceful, all-blissful. There is no difference between the Atman and bliss. The Atman is bliss itself. God, perfection, peace, immortality, bliss are one. The goal of life is to attain perfection, immortality or God. The nearer one approaches the Truth, the happier one becomes. For, the essential nature of Truth is positive, absolute bliss. There is no bliss in the finite. Bliss is only in the Infinite. Eternal bliss can be had only from the eternal Self. To know the Self is to enjoy eternal bliss and everlasting peace. Self-realisation bestows eternal existence, absolute knowledge, and perennial bliss. None can be saved without Self-realisation. The quest for the Absolute should be undertaken even sacrificing the dearest object, even life, even courting all pain. Study philosophical books as much as you like, deliver lectures and lectures throughout your global tour, remain in a Himalayan cave for one hundred years, practise Pranayama for fifty years, you cannot attain emancipation without the realisation of the oneness of the Self." - Swami Sivananda

Baptism: From Greek baptizein or baptizo, "I wash," which originates from bapto, "to dip." An ancient ritual visible in some form within all the world's religions. While baptism is usually associated with Christianity, it is derived from the Jewish tevilah, a full body immersion in a mikveh.

Baptism or ritual immersion in water symbolizes the descent of the energy of the "water of life" or primeval womb (chaos) as a blessing upon the soul who seeks to become pure of blemish. The ritual bath or immersion represents a pact of sexual purity, in which the soul promises to become clean of animal lust. In the esoteric aspect, baptism is the absorption of the image of God (Tzalem) by means of sexual transmutation.

"The Baptism is a pact of sexual magic. When we fulfill the pact of sexual magic, then we reach the Self-realization of the Being." - Samael Aun Weor, *The Gnostic Bible: The Pistis Sophia Unveiled*

Bodhisattva: (Sanskrit; Tibetan: changchub sempa) Literally, Bodhi means "enlightenment" or "wisdom." Sattva means "essence" or "goodness," therefore the term Bodhisattva literally means "essence of wisdom." In the esoteric or secret teachings of Tibet and Gnosticism, a Bodhisattva is a human being who has reached the Fifth Initiation of Fire (Tiphereth) and has chosen to continue working by means of the Straight Path, renouncing the easier Spiral Path (in Nirvana), and returning instead to help suffering humanity. By means of this sacrifice, this individual incarnates the Christ (Avalokitesvara), thereby embodying the supreme source of wisdom and compassion. This is the entrance to the Direct Path to complete liberation from the ego, a route that only very few take, due to the fact that one must pay the entirety of one's karma in one life. Those who have taken this road have been the most remarkable figures in human history: Jesus, Buddha, Mohammed, Krishna, Moses, Padmasambhava, Milarepa, Joan of Arc, Fu-Ji, and many others whose names are not remembered or known. Of course, even among bodhisattvas there are many levels of Being: to be a bodhisattva does not mean that one is enlightened. Interestingly, the Christ in Hebrew is called Chokmah, which means "wisdom," and in Sanskrit the same is Vishnu, the root of the word "wisdom." It is Vishnu who sent his Avatars into the world in order to guide humanity. These avatars were Krishna, Buddha, Rama, and the Avatar of this age: the Avatar Kalki.

Bons: (or Bhons) The oldest religion in Tibet. It was largely overshadowed (some say persecuted) by the arrival of Buddhism. Samael Aun Weor had accepted the statements of earlier investigators which described the Bon religion as essentially black; but upon further investigation he discovered that they are not necessarily black, just extreme in some practices.

Brahmanadi: "The Brahmanadi or "canalis centralis" within which the Kundalini ascends exists throughout the length of the spinal medulla...

Each one of our seven bodies has its own spinal medulla and its Brahmanadi." - Samael Aun Weor, *Kundalini Yoga*

"Within the Sushumna Nadi there is a Nadi by name Vajra. Chitra Nadi, a minute canal, which is also called Brahmanadi, is within this Vajra Nadi. Kundalini, when awakened, passes through Chitra Nadi." - Swami Sivananda, *Kundalini Yoga*

Brahmarandhra: (Sanskrit) "'Brahma-randhra' means the hole of Brahman. It is the dwelling house of the human soul. This is also known as "Dasamadvara," the tenth opening or the tenth door. The hollow place in the crown of the head known as anterior fontanelle in the new-born child is the Brahmarandhra. This is between the two parietal and occipital bones. This portion is very soft in a babe. When the child grows, it gets obliterated by the growth of the bones of the head. Brahma created the physical body and entered (Pravishat) the body to give illumination inside through this Brahmarandhra. In some of the Upanishads, it is stated like that. This is the most important part. It is very suitable for Nirguna Dhyana (abstract meditation). When the Yogi separates himself from the physical body at the time of death, this Brahmarandhra bursts open and Prana comes out through this opening (Kapala Moksha). "A hundred and one are the nerves of the heart. Of them one (Sushumna) has gone out piercing the head; going up through it, one attains immortality" (Kathopanishad)." - Swami Sivananda, *Kundalini Yoga*

Buddha: (Sanskrit) n. "awakened one, enlightened, sage, knowledge, wise one." adj. "awake, conscious, wise, intelligent, expanded."

Commonly used to refer simply to the Buddha Shakyamuni (the "founder" of Buddhism), the term Buddha is actually a title. There are a vast number of Buddhas, each at different levels of attainment. At the ultimate level, a Buddha is a being who has become totally free of suffering. The Inner Being (Hebrew: Chesed; Sanskrit: Atman) first becomes a Buddha when the Human Soul completes the work of the Fourth Initiation of Fire (related to Netzach, the mental body).

One of the Three Jewels (Tri-ratna), which are Buddha (the awakened one, our own inner Being), Dharma (the teaching he gives to perfect us), Sangha (the community of awakened masters who can help us awaken).

The historical Buddha Shakyamuni is a very great master who continues to aid humanity. Nevertheless, he is not the only Buddha.

"Much has been said of the Buddhas. There is no doubt that there are Contemplation Buddhas and Manifestation Buddhas. Manifestation Buddhas are creatures who dominated the mind, who destroyed the ego, who did not let negative emotions enter their hearts, who did not create mental effigies in their own mind nor in the minds of others. Let us remember Tsong Khapa who reincarnated in Tibet; he was the Buddha Gautama previously. The Buddha of Buddha Amitabha is another thing, his true divine prototype. Amitabha is the Contemplation Buddha, and Gautama, we could say, is the Manifestation Buddha, the worldly

Buddha or Bodhisattva. We cannot deny that Amitabha expressed himself brilliantly through Gautama. We cannot deny that later Amitabha
sent Gautama (the Bodhisattva or worldly Buddha) directly to a new
reincarnation. Then he expressed himself as Tsong Khapa. These are
Contemplation Buddhas, they are masters of their mind, creatures who
liberated themselves from the mind. The Lords worship the Great Buddha
that we also know as the Logos and they pray to him." - Samael Aun Weor
from the lecture entitled Mental Representations

"We know very well that Atman-Buddhi is the Inner Buddha, the Buddha,
the Innermost; this is how it is written in the Sanskrit books. Now
then, we know that Christ is the Second Logos; since the First Logos is
Brahma, the Second is Vishnu (the Son) and Shiva is the Third Logos
(the Holy Spirit). Therefore, the Inner Christ, evidently and within the
levels of the Being, or better said, within the levels of our Superlative and
Transcendental Being, is beyond our Inner Buddha, yet they complement
each other. Two types of Buddhas exist; yes, we know this. There exist the
Transitory Buddhas and the Permanent Buddhas. A Transitory Buddha
is a Buddha who still has not achieved within himself the incarnation of
the Inner Christ. A Permanent Buddha or Buddha of Contemplation is a
Buddha who has already Christified himself, a Buddha that has already
received the Inner Christ within his own internal nature. This type of
Buddha is a Buddha Maitreya, since it is a Buddha who incarnated the
Inner Christ (this is how the term "Maitreya" should be understood). So,
Buddha Maitreya is not a person: Buddha Maitreya is a title, a degree,
which indicates any given Buddha who already achieved Christification." -
Samael Aun Weor, The Esoteric Path

"The Buddha appears in the world so that sentient beings may obtain the
gnosis that he himself obtained. Thus, the Buddha's demonstrations of
the path are strictly means to lead sentient beings to buddhahood." - The
Fourteenth Dalai Lama [http://www.dalailama.com/page.22.htm]

Buddhata: Derived from "buddhadatu or buddhadhatu" (Sanskrit), which
means "essence of the Buddha," (from dhatu, "element, primary element,
cause, mineral"). The term buddhadhatu appeared in Mahayana scripture
as a reference to tathagatagarbha, the "embryo of the Buddha," also called
Buddha Nature. In general use, this describes that element in us that has
the potential to become a Buddha, an "awakened one."

Buddhi: (Sanskrit, literally "intelligence") An aspect of mind.

"Buddhi is pure [superior] reason. The seat of Buddhi is just below the
crown of the head in the Pineal Gland of the brain. Buddhi is manifested
only in those persons who have developed right intuitive discrimination
or Viveka. The ordinary reason of the worldly people is termed practical
reason, which is dense and has limitations... Sankhya Buddhi or Buddhi
in the light of Sankhya philosophy is will and intellect combined. Mind is
microcosm. Mind is Maya. Mind occupies an intermediate state between

Prakriti and Purusha, matter and Spirit." - Swami Sivananda, *Yoga in Daily Life*

"When the diverse, confining sheaths of the Atma have been dissolved by Sadhana, when the different Vrittis of the mind have been controlled by mental drill or gymnastic, when the conscious mind is not active, you enter the realm of spirit life, the super-conscious mind where Buddhi and pure reason and intuition, the faculty of direct cognition of Truth, manifest. You pass into the kingdom of peace where there is none to speak, you will hear the voice of God which is very clear and pure and has an upward tendency. Listen to the voice with attention and interest. It will guide you. It is the voice of God." - Swami Sivananda, *Essence of Yoga*

In Kabbalah: The feminine Spiritual Soul, related to the sephirah Geburah. Symbolized throughout world literature, notably as Helen of Troy, Beatrice in The Divine Comedy, and Beth-sheba (Hebrew, literally "daughter of seven") in the Old Testament. The Divine or Spiritual Soul is the feminine soul of the Innermost (Atman), or his "daughter." All the strength, all the power of the Gods and Goddesses resides in Buddhi / Geburah, Cosmic Consciousness, as within a glass of alabaster where the flame of the Inner Being (Gedulah, Atman the Ineffable) is always burning. Centers: The human being has seven centers of psychological activity. The first five are the Intellectual, Emotional, Motor, Instinctive, and Sexual Centers. However, through inner development one learns how to utilize the Superior Emotional and Superior Intellectual Centers. Most people do not use these two at all.

The seven centers are also referred to as three centers: Intellectual, Emotional, and Motor-Instinctive-Sexual.

Causal Body: The body of conscious will, related to the sixth dimension, the sephirah Tiphereth, and the Human Soul. In Hindu philosophy, it is called Anandamaya kosha (sheath / body of bliss).

Chaos: (Greek) There are three primary applications of this term.

"The first Chaos from which the cosmos emerged is between the Sephiroth Binah and Chesed. The second Chaos, from where the fundamental principles of the human being emerged, exists within Yesod-Mercury, which is the sexual human center. The third Chaos, the Infernal Worlds, exists below the Thirteenth Aeons in the region of Klipoth, in the underworld." - Samael Aun Weor, *The Gnostic Bible: The Pistis Sophia Unveiled*

The Abyss (not the Inferior Abyss), or the "Great Deep." Personified as the Egyptian Goddess Neith. The Great Mother, the Immaculate Virgin from which arises all matter. The Chaos is WITHIN the Ain Soph. The primitive state of the universe. Esoterically, a reference to the semen, both in the microcosm and the macrocosm. Alchemically, it is said to be a mixture of water & fire, and it holds the seeds of the cosmos.

Chakra: (Sanskrit) Literally, "wheel." The chakras are subtle centers of energetic transformation. There are hundreds of chakras in our hidden physiology, but seven primary ones related to the awakening of consciousness.

"The Chakras are centres of Shakti as vital force... The Chakras are not perceptible to the gross senses. Even if they were perceptible in the living body which they help to organise, they disappear with the disintegration of organism at death." - Swami Sivananda, *Kundalini Yoga*

"The chakras are points of connection through which the divine energy circulates from one to another vehicle of the human being." - Samael Aun Weor, *Aztec Christic Magic*

Chastity: Although modern usage has rendered the term chastity virtually meaningless to most people, its original meaning and usage clearly indicate "moral purity" upon the basis of "sexual purity." Contemporary usage implies "repression" or "abstinence," which have nothing to do with real chastity. True chastity is a rejection of impure sexuality. True chastity is pure sexuality, or the activity of sex in harmony with our true nature, as explained in the secret doctrine. Properly used, the word chastity refers to sexual fidelity or honor.

"The generative energy, which, when we are loose, dissipates and makes us unclean, when we are continent invigorates and inspires us. Chastity is the flowering of man; and what are called Genius, Heroism, Holiness, and the like, are but various fruits which succeed it." - Henry David Thoreau, *Walden*

Christ: Derived from the Greek Christos, "the Anointed One," and Krestos, whose esoteric meaning is "fire." The word Christ is a title, not a personal name.

"Indeed, Christ is a Sephirothic Crown (Kether, Chokmah and Binah) of incommensurable wisdom, whose purest atoms shine within Chokmah, the world of the Ophanim. Christ is not the Monad, Christ is not the Theosophical Septenary; Christ is not the Jivan-Atman. Christ is the Central Sun. Christ is the ray that unites us to the Absolute." - Samael Aun Weor, *Tarot and Kabbalah*

"The Gnostic Church adores the saviour of the world, Jesus. The Gnostic Church knows that Jesus incarnated Christ, and that is why they adore him. Christ is not a human nor a divine individual. Christ is a title given to all fully self-realized masters. Christ is the Army of the Voice. Christ is the Verb. The Verb is far beyond the body, the soul and the Spirit. Everyone who is able to incarnate the Verb receives in fact the title of Christ. Christ is the Verb itself. It is necessary for everyone of us to incarnate the Verb (Word). When the Verb becomes flesh in us we speak with the verb of light. In actuality, several masters have incarnated the Christ. In secret India, the Christ Yogi Babaji has lived for millions of years; Babaji is immortal. The great master of wisdom Kout Humi also incarnated the Christ. Sanat Kumara, the founder of the great College of Initiates of the White Lodge, is another living Christ. In the past, many incarnated the Christ. In the present, some have incarnated the Christ. In the future many will incarnate the Christ. John the Baptist also incarnated the Christ. John the Baptist is a living Christ. The difference between Jesus and the other masters that also incarnated the Christ has to do with hierarchy. Jesus is the highest Solar initiate of the cosmos..." - Samael Aun Weor, *The Perfect Matrimony*

Clairvoyance: A term invented by occultists, derived from the French clair "clear," and voyance "seeing."

"There exist clairvoyance and pseudo-clairvoyance. The Gnostic student must make a clear differentiation between these two forms of extrasensory perception. Clairvoyance is based on objectivity. However, pseudo-clair-voyance is based on subjectivity. Understand that by objectivity we mean spiritual reality, the spiritual world. Understand that by subjectivity we mean the physical world, the world of illusion, that which has no reality. An intermediate region also exists, this is the astral world, which can be objective or subjective according to the degree of spiritual development of each person." - Samael Aun Weor, *The Perfect Matrimony*

"Positive clairvoyance is achieved only with a great intellectual culture and a great esoteric discipline. The highest cultured people, who are submit-ted to the most rigorous intellectual disciplines, only achieve the truly positive clairvoyance. The illuminated intellect is the outcome of positive clairvoyance." - Samael Aun Weor, *Fundamental Notions of Endocrinology and Criminology*

The two main categories of consciousness are objective (positive, related with free consciousness) and subjective (negative, related to the deluded perception and opinions of the psychological "I"s). Further, there are five types of clairvoyance, as explained in *Fundamental Notions of Endocrinology and Criminology.*

1. Conscious clairvoyance: to perceive any given phenomenon (whether internal phenomenon related with the psyche and internal worlds or external phenomenon related to the circumstances of the physical world and nature) through the intelligence of the Monad which is essence or consciousness. Conscious clairvoyance is experienced when one is able to perceive a physical or psychological phenomenon how it really is, in all of its causes and multiple dimensions.

2. Supra-conscious clairvoyance: This is the level of Logoic consciousness. This is only for those venerable masters who finish The Great Work. This level of consciousness is Turiya, those masters who have no ego, who have resurrected, and for those who never dream.

3. Subconscious clairvoyance: This is related to the perception of the egos who are related with memories of past experience. These egos are the most superficial egos whose inherent pattern was defined during the formation of the personality (birth to seven years old). These egos can be created at any time in our lives but the pattern is related to the false personality and the PCPF. An example of a subconscious ego is the one who avoids broc-coli for their entire lives because they remember the disgust they had when

they were forced to eat it by their parents. Remember that subconscious clairvoyance is the way the ego perceives that particular experience; as in the example, it was the way the ego perceives the impression of broccoli and that example.

4. Unconscious clairvoyance: This is the type of perception that develops through the frustration of desires. Pride constantly talks about himself and how great he is because it if frustrated that nobody else talks about him; this is an unconscious habit. Lust becomes frustrated because it was never able to satisfy its sexual desire to fornicate with a particular movie star, etc. This desire becomes frustrated and in the astral plane projects its frustrated desires in the form of sexual dreams with the image/impression of the movie star.

5. Infra-conscious clairvoyance: The deepest aspects of our egos, related to the spheres of Lilith in the Klipoth. Remember that everything in the universe has its antithesis. The antithesis of the angel of love, Anael, is Lilith, the demon of fornication, black magic and homosexuality. This region is usually only experienced during nightmares. A minority of people bring these egos to the surface, incorporating these elements in action and with the personality. Sadly, this humanity has more and more people who bring the elements of black magic, homosexuality and brutality to the surface of their psychological world.

Consciousness: "Wherever there is life, there is consciousness. Consciousness is inherent to life as humidity is inherent to water." - Samael Aun Weor, *Fundamental Notions of Endocrinology and Criminology*

From various dictionaries: 1. The state of being conscious; knowledge of one's own existence, condition, sensations, mental operations, acts, etc. 2. Immediate knowledge or perception of the presence of any object, state, or sensation. 3. An alert cognitive state in which you are aware of yourself and your situation. In universal Gnosticism, the range of potential consciousness is allegorized in the Ladder of Jacob, upon which the angels ascend and descend. Thus there are higher and lower levels of consciousness, from the level of demons at the bottom, to highly realized angels in the heights.

"It is vital to understand and develop the conviction that consciousness has the potential to increase to an infinite degree." - The 14th Dalai Lama

"Light and consciousness are two phenomena of the same thing; to a lesser degree of consciousness, corresponds a lesser degree of light; to a greater degree of consciousness, a greater degree of light." - Samael Aun Weor, *The Esoteric Treatise of Hermetic Astrology*

Cteis: (Greek Kteis) Alternatively spelled "ecteis." Literally, "comb" (of a loom), used for rake, horn, fingers, ribs, scallop, vagina, yoni.

"The Cteis was a circular and concave pedestal, or receptacle, on which the Phallus, or column [obelisk] rested. The union of these two, as the generative and producing principles of nature, in one compound figure, was the most usual mode of representation. Here we find the origin of the point within a circle, a symbol which was first adopted by the

old sun worshipers. The Compass arranged above the Square symbolizes the (male) Sun, impregnating the passive (female) Earth with its
life-producing rays. The true meanings, then are two-fold: the earthly
(human) representations are of the man and his phallus, and the woman
with her receptive cteis (vagina). The male-female divinities were commonly symbolized by the generative parts of man and woman... The
Phallus and Cteis (vagina), emblems of generation and production, and
which, as such, appeared in the Mysteries. The Indian Lingam was the
union of both, as were the Boat and Mast, and the Point within the Circle.
The Cteis was symbolized as the moon. The female personification of
the productive principle. It generally accompanied the Phallus... and as a
symbol of the prolific powers of nature, and was extensively venerated by
the nations of antiquity." - *Morals and Dogma,* by Albert Pike, [1871]

"The kteis, or female organ, as the symbol of the passive or reproductive
powers of nature, generally occurs on ancient Roman monuments as the
concha Veneris, a fig, barley, corn and the letter delta." - *PRIAPEIA, sive
diversorum poetarum in Priapum lusus,* translation by Leonard C. Smithers
and Sir Richard Burton [1890]

Divine Mother: "Among the Aztecs, she was known as Tonantzin, among the
Greeks as chaste Diana. In Egypt she was Isis, the Divine Mother, whose
veil no mortal has lifted. There is no doubt at all that esoteric Christianity
has never forsaken the worship of the Divine Mother Kundalini. Obviously
she is Marah, or better said, RAM-IO, MARY. What orthodox religions did
not specify, at least with regard to the exoteric or public circle, is the aspect
of Isis in her individual human form. Clearly, it was taught only in secret
to the Initiates that this Divine Mother exists individually within each
human being. It cannot be emphasized enough that Mother-God, Rhea,
Cybele, Adonia, or whatever we wish to call her, is a variant of our own
individual Being in the here and now. Stated explicitly, each of us has our
own particular, individual Divine Mother." - Samael Aun Weor, *The Great
Rebellion*

"Devi Kundalini, the Consecrated Queen of Shiva, our personal Divine
Cosmic Individual Mother, assumes five transcendental mystic aspects in
every creature, which we must enumerate:

1. The unmanifested Prakriti

2. The chaste Diana, Isis, Tonantzin, Maria or better said Ram-Io

3. The terrible Hecate, Persephone, Coatlicue, queen of the infemos and
death; terror of love and law

4. The special individual Mother Nature, creator and architect of our
physical organism

5. The Elemental Enchantress to whom we owe every vital impulse, every
instinct." - Samael Aun Weor, *The Mystery of the Golden Blossom*

Drukpa: (Also known variously as Druk-pa, Dugpa, Brugpa, Dag dugpa or
Dad dugpa) The term Drukpa comes from from Dzongkha and Tibetan
('brug yul), which means "country of Bhutan," and is composed of Druk,

"dragon," and pa, "person." In Asia, the word refers to the people of Bhutan, a country between India and Tibet.

Drukpa can also refer to a large sect of Buddhism which broke from the Kagyug-pa "the Ones of the Oral Tradition." They considered themselves as the heirs of the Indian Gurus: their teaching, which goes back to Vajradhara, was conveyed through Dakini, from Naropa to Marpa and then to the ascetic and mystic poet Milarepa. Later on, Milarepa's disciples founded new monasteries, and new threads appeared, among which are the Karmapa and the Drukpa. All those schools form the Kagyug-pa order, in spite of episodic internal quarrels and extreme differences in practice. The Drukpa sect is recognized by their ceremonial large red hats, but it should be known that they are not the only "Red Hat" group (the Nyingmas, founded by Padmasambhava, also use red hats). The Drukpas have established a particular worship of the Dorje (Vajra, or thunderbolt, a symbol of the phallus).

Samael Aun Weor wrote repeatedly in many books that the "Drukpas" practice and teach Black Tantra, by means of the expelling of the sexual energy. If we analyze the word, it is clear that he is referring to "Black Dragons," or people who practice Black Tantra. He was not referring to all the people of Bhutan, or all members of the Buddhist Drukpa sect. Such a broad condemnation would be as ridiculous as the one made by those who condemn all Jews for the crucifixion of Jesus.

"In 1387, with just reason, the Tibetan reformer Tsong Khapa cast every book of necromancy that he found into flames. As a result, some discontent Lamas formed an alliance with the aboriginal Bhons, and today they form a powerful sect of black magic in the regions of Sikkim, Bhutan, and Nepal, submitting themselves to the most abominable black rites." - Samael Aun Weor, *The Revolution of Beelzebub*

Ego: The multiplicity of contradictory psychological elements that we have inside are in their sum the "ego." Each one is also called "an ego" or an "I." Every ego is a psychological defect which produces suffering. The ego is three (related to our Three Brains or three centers of psychological processing), seven (capital sins), and legion (in their infinite variations).

"The ego is the root of ignorance and pain." - Samael Aun Weor, *The Esoteric Treatise of Hermetic Astrology*

"The Being and the ego are incompatible. The Being and the ego are like water and oil. They can never be mixed... The annihilation of the psychic aggregates (egos) can be made possible only by radically comprehending our errors through meditation and by the evident Self-reflection of the Being." - Samael Aun Weor, *The Gnostic Bible: The Pistis Sophia Unveiled*

Elemental: The intelligence or soul of non-human creatures, whose physical bodies are the minerals, plants and animals, but whose souls are called variously gnomes, sprites, elves, fairies, devas, etc. (Strictly speaking, even intellectual animals remain as elementals until they create the soul; however in common usage the term elementals refers to the creatures of the three lower kingdoms: mineral, plant, and animal).

"In the times of King Arthur and the Knights of the Round Table, elementals of Nature were manifest everywhere, deeply penetrating our physical atmosphere. Many are the tales of elves, leprechauns and fairies, which still abound in green Erin, Ireland. Unfortunately, all these things of innocence, all this beauty from the soul of the Earth, is no longer perceived by humanity. This is due to the intellectual scoundrel's pedantries and the animal ego's excessive development." –Samael Aun Weor, *The Great Rebellion*

Elohim: [אלהים] An Hebrew term with a wide variety of meanings. In Christian translations of scripture, it is one of many words translated to the generic word "God," but whose actual meaning depends upon the context. For example:

1. In Kabbalah, אלהים is a name of God the relates to many levels of the Tree of Life. In the world of Atziluth, the word is related to divnities of the sephiroth Binah (Jehovah Elohim, mentioned especially in Genesis), Geburah, and Hod. In the world of Briah, it is related beings of Netzach and Hod.

2. El [אל] is "god," Eloah [אלה] is "goddess," therefore the plural Elohim refers to "gods and goddesses," and is commonly used to refer to Cosmocreators or Dhyan-Choans.

3. אלה Elah or Eloah is "goddess." Yam [ים] is "sea" or "ocean." Therefore אלהים Elohim can be אלה-ים "the sea goddess" [i.e. Aphrodite, Stella Maris, etc.]

There are many more meanings of "Elohim." In general, Elohim refers to high aspects of divinity.

"Each one of us has his own Interior Elohim. The Interior Elohim is the Being of our Being. The Interior Elohim is our Father-Mother. The Interior Elohim is the ray that emanates from Aelohim." - Samael Aun Weor, *The Gnostic Bible: The Pistis Sophia Unveiled*

Ens Seminis: (Latin) Literally, "the entity of semen." A term used by Paracelsus.

Ens Virtutis: (Latin) A term used by Paracelsus. Literally, ens is "army; host; mighty works (pl.);" and virtutis is "strength/power; courage/bravery; worth/manliness/virtue/character/excellence." Virtutis is derived from Latin vir, "man." So, we can translate this as "power entity."

Paracelsus stated that the ens virtutis must be extracted from the ens seminis, thus saying that all virtue and excellence is developed from the force within the sexual waters.

Essence: "Without question the Essence, or Consciousness, which is the same thing, sleeps deeply... The Essence in itself is very beautiful. It came from above, from the stars. Lamentably, it is smothered deep within all these "I's" we carry inside. By contrast, the Essence can retrace its steps, return to the point of origin, go back to the stars, but first it must liberate itself from its evil companions, who have trapped it within the slums of perdition. Human beings have three percent free Essence, and the other ninety-seven percent is imprisoned within the "I's"." - Samael Aun Weor, The Great Rebellion

"A percentage of psychic Essence is liberated when a defect is disintegrated. Thus, the psychic Essence which is bottled up within our defects will be completely liberated when we disintegrate each and every one of our false values, in other words, our defects. Thus, the radical transformation of ourselves will occur when the totality of our Essence is liberated. Then, in that precise moment, the eternal values of the Being will express themselves through us. Unquestionably, this would be marvelous not only for us, but also for all of humanity." - Samael Aun Weor, *The Revolution of the Dialectic*

Fohat: (Theosophical/Tibetan) A term used by H.P. Blavatsky to represent the active (male) potency of the Shakti (female sexual power) in nature, the essence of cosmic electricity, vital force. As explained in *The Secret Doctrine*, "He (Fohat) is, metaphysically, the objectivised thought of the gods; the "Word made flesh" on a lower scale, and the messenger of Cosmic and human ideations: the active force in Universal Life.... In India, Fohat is connected with Vishnu and Surya in the early character of the (first) God; for Vishnu is not a high god in the Rig Veda. The name Vishnu is from the root vish, "to pervade," and Fohat is called the "Pervader" and the Manufacturer, because he shapes the atoms from crude material..." The term fohat has recently been linked with the Tibetan verb phro-wa and the noun spros-pa. These two terms are listed in Jäschke's Tibetan-English Dictionary (1881) as, for phro-wa, "to proceed, issue, emanate from, to spread, in most cases from rays of light..." while for spros-pa he gives "business, employment, activity."

Fornication: Originally, the term fornication was derived from the Indo-European word gwher, whose meanings relate to heat and burning (the full explanation can be found online at http://sacred-sex.org/terminology/fornication). Fornication means to make the heat (solar fire) of the seed (sexual power) leave the body through voluntary orgasm. Any voluntary orgasm is fornication, whether between a married man and woman, or an unmarried man and woman, or through masturbation, or in any other case; this is explained by Moses: "A man from whom there is a discharge of semen, shall immerse all his flesh in water, and he shall remain unclean until evening. And any garment or any leather [object] which has semen on it, shall be immersed in water, and shall remain unclean until evening. A woman with whom a man cohabits, whereby there was [a discharge of] semen, they shall immerse in water, and they shall remain unclean until evening." - Leviticus 15:16-18

To fornicate is to spill the sexual energy through the orgasm. Those who "deny themselves" restrain the sexual energy, and "walk in the midst of the fire" without being burned. Those who restrain the sexual energy, who renounce the orgasm, remember God in themselves, and do not defile themselves with animal passion, "for the temple of God is holy, which temple ye are."

"Whosoever is born of God doth not commit sin; for his seed remaineth in him: and he cannot sin, because he is born of God." - 1 John 3:9

This is why neophytes always took a vow of sexual abstention, so that they could prepare themselves for marriage, in which they would have sexual relations but not release the sexual energy through the orgasm. This is why Paul advised:

"...they that have wives be as though they had none..." - I Corinthians 7:29

"A fornicator is an individual who has intensely accustomed his genital organs to copulate (with orgasm). Yet, if the same individual changes his custom of copulation to the custom of no copulation, then he transforms himself into a chaste person. We have as an example the astonishing case of Mary Magdalene, who was a famous prostitute. Mary Magdalene became the famous Saint Mary Magdalene, the repented prostitute. Mary Magdalene became the chaste disciple of Christ." - Samael Aun Weor, *The Revolution of Beelzebub*

Gnosis: (Greek) Knowledge.

1. The word Gnosis refers to the knowledge we acquire through our own experience, as opposed to knowledge that we are told or believe in. Gnosis - by whatever name in history or culture - is conscious, experiential knowledge, not merely intellectual or conceptual knowledge, belief, or theory. This term is synonymous with the Hebrew "daath" and the Sanskrit "jna."

2. The tradition that embodies the core wisdom or knowledge of humanity.

"Gnosis is the flame from which all religions sprouted, because in its depth Gnosis is religion. The word "religion" comes from the Latin word "religare," which implies "to link the Soul to God"; so Gnosis is the very pure flame from where all religions sprout, because Gnosis is knowledge, Gnosis is wisdom." - Samael Aun Weor from the lecture entitled The Esoteric Path

"The secret science of the Sufis and of the Whirling Dervishes is within Gnosis. The secret doctrine of Buddhism and of Taoism is within Gnosis. The sacred magic of the Nordics is within Gnosis. The wisdom of Hermes, Buddha, Confucius, Mohammed and Quetzalcoatl, etc., etc., is within Gnosis. Gnosis is the doctrine of Christ." - Samael Aun Weor, *The Revolution of Beelzebub*

Hasnamuss: Plural "hasnamussen." A term used by Gurdjieff in reference to a person with a divided consciousness: part of it is free and natural, and part is trapped in the ego. In synthesis, everyone who has ego is a Hasnamuss. Although there are many variations and kinds of Hasnamuss, generally four primary types are described:

· mortal: the common person
· those with the solar astral body
· those with the solar bodies created

· fallen angels

These are described in detail by Samael Aun Weor in his lecture "The Master Key."

"The Twice-born who does not reduce his lunar ego to cosmic dust converts himself into an abortion of the Cosmic Mother. He becomes a Marut, and there exist thousands of types of Maruts. Certain oriental sects and some Muslim tribes commit the lamentable error of rendering cult to all of those families of Maruts. Every Marut, every hasnamuss has in fact two personalities: one white and another black (one solar and another lunar). The Innermost, the Being dressed with the solar electronic bodies, is the white personality of the hasnamuss, and the pluralized "I" dressed with the protoplasmic lunar bodies is the hasnamuss' black personality. Therefore, these Maruts have a double center of gravity." - Samael Aun Weor

Gurdjieff described these qualities of the Hasnamuss:

· Every kind of depravity, conscious as well as unconscious
· The feeling of self-satisfaction from leading others astray
· The irresistible inclination to destroy the existence of other breathing creatures
· The urge to become free from the necessity of actualizing the being-efforts demanded by Nature
· The attempt by every kind of artificiality to conceal from others what in their opinion are one's physical defects
· The calm self-contentment in the use of what is not personally deserved
· The striving to be not what one is.

Although the origin of this term is uncertain and has interesting meanings when analyzed in Arabic, Hebrew, etc., in Sanskrit we find Hasnamuss can be derived from हा Ha: a Sanskrit particle expressing sorrow, dejection, pain; अशन asna: voracious, eating, consuming; or, a stone; मूष् mus: mouse, thief

Holy Spirit: The Christian name for the third aspect of the Holy Trinity, or "God." This force has other names in other religions. In Kabbalah, the third sephirah, Binah. In Buddhism, it is related to Nirmanakaya, the "body of formation" through which the inner Buddha works in the world.

"The Holy Spirit is the Fire of Pentecost or the fire of the Holy Spirit called Kundalini by the Hindus, the igneous serpent of our magical powers, Holy Fire symbolized by Gold..." - Samael Aun Weor, *The Perfect Matrimony*

"It has been said in *The Divine Comedy* with complete clarity that the Holy Spirit is the husband of the Divine Mother. Therefore, the Holy Spirit unfolds himself into his wife, into the Shakti of the Hindus. This must be known and understood. Some, when they see that the Third Logos is unfolded into the Divine Mother Kundalini, or Shakti, She that has many names, have believed that the Holy Spirit is feminine, and they have been mistaken. The Holy Spirit is masculine, but when He unfolds Himself into She, then the first ineffable Divine Couple is formed, the Creator Elohim, the Kabir, or Great Priest, the Ruach Elohim, that in accordance to Moses, cultivated the waters in the beginning of the world." - Samael Aun Weor, *Tarot and Kabbalah*

"The Primitive Gnostic Christians worshiped the lamb, the fish and the white dove as symbols of the Holy Spirit." - Samael Aun Weor, *The Perfect Matrimony*

Hydrogen: Grom Greek hydr-, stem of hydor "water" + French -gène "producing," from gen: generate, genes, genesis, genetic, etc.

Hydrogen is the simplest element on the periodic table, and is the building block of all forms of matter. Hydrogen is a packet of solar light. The solar light (the light that comes from the sun) is the reflection of the cosmic solar intelligence, the Okidanok, the Cosmic Christ, which creates and sustains every world.

Hydrogen is "fecundated water, generated water" (hydro). The water is the source of all life. Everything that we eat, breathe and all of the impressions that we receive are in the form of various structures of hydrogen.

"It is urgent to know that there are twelve fundamental basic hydrogens in the universe. The twelve basic hydrogens are arranged in tiers in accordance with the twelve categories of matter. The twelve categories of matter exist in all creation; let us remember the twelve salts of the zodiac, the twelve spheres of cosmic vibration within which a solar humanity must be developed. All the secondary hydrogens, whose varied densities go from 6 to 12283, are derived from the twelve basic hydrogens. In Gnosticism, the term hydrogen has a very extensive significance. Indeed, any simple element is hydrogen of a certain density. Hydrogen 384 is found in water, 192 in the air, while 96 is wisely deposited in the animal magnetism, emanations of the human body, X-rays, hormones, vitamins, etc." - Samael Aun Weor, *Light from Darkness*

"...hydrogen in itself is the first emanation of the universal primordial matter (Mulaprakriti)." - Samael Aun Weor, *Cosmic Teachings of a Lama*

"Every substance is transformed into a specific type of hydrogen. Thus, just as the substances and life forms are infinite, likewise the hydrogens are infinite." - Samael Aun Weor, *The Perfect Matrimony*

Samael Aun Weor will place a note (Do, Re, Mi...) and a number related with the vibration and atomic weight (level of complexity) with a particular hydrogen. For example, he constantly refers to the Hydrogen Si-12. "Si" is the highest note in the octave and it is the result of the notes that come before it. This particular hydrogen is always related to the forces of Yesod, which is the synthesis and coagulation of all food, air and impressions that we have previously received. Food begins at Do-768, air begins at Do-384, and impressions begin at Do-48.

"In all the elements of Nature, in every chemical substance, in every fruit, exists its corresponding type of Hydrogen, and the Hydrogen of sex is Si-12... Within the seven notes of the musical scale, all the biological and physiological processes are carried out, and the final result is that marvelous elixir called semen [sexual energy, regardless of gender]. The process is initiated with the note Do from the moment in which the food enters the mouth, and continues with the notes Re-Mi-Fa-Sol-La, and when the musical Si resounds, the extraordinary elixir called semen is already prepared." - Samael Aun Weor, *Practical Astrology*

Infrasexual: From infra, "below, underneath, beneath; later than, smaller, inferior to," from *ndher "under." As opposed to "supra."

Sexuality has three basic levels:

Suprasexuality: sexual transmutation to create the soul and the perfect human being. Christ, Buddha, Dante, Zoroaster, Mohammed, Hermes, Quetzalcoatl, and many other great masters were suprasexual.

Normal sexuality: sexuality for procreation and the continuity of the species.

Infrasexuality: sexuality of the underworld, hell, the abyss, which has now infected humanity worldwide. The degeneration in the use or function of the sexual organs or energy. This includes all forms of sexual perversion, such as sexual violence, sex as power or addiction, pornography, prostitution, masturbation, homosexuality, hatred of sex (such as among religious people), etc.

"It is obvious that the infernal worlds are infrasexual. It is evident that infrasexuality reigns with sovereignty within humanity." - Samael Aun Weor, *Tarot and Kabbalah*

"It is necessary to remember that infrasexuality hates normal sex and suprasex. In all ages, infrasexual ones have blasphemed against the Third Logos, considering sex to be taboo, a sin, a cause for shame, clandestine, etc. Infrasexual people have schools where they teach people to hate sex. Infrasexual people consider themselves to be Mahatmas, hierophants, etc." - Samael Aun Weor, *The Perfect Matrimony*

"Kabbalistic traditions state that Adam had two wives: Lilith and Nahemah. Lilith is the mother of abortions, homosexuality and in general, all kinds of crimes against Nature. Nahemah is the mother of malignant beauty, passion and adultery. Thus, the Abyss is divided into two large regions: the spheres of Lilith and Nahemah. Infrasexuality reigns sovereign in these two large regions. [...] The sphere of Lilith is characterized by its cruelty. The psychology of this sphere has various aspects: monks and nuns who hate sex, homosexuality in convents, homosexuality outside of monastic life, induced abortions, people who love masturbation, criminals of the brothel, people who enjoy torturing others, etc. In this sphere we find the most horrible crimes reported in police records: horrible cases of bloody crimes of homosexual origin, terrifying acts of sadism, homosexuality in jails, lesbianism, terrifying

psychotic criminals, those who enjoy making their loved one suffer, horrible infanticides, patricides, matricides, etc. In this sphere we also find
pseudo-occultists who would rather suffer from nocturnal pollution
than get married, people who mortally hate the Arcanum A. Z. F. and the
Perfect Matrimony, people who believe that they can reach God while
hating sex, anchoritic people who abhor sex and who consider it vulgar
and gross. [...] The sphere of Nahemah seduces with the enchantment of
her malignant beauty. In this infrasexual sphere we find the "Don Juans
and femme fatales." The world of prostitution unfolds in this sphere.
The infrasexual men of Nahemah feel very manly. Men who have many
women live in this sphere. They feel happy in adultery. They believe
themselves to be very manly; they are unaware that they are infrasexual.
In the sphere of Nahemah we also find millions of prostitutes. These
poor women are victims of the fatal charm of Nahemah. In the sphere
of Nahemah we find elegant ladies of high social standing. These people
are very happy within adultery. That is their world. In the infrasexual
region of Nahemah we find a sweetness that moves the soul: virgins
that seduce with the charm of their tenderness, very beautiful seductive
women, men who abandon their homes bewitched by the enchantment
of these most precious beauties. In this region we also find indescribable
beauty, uncontrollable passions, beautiful salons, elegant cabarets, soft
beds, delightful dances, orchestras of the Abyss, unforgettable romantic
words that cannot be forgotten, etc. The infrasexual people of Nahemah
sometimes accept the Arcanum A.Z.F. (Sexual Magic) but fail because
they are unable to avoid the ejaculation of semen. They almost always
withdraw from the Perfect Matrimony uttering horrible things against it.
We have heard them saying: "I practiced Sexual Magic and sometimes I
was able to remain without spilling the semen. I was an animal enjoying
the delicious passions of sex." After withdrawing from the path of the
razor's edge, represented by the spinal medulla, they seek refuge in some
seductive doctrine of Nahemah. If they are lucky enough not to fall into
the sphere of Lilith, they continue ejaculating the seminal liquor. Such is
their infrasexual world." - Samael Aun Weor, *The Perfect Matrimony*

"Infrasexuals and perverts mortally hate the doctrine of Peter. Many
are the sincerely mistaken ones who believe that they can Self-realize
by excluding sex. Many are the ones that talk against sex, the ones that
insult sex, the ones that spit all of their slanderous drivel on the sacred
sanctuary of the Third Logos. Those that hate sex, those that say that
sex is gross, filthy, animalistic, bestial, are the insulters, the ones that
blaspheme against the Holy Spirit. Flee fornication (spilling of semen),
every sin that a man doeth is without the body but he that committeth
fornication sinneth against his own body. [1 Corinthians 6:18] Wherefore
I say unto you, all manner of sin and blasphemy shall be forgiven unto
men but the blasphemy against the Holy Ghost shall not be forgiven
unto men...neither in this world, neither in the world to come. [Matthew
12:31-32; see also Mark 3:28-29] For if we sin wilfully after that we have
received the knowledge of the truth, there remaineth no more sacrifice for

sins. [Hebrews 10:26; see also Hebrews 10:27-31] Whosoever pronounces himself against Sexual Magic, whosoever spits their infamy against the sanctuary of the Third Logos, cannot ever reach the Second Birth. In the Occidental world, many people exist that mortally hate Sexual Magic. Those people justify their absurd hatred with many pretexts. They say that the Maithuna is only for Oriental people, and that we the occidentals are not prepared. Such people affirm that with this doctrine of sex yoga, the unique thing that can result is a harvest of black magicians. What is interesting about all of this is that such people of a reactionary, conservative, regressive and retarded type do not say a single word against fornication, against adultery, against prostitution, against homosexuality, against masturbation, etc., etc. All of this seems normal to them, and they do not have any inconvenience in miserably squandering the sexual energy. Sex must be in itself the most elevated creative function. Disgracefully, ignorance reigns with sovereignty and humanity is very distant from comprehending the great mysteries of sex." - Samael Aun Weor, *Tarot and Kabbalah*

"Really, it causes pain to see those poor infrasexuals in the Molecular World (Astral Plane) after death. Their lunar bodies convert them into lunar women who wander throughout the Molecular World as somnambulists, asleep, cold, and unconscious creatures. What was the good of all of the subjective practices of these infrasexuals? What was the good of all of their beliefs, systems, orders, etc.? To no avail, the infrasexuals will try to gain their liberation by despising sex, by renouncing the Maithuna (Sexual Magic), by abstinence, by abuse, or by following the degenerated path of the homosexuals and masturbators, etc. Uselessly, the mistaken, sincere ones try to create the Solar Bodies by practicing respiratory exercises, yoga without Maithuna, or similar exercises, or with vegetarian diets, etc. It is completely demonstrated that we are children of sex and that only through [pure, upright] sex can we create. Really, we can only create the Solar Bodies with sex. We can convert ourselves into Solar Spirits only with the marvelous force of the Third Logos." - Samael Aun Weor, *The Revolution of Beelzebub*

Initiation: The process whereby the Innermost (the Inner Father) receives recognition, empowerment and greater responsibilities in the Internal Worlds, and little by little approaches His goal: complete Self-realization, or in other words, the return into the Absolute. Initiation NEVER applies to the "I" or our terrestrial personality.

"There are Nine Initiations of Minor Mysteries and seven great Initiations of Major Mysteries. The Innermost is the one who receives all of these Initiations. The Testament of Wisdom says: "Before the dawning of the false aurora upon the earth, the ones who survived the hurricane and the tempest were praising the Innermost, and the heralds of the aurora appeared unto them." The psychological "I" does not receives Initiations. The human personality does not receive anything. Nonetheless, the "I" of some Initiates becomes filled with pride when saying 'I am a Master, I have such Initiations.' Thus, this is how the "I" believes itself to be an Initiate and keeps reincarnating in order to "perfect itself", but, the "I" never ever perfects itself. The "I" only reincarnates in order to satisfy desires. That is all." - Samael Aun Weor, *The Aquarian Message*

Innermost: "Our real Being is of a universal nature. Our real Being is neither a kind of superior nor inferior "I." Our real Being is impersonal, universal, divine. He transcends every concept of "I," me, myself, ego, etc., etc." - Samael Aun Weor, *The Perfect Matrimony*

Also known as Atman, the Spirit, Chesed, our own individual interior divine Father.

"The Innermost is the ardent flame of Horeb. In accordance with Moses, the Innermost is the Ruach Elohim (the Spirit of God) who sowed the waters in the beginning of the world. He is the Sun King, our Divine Monad, the Alter-Ego of Cicerone." - Samael Aun Weor, *The Revolution of Beelzebub*

Intellectual Animal: When the Intelligent Principle, the Monad, sends its spark of consciousness into Nature, that spark, the anima, enters into manifestation as a simple mineral. Gradually, over millions of years, the anima gathers experience and evolves up the chain of life until it perfects itself in the level of the mineral kingdom. It then graduates into the plant kingdom, and subsequently into the animal kingdom. With each ascension the spark receives new capacities and higher grades of complexity. In the animal kingdom it learns procreation by ejaculation. When that animal intelligence enters into the human kingdom, it receives a new capacity: reasoning, the intellect; it is now an anima with intellect: an Intellectual Animal. That spark must then perfect itself in the human kingdom in order to become a complete and perfect human being, an entity that has conquered and transcended everything that belongs to the lower kingdoms. Unfortunately, very few intellectual animals perfect themselves; most remain enslaved by their animal nature, and thus are reabsorbed by Nature, a process belonging to the devolving side of life and called by all the great religions "Hell" or the Second Death.

"The present manlike being is not yet human; he is merely an intellectual animal. It is a very grave error to call the legion of the "I" the "soul." In fact, what the manlike being has is the psychic material, the material for the soul within his Essence, but indeed, he does not have a Soul yet." - Samael Aun Weor, *The Revolution of the Dialectic*

Internal Worlds: The many dimensions beyond the physical world. These dimensions are both subjective and objective. To know the objective internal worlds (the astral plane, or Nirvana, or the Klipoth) one must first know one's own personal, subjective internal worlds, because the two are intimately associated.

"Whosoever truly wants to know the internal worlds of the planet Earth or of the solar system or of the galaxy in which we live, must previously know his intimate world, his individual, internal life, his own internal worlds. Man, know thyself, and thou wilt know the universe and its gods.

The more we explore this internal world called "myself," the more we will comprehend that we simultaneously live in two worlds, in two realities, in two confines: the external and the internal. In the same way that it is indispensable for one to learn how to walk in the external world so as not to fall down into a precipice, or not get lost in the streets of the city, or to select one's friends, or not associate with the perverse ones, or not eat poison, etc.; likewise, through the psychological work upon oneself we learn how to walk in the internal world, which is explorable only through Self-observation." - Samael Aun Weor, *Treatise of Revolutionary Psychology*

Through the work in Self-observation, we develop the capacity to awaken where previously we were asleep: including in the objective internal worlds.

Judas: The name Judas (Greek) is a translation from the Hebrew name Judah, the most exalted tribe of Israel. In Hebrew, Judah is יהודה, a very significant name that joins the most holy name of God (יהוה) with the letter ד Daleth, which represents a doorway and is the first letter of the word Daath (knowledge), indicating the secret teachings. The name Judas is most known in relation to two disciples of Jesus, particularly Judas Iscariot, who led the Rabbis to Jesus and began the process of his torture and crucifixion, a role that has since associated the name Judas with betrayal.

"Judas Iscariot is not as many think, a man who betrayed his Master. No! Judas Iscariot performed a script taught by his Master, and that is all! Jesus of Nazareth himself prepared him, and Judas learned this script by memory, thus, consciously, he played his role in public. The doctrine of Judas signifies the elimination of all our psychological aggregates: death to the ego. This is why Judas "hung himself," in order to indicate that the ego must be reduced to ashes. Judas followed a script, and nothing else. He prepared himself conscientiously in order to not contradict at all the sacred scriptures. Just as any actor performs his role, Judas rehearsed it many times before performing it in public, and nothing more. Judas is and continues to be the most exalted disciple of Jesus of Nazareth. Judas achieved Christification." - Samael Aun Weor, *Kabbalah of the Mayan Mysteries* (1977)

Kabbalah: (Hebrew קבלה) Alternatively spelled Cabala, Qabalah from the Hebrew קבל KBLH or QBL, "to receive." An ancient esoteric teaching hidden from the uninitiated, whose branches and many forms have reached throughout the world. The true Kabbalah is the science and language of the superior worlds and is thus objective, complete and without flaw; it is said that "All enlightened beings agree," and their natural agreement is a function of the awakened consciousness. The Kabbalah is the language of that consciousness, thus disagreement regarding its meaning and interpretation is always due to the subjective elements in the psyche.

"The objective of studying the Kabbalah is to be skilled for work in the internal worlds... One that does not comprehend remains confused in the internal worlds. Kabbalah is the basis in order to understand the language of these worlds." - Samael Aun Weor, *Tarot and Kabbalah*

"In Kabbalah we have to constantly look at the Hebrew letters." - Samael Aun Weor, *Tarot and Kabbalah*

Karma: (Sanskrit, literally "deed"; derived from kri, "to do, make, cause, effect.") Causality, the Law of Cause and Effect.

"Be not deceived; God is not mocked: for whatsoever a man soweth, that shall he also reap." - Galatians 6:7

"Buddha said there are three eternal things in life: 1. The Law (Karma), 2. Nirvana, 3. Space." - Samael Aun Weor, *Tarot and Kabbalah*

Kundabuffer: Originally a useful organ that served the function of helping ancient humanity become focused on material, physical existence, it became corrupted by desire and sexual fall, thus resulting in the emergence of the ego and the fortification of the sexual energy in a negative polarity, and has since been symbolized by the tail of the devils, the tail of Satan.

"It is necessary to know that the Kundabuffer Organ is the negative development of the fire. This is the descending serpent, which precipitates itself from the coccyx downwards, towards the atomic infernos of the human being. The Kundabuffer Organ is the horrifying tail of Satan, which is shown in the "body of desires" of the Intellectual Animal, who in the present times is falsely called man." - Samael Aun Weor, *The Elimination of Satan's Tail*

"The diabolic type whose seduction is here, there and everywhere under the pretext of working in the Ninth Sphere, who abandons his wife because he thinks she will not be useful to him for the work in the Fiery Forge of Vulcan, instead of awakening Kundalini, will awaken the abominable Kundabuffer organ. A certain Initiate, whose name will not be mentioned in this Treatise, commits the error of attributing to the Kundalini all the sinister qualities of the Kundabuffer organ... When the Fire is cast downwards from the chakra of the coccyx, the tail of Satan appears; the abominable Kundabuffer organ. The hypnotic power of the organ of Witches' Sabbath holds the human multitude asleep and depraved. Those who commit the crime of practicing Black Tantra (Sexual Magic with Seminal Ejaculation) clearly awaken and develop the organ of all fatalities. Those who betray their Guru or Master, even if practicing White Tantra (without seminal ejaculation), will obviously activate the organ of all evils. Such sinister power opens the seven doorways of the lower abdomen (the seven infernal chakras) and converts us into terribly perverse demons." - Samael Aun Weor, *The Mystery of the Golden Blossom*

Kundalini: "Kundalini, the serpent power or mystic fire, is the primordial energy or Sakti that lies dormant or sleeping in the Muladhara Chakra, the centre of the body. It is called the serpentine or annular power on account of serpentine form. It is an electric fiery occult power, the great pristine force which underlies all organic and inorganic matter. Kundalini is the cosmic power in individual bodies. It is not a material force like electricity, magnetism, centripetal or centrifugal force. It is a

spiritual potential Sakti or cosmic power. In reality it has no form. [...]
O Divine Mother Kundalini, the Divine Cosmic Energy that is hidden
in men! Thou art Kali, Durga, Adisakti, Rajarajeswari, Tripurasundari,
Maha-Lakshmi, Maha-Sarasvati! Thou hast put on all these names and
forms. Thou hast manifested as Prana, electricity, force, magnetism,
cohesion, gravitation in this universe. This whole universe rests in Thy
bosom. Crores of salutations unto thee. O Mother of this world! Lead
me on to open the Sushumna Nadi and take Thee along the Chakras to
Sahasrara Chakra and to merge myself in Thee and Thy consort, Lord
Siva. Kundalini Yoga is that Yoga which treats of Kundalini Sakti, the
six centres of spiritual energy (Shat Chakras), the arousing of the sleeping Kundalini Sakti and its union with Lord Siva in Sahasrara Chakra,
at the crown of the head. This is an exact science. This is also known as
Laya Yoga. The six centres are pierced (Chakra Bheda) by the passing of
Kundalini Sakti to the top of the head. 'Kundala' means 'coiled'. Her form
is like a coiled serpent. Hence the name Kundalini." - Swami Sivananda,
Kundalini Yoga

"Kundalini is a compound word: Kunda reminds us of the abominable
"Kundabuffer organ," and lini is an Atlantean term meaning termination. Kundalini means "the termination of the abominable Kundabuffer
organ." In this case, it is imperative not to confuse Kundalini with
Kundabuffer." - Samael Aun Weor, *The Great Rebellion*

These two forces, one positive and ascending, and one negative and
descending, are symbolized in the Bible in the book of Numbers (the
story of the Serpent of Brass). The Kundalini is "The power of life."- from
the Theosophical Glossary. The Sexual Fire that is at the base of all life.

"The ascent of the Kundalini along the spinal cord is achieved very slowly
in accordance with the merits of the heart. The fires of the heart control
the miraculous development of the Sacred Serpent. Devi Kundalini is
not something mechanical as many suppose; the Igneous Serpent is only
awakened with genuine Love between husband and wife, and it will never
rise up along the medullar canal of adulterers." - Samael Aun Weor, *The
Mystery of the Golden Blossom*

"The decisive factor in the progress, development and evolution of the
Kundalini is ethics." - Samael Aun Weor, *The Revolution of Beelzebub*

"Until not too long ago, the majority of spiritualists believed that on
awakening the Kundalini, the latter instantaneously rose to the head and
the initiate was automatically united with his Innermost or Internal God,
instantly, and converted into Mahatma. How comfortable! How comfort-
ably all these theosophists, Rosicrucians and spiritualists, etc., imagined
High Initiation." - Samael Aun Weor, *The Zodiacal Course*

"There are seven bodies of the Being. Each body has its "cerebrospinal"
nervous system, its medulla and Kundalini. Each body is a complete
organism. There are, therefore, seven bodies, seven medullae and seven
Kundalinis. The ascension of each of the seven Kundalinis is slow and

difficult. Each canyon or vertebra represents determined occult powers and this is why the conquest of each canyon undergoes terrible tests." - Samael Aun Weor, *The Zodiacal Course*

Left-hand: In traditional cultures (especially Asian), the right hand is utilized for positive, clean, upright actions, such as eating, making offerings, etc., while the left hand is used for hidden, unclean, or harmful actions. This tradition emerged from the ancient esoteric knowledge, unknown to the public, in which the followers of the light (divinity, purity) correspond to the "right-hand of God" while the adherents of impurity and desire fall to the left, into disgrace. These contrary paths are rooted in Sanskrit terms. Dakshinachara (Sanskrit) literally means "upright in conduct" but is interpreted as "Right-Hand Path." Vamacara literally means "black magic," or "behaving badly or in the wrong way," and is used to refer to "Left-Hand Path" or "Left-path" (Sanskrit: Vamamarga). These two paths are explained in Kabbalah as well.

In modern times, those who follow the left-hand path have worked hard to make their path seem respectable and equal to the right, by claiming the two need each other to exist. This argument is based on the lie that left-hand initiates pursue the darkness of the Uncreated Light, the Absolute (which is pure, divine), yet the reality is that their degeneration and harmful acts propel them into the darkness of the abyss, the hell realms, to be cleansed of their impurity. Followers of the left-hand path believe they can outwit Divinity.

"And he shall separate them one from another, as a shepherd divideth his sheep from the goats. And he shall set the sheep on his right, but the goats on his left." —Matthew 25: 32-33

"Then the people of the right hand —Oh! how happy shall be the people of the right hand! And the people of the left hand —Oh! how wretched shall be the people of the left hand!" —Qur'an, Surah Al-Waqiah (The Inevitable) [56:8-9]

The widespread of the use of these terms in the West originated with H. P. Blavatsky.

It is important to note that physical handedness has nothing to do with one's spiritual level, value, or destiny. The persecution of left-handedness is just an ignorant form of discrimination.

"In symbolism the body is divided vertically into halves, the right half being considered as light and the left half as darkness. By those unacquainted with the true meanings of light and darkness the light half was denominated spiritual and the left half material. Light is the symbol of objectivity; darkness of subjectivity. Light is a manifestation of life and is therefore posterior to life. That which is anterior to light is darkness, in which light exists temporarily but darkness permanently. As life precedes light, its only symbol is darkness, and darkness is considered as the veil which must eternally conceal the true nature of abstract and undifferentiated Being.

"In ancient times men fought with their right arms and defended the vital centers with their left arms, on which was carried the protecting shield. The right half of the body was regarded therefore as offensive and the left half defensive. For this reason also the right side of the body was considered masculine and the left side feminine. Several authorities are of the opinion that the present prevalent right-handedness of the race is the outgrowth of the custom of holding the left hand in restraint for defensive purposes. Furthermore, as the source of Being is in the primal darkness which preceded light, so the spiritual nature of man is in the dark part of his being, for the heart is on the left side.

"Among the curious misconceptions arising from the false practice of associating darkness with evil is one by which several early nations used the right hand for all constructive labors and the left hand for only those purposes termed unclean and unfit for the sight of the gods. For the same reason black magic was often referred to as the left-hand path, and heaven was said to be upon the right and hell upon the left. Some philosophers further declared that there were two methods of writing: one from left to right, which was considered the exoteric method; the other from right to left, which was considered esoteric. The exoteric writing was that which was done out or away from the heart, while the esoteric writing was that which--like the ancient Hebrew--was written toward the heart." —Manly P. Hall, *The Secret Teachings of All Ages*

Lilith: (also Lilit; Hebrew) An ancient symbol appearing in Sumerian mythology (4000 BC), later known in Kabbalah as the feminine half or the first "wife" of Adam. After the division, she because the source of many demonic spirits who continue to plague mankind, including the sucubi and incubi generated by masturbation and sexual fantasy.

"In a hole by the great, supernal abyss, there is a certain female, a spirit above all spirits. We have explained that its name is Lilit. She was first with Adam, being his wife... In ancient books, it has been said that Lilit fled from Adam before that, namely before Eve was prepared. We did not understand it this way, because this female, Lilit, was with him. As long as this woman, Eve, was not made to be with Adam, Lilit was with him. When Eve was designed to be with him, Lilit fled to the sea, destined to harm the world." - Zohar

1) "Lilith is the mother of abortions, homosexuality, and in general, all kinds of crimes against Nature." - Samael Aun Weor, *The Perfect Matrimony*

2) "Another small moon called Lilith by astronomers also exists. Lilith is the black moon. The souls that have already totally separated themselves from their Monad formed by Atman-Buddhi-Manas, go there." - Samael Aun Weor, *The Zodiacal Course*

Logos: (Greek) means Verb or Word. In Greek and Hebrew metaphysics, the unifying principle of the world. The Logos is the manifested deity of every nation and people; the outward expression or the effect of the cause which is ever concealed. (Speech is the "logos" of thought). The

Logos has three aspects, known universally as the Trinity or Trimurti. The First Logos is the Father, Brahma. The Second Logos is the Son, Vishnu. The Third Logos is the Holy Spirit, Shiva. One who incarnates the Logos becomes a Logos.

"The Logos is not an individual. The Logos is an army of ineffable beings." - Samael Aun Weor, *Fundamental Notions of Endocrinology & Criminology*

Lucifer: (Latin: lux, lucis, luce, luci, and lucu: "light"; fer, fero: "to bear, carry, support, lift, hold, take up"; these synthesize as "Bearer of Light") Before Milton (17th c), Lucifer had never been a name of the devil. One of the early Popes of Rome bore that name, and there was even a Christian sect in the fourth century which was called the Luciferians. Lucifer, the "carrier of the light," is Prometheus, the divinity who brings the life-giving fire to humanity, yet is punished for this act, and is only freed when that fire incarnates as Herakles ("the aura of Hera"), the hero (bodhisattva; i.e. Jesus, Krishna, Moses, etc) who liberates the Christic fire from its bondage in the stone (the mountain / Mercury).

"We need to whitewash the devil with maximum expedited urgency. This is only possible through fighting against our own selves, by dissolving all those conjunctions of psychological aggregates that constitute the "I," the "myself," the "itself." Only by dying in ourselves can we whitewash the brass and contemplate the Sun of the Middle Night (the Father). This signifies that we must defeat all temptations and eliminate all of the inhuman elements that we carry within (anger, greed, lust, envy, pride, laziness, gluttony, etc, etc, etc.). A trainer in the psychological gymnasium of human existence is always required. The divine Daimon, quoted many times by Socrates, is the very shadow of our own individual Spirit. He is the most extraordinary psychological trainer that each one of us carries within. He delivers us into temptation with the purpose of training us, teaching us. Only in this way is it possible for the precious gems of virtue to sprout from our psyche. Now I question myself and I question you. Where is the evil of Lucifer? The results speak for themselves. If there are no temptations there are no virtues. Virtues are more grandiose when temptations are stronger. What is important is not to fall into temptation. That is why we have to pray to our Father, saying, "Lead us not into temptation." - Samael Aun Weor, *Tarot and Kabbalah*

Lumisial: "A place of light." A Gnostic Lumisial is a generator of spiritual energy, a Gnostic school which maintains the ancient initiatic Three Chamber structure. The source of power is the Cosmic Christ, and the means to receive and transform it are within the Second and Third Chambers.

"We are therefore working, my dear brethren, to initiate the Era of Aquarius. We are working in order to save what is possible, meaning, those who allow themselves to be saved. This is why it is necessary that we shape our Gnostic Movements and that we organize them each time better; that we establish the Three Chambers. Our Gnostic Movements must have exactly Three Chambers. Each Lumisial must have Three Chambers for the instruction of our students. Our Gnostic Centers receive a name in a very pure language that flows like a river of gold that runs in the sunny, thick jungle; that name is LUMISIALS." - Samael Aun Weor, The Final Catastrophe and the Extraterrestrials

Magic: The word magic is derived from the ancient word "mag" that means priest. Real magic is the work of a priest. A real magician is a priest.

"Magic, according to Novalis, is the art of influencing the inner world consciously." - Samael Aun Weor, *The Mystery of the Golden Blossom*

"When magic is explained as it really is, it seems to make no sense to fanatical people. They prefer to follow their world of illusions." - Samael Aun Weor, *The Revolution of Beelzebub*

Mahamanvantara: (Sanskrit) "The Great Day." A period of universal activity, as opposed to a mahapralaya, a cosmic night or period of rest.

"Truthfully, the quantities of years assigned to a cosmic day are symbolic. The cosmic night arrives when the ingathering of the perfect souls is complete, which means, when the cosmic day is absolutely perfected." - Samael Aun Weor, *The Pistis Sophia Unveiled*

"I was absorbed within the Absolute at the end of that Lunar mahamanvantara, which endured 311,040,000,000,000 years, or, in other words, an age of Brahma." - Samael Aun Weor, *The Revolution of Beelzebub*

Maithuna: Sanskrit, "sacramental intercourse."

The Sanskrit word Maithuna is used in Hindu Tantras (esoteric scriptures) to refer to the sacrament (sacred ritual) of sexual union between husband and wife.

Maithuna or Mithuna has various appearances in scripture:

· Mithuna: paired, forming a pair; copulation; the zodiacal sign of Gemini in Vedic Astrology, which is depicted as a man and woman in a sexual embrace

· Mithunaya: to unite sexually

· Mithuni: to become paired, couple or united sexually

By means of the original Tantric Maithuna, after being prepared psychologically and spiritually and initiated by a genuine teacher (guru), the couple learns how to utilize their love and spiritual aspiration in order to transform their natural sexual forces to purify the mind, eliminate psychological defects, and awaken the latent powers of the Consciousness. The man represents Shiva, the masculine aspect of the creative divine, and the woman represents Shakti, the feminine aspect and the source of the power of creation.

This method was kept in strictest secrecy for thousands of years in order to preserve it in its pure form, and to prevent crude-minded people from deviating the teaching, other people, or harming themselves. Nonetheless, some degenerated traditions (popularly called "left-hand" traditions, or black magic) interpret Maithuna or sacramental sexuality according to their state of degeneration, and use these sacred teachings to justify their lust, desire, orgies, and other types of deviations from pure, genuine Tantra.

Krishna: "And I am the strength of the strong, devoid of lust and attachment. O best of the Bharatas, I am sex not contrary to dharma." (Bhagavad Gita 7.11)

Manas: (Sanskrit) In general use, "mind." However, in Sanskrit the word manas can mean "imagination, intellect, inclination, will, excogitation, temper, understanding, intention, mind, spirit or spiritual principle, mood, perception, opinion, intelligence, breath or living soul which escapes from the body at death, desire, sense, reflection, thought, affection, conscience, invention, spirit."

Manas is derived from the Sanskrit root man, "to think." Manas is the root of the English term "man."

In Hinduism, the word manas is used with great flexibility and range, and thus can be applied in a variety of ways in the understanding of our psyche. In most cases it refers to the undisciplined mind of the common person, that is ruled by desires and ignorant of the true nature of the self (Atman). Manas is understood as the capacity for thought, which is one aspect of the antahkarana, the "inner organ."

The Vedas posit two forms of manas:

buddhi manas

kama manas

The Upanishads also present two forms of manas:

"Manas (mind) is said to be of two kinds, the pure and the impure. That which is associated with the thought of desire is the impure, while that which is without desire is the pure. To men, their mind alone is the cause of bondage or emancipation. That mind which is attracted by objects of sense tends to bondage, while that which is not so attracted tends to emancipation." - Amritabindu Upanishad

"Suddha Manas or Sattvic mind (pure mind) and Asuddha (impure) Manas or the instinctive mind or desire-mind as it is called are the two kinds of mind according to Upanishadic teaching. There is the lower mind filled with passion. There is the higher mind filled with Sattva (purity). There are two minds. You will have to make it into one — Sattvic mind only — if you want to meditate. It is through the higher or Sattvic mind that you will have to control the lower or instinctive mind of passions and emotions." - Swami Sivananda

In Buddhism, manas is used to refer to "mind" or "intelligence," in terms of mental function and activity.

Samael Aun Weor uses the term manas primarily in two ways:

Superior Manas: the Human Soul, the Causal Body, the sephirah Tiphereth

Inferior Manas: the intellect, the mental body, the sephirah Netzach

Mantra: (Sanskrit, literally "mind protection") A sacred word or sound. The use of sacred words and sounds is universal throughout all religions and mystical traditions, because the root of all creation is in the Great Breath or the Word, the Logos. "In the beginning was the Word..."

Marut: (Sanskrit मरुत्) Literally, "wind, air, storm god, beauty, gold, god of wind."

An alternate name of Vayu, the god of the wind or air.

In the Vedas, the word is a reference to "the storm gods" or gods of the wind. "...the Maruts have themselves glorified their greatness." - Vedas

Samael Aun Weor uses the term Marut to refer to people who have solar bodies but also have the ego alive, therefore they are very dangerous.

"The Twice-born who does not reduce his lunar ego to cosmic dust converts himself into an abortion of the cosmic mother. He becomes a marut, and there are thousands of types of maruts. Certain Asian sects and some Muslim tribes commit the lamentable error of rendering cult to all of those families of maruts. Every marut, every hasnamuss [plural: hasnamussen] has in fact two personalities: one white and another black (one solar and another lunar). The Innermost, the Being dressed with the electronic solar bodies, is the white personality of the hasnamuss, and the pluralized "I" dressed with the protoplasmic lunar bodies is the hasna-muss' black personality. Therefore, these maruts have a double center of gravity." —Samael Aun Weor

"[The Divine Mother Earth Goddess] Diti, having lost her children [because they were killed by Storm God Indra / Zeus], propitiated [the master] Kasyapa; and the best of ascetics, being pleased with her, prom-ised her a boon; on which she prayed for a son of irresistible prowess and valour, who should destroy Indra. The excellent Muni granted his wife the great gift she had solicited, but with one condition: "You shall bear a son," he said, "who shall slay Indra, if with thoughts wholly pious, and person entirely pure [chaste], you carefully carry the babe in your womb for a hundred years." Having thus said, Kasyapa departed; and the dame conceived, and during gestation assiduously observed the rules of mental and personal purity [brahmacharya]. When the king of the immortals [Indra], learnt that Diti bore a son destined for his destruction, he came to her, and attended upon her with the utmost humility, watching for an opportunity to disappoint her intention. At last, in the last year of the century, the opportunity occurred. Diti retired one night to rest without performing the prescribed ablution of her feet, and fell asleep [ie. she failed in her spiritual duties]; on which the thunderer divided with his thunderbolt the embryo in her womb into seven portions. The child, thus mutilated, cried bitterly; and Indra repeatedly attempted to console and silence it [by saying "Ma ruda," which means "Cry not."], but in vain: on which the god, being incensed, again divided each of the seven portions into seven [thereby making them 49], and thus formed the swift-moving deities called Márutas [Maruts]." —Vishnu Purana 21

Meditation: "When the esotericist submerges himself into meditation, what he seeks is information." - Samael Aun Weor

"It is urgent to know how to meditate in order to comprehend any psychic aggregate, or in other words, any psychological defect. It is indispensable to know how to work with all our heart and with all our soul, if we want the elimination to occur." - Samael Aun Weor, *The Gnostic Bible: The Pistis Sophia Unveiled*

"1. The Gnostic must first attain the ability to stop the course of his thoughts, the capacity to not think. Indeed, only the one who achieves that capacity will hear the Voice of the Silence.

"2. When the Gnostic disciple attains the capacity to not think, then he must learn to concentrate his thoughts on only one thing.

"3. The third step is correct meditation. This brings the first flashes of the new consciousness into the mind.

"4. The fourth step is contemplation, ecstasy or Samadhi. This is the state of Turiya (perfect clairvoyance). - Samael Aun Weor, *The Perfect Matrimony*

Mental Body: One of the seven bodies of the human being. Related to Netzach, the seventh sephirah of the Tree of Life; corresponds to the fifth dimension. In Egyptian mysticism, it is called Ba. In Hinduism, is it called vijnanmayakosha or kama manas (some Hindu teachers think the mental body is "manomayakosha," but that is the astral body).

"The mental body is a material organism, yet it is not the physical organism. The mental body has its ultra-biology and its internal pathology, which is completely unknown to the present men of science." - Samael Aun Weor, *The Revolution of Beelzebub*

Monad: (Latin) From monas, "unity; a unit, monad." The Monad is the Being, the Innermost, our own inner Spirit.

"We must distinguish between Monads and Souls. A Monad, in other words, a Spirit, is; a Soul is acquired. Distinguish between the Monad of a world and the Soul of a world; between the Monad of a human and the Soul of a human; between the Monad of an ant and the Soul of an ant. The human organism, in final synthesis, is constituted by billions and trillions of infinitesimal Monads. There are several types and orders of primary elements of all existence, of every organism, in the manner of germs of all the phenomena of nature; we can call the latter Monads, employing the term of Leibnitz, in the absence of a more descriptive term to indicate the simplicity of the simplest existence. An atom, as a vehicle of action, corresponds to each of these genii or Monads. The Monads attract each other, combine, transform themselves, giving form to every organism, world, micro-organism, etc. Hierarchies exist among the Monads; the Inferior Monads must obey the Superior ones that is the Law. Inferior Monads belong to the Superior ones. All the trillions of Monads that animate the human organism have to obey the owner, the chief, the Principal Monad. The regulating Monad, the Primordial Monad permits the activity of all of its subordinates inside the human organism, until the time indicated by the Law of Karma." - Samael Aun Weor, *The Esoteric Treatise of Hermetic Astrology*

"(The number) one is the Monad, the Unity, Iod-Heve or Jehovah, the Father who is in secret. It is the Divine Triad that is not incarnated within a Master who has not killed the ego. He is Osiris, the same God, the Word." - Samael Aun Weor, *Tarot and Kabbalah*

"When spoken of, the Monad is referred to as Osiris. He is the one who has to Self-realize Himself... Our own particular Monad needs us and we need it. Once, while speaking with my Monad, my Monad told me, 'I am self-realizing Thee; what I am doing, I am doing for Thee.' Otherwise, why are we living? The Monad wants to Self-realize and that is why we are here. This is our objective." - Samael Aun Weor, *Tarot and Kabbalah*

"The Monads or vital genii are not exclusive to the physical organism; within the atoms of the Internal Bodies there are found imprisoned many orders and categories of living Monads. The existence of any physical or supersensible, Angelic or Diabolical, Solar or Lunar body, has billions and trillions of Monads as their foundation." - Samael Aun Weor, *The Esoteric Treatise of Hermetic Astrology*

Ninth Sphere: In Kabbalah, a reference to the sephirah Yesod of the Tree of Life (Kabbalah). When you place the Tree of Life over your body, you see that Yesod is related to your sexual organs.

"The Ninth Sphere of the Kabbalah is sex." - Samael Aun Weor, *The Perfect Matrimony*

The Ninth Sphere also refers to the sephirah Yesod and to the lowest sphere of the Klipoth.

"The great Master Hilarion IX said that in ancient times, to descend into the Ninth Sphere was the maximum ordeal for the supreme dignity of the Hierophant. Hermes, Buddha, Jesus Christ, Dante, Zoroaster, Mohammed, Rama, Krishna, Pythagoras, Plato and many others, had to descend into the Ninth Sphere in order to work with the fire and the water which is the origin of worlds, beasts, human beings and Gods. Every authentic white initiation begins here." - Samael Aun Weor, *The Aquarian Message*

Nirvana: (Sanskrit निर्वाण, "extinction" or "cessation"; Tibetan: nyangde, literally "the state beyond sorrow") In general use, the word nirvana refers to the permanent cessation of suffering and its causes, and therefore refers to a state of consciousness rather than a place. Yet, the term can also apply to heavenly realms, whose vibration is related to the cessation of suffering. In other words, if your mind-stream has liberated itself from the causes of suffering, it will naturally vibrate at the level of Nirvana (heaven).

"When the Soul fuses with the Inner Master, then it becomes free from Nature and enters into the supreme happiness of absolute existence. This state of happiness is called Nirvana. Nirvana can be attained through millions of births and deaths, but it can also be attained by means of a shorter path; this is the path of "initiation." The Initiate can reach Nirvana in one single life if he so wants it." - Samael Aun Weor, *The Zodiacal Course*

"Nirvana is a region of Nature where the ineffable happiness of the fire reigns. The Nirvanic plane has seven sub-planes. A resplendent hall exists in each one of these seven sub-planes of Nirvanic matter where the Nirmanakayas study their mysteries. This is why they call their sub-planes "halls" and not merely "sub-planes" as the Theosophists do. The Nirvanis say: "We are in the first hall of Nirvana or in the second hall of Nirvana, or in the third, or in the fourth, or fifth, or sixth, or in the seventh hall of Nirvana." To describe the ineffable joy of Nirvana is impossible. There, the music of the spheres reigns and the soul is enchanted within a state of bliss, which is impossible to describe with words." - Samael Aun Weor, *The Revolution of Beelzebub*

Octave: The word octave comes from Medieval Latin octava, from Latin, feminine of octavus eighth, from octo "eight," and refers to the difference in sound between the first and eighth notes on a musical scale, thus indicating that the eighth note repeats the first, but higher or lower. To symbolize this, humanity has long used a scale to represent the steps between the first and eighth notes:

DO-RE-MI-FA-SOL-LA-SI-DO

The first and last DO are an octave apart, and they sound very similar, almost like the same note, except that the top note is higher because it vibrates twice as fast, while lower octaves vibrate at half the speed, thus sounding lower.

This musical example illustrates a law that functions throughout nature, from the microcosmic level to the macrocosmic level.

"While making a list of the elements in the ascending order of their atomic weights, John A. Newlands discovered at every eighth element a distinct repetition of properties. This discovery is known as the law of octaves in modern chemistry." — Manly P. Hall

While the seven-note scale is very ancient and its origins unknown by modern humanity, the names DO-RE-MI were invented in the eleventh century.

Ojas: (Sanskrit, literally "power or force of life") The energy that results from positive, pure spiritual transmutation, achieved through very specific techniques.

"Sublimation is not a matter of suppression or repression, but a positive, dynamic, conversion process. It is the process of controlling the sex energy, conserving it, then diverting it into higher channels, and finally, converting it into spiritual energy or Ojas Sakti. The material energy is changed into spiritual energy, just as heat is changed into light and electricity. Just as a chemical substance is sublimated or purified by raising the substance through heat into vapour which again is condensed into solid form, so also, the sexual energy is purified and changed into divine energy by spiritual Sadhana." - Swami Sivananda, *Brahmacharya*

"The Sanskrit term Ojas means "transmuted sexual energy," a type of Christic force. The semen is transmuted by means of Maithuna into subtle vapors, and these in turn convert themselves into energies that bipolarize in order to rise through Ida and Pingala up to the brain. To be converted into Ojas (Christic force) the semen must become "cerebrated." In order to be charged with Ojas (Christic force), the brain must become "semenized."" - Samael Aun Weor, *The Doomed Aryan Race*

Personality: (Latin personae: mask) There are two fundamental types of personality:

1. Solar: the personality of the inner Being. This type is only revealed through the liberation of the mind from samsara.

2. Lunar: the terrestrial, perishable personality. We create a new lunar personality in the first seven years of each new physical body, in accordance with three influences: genotype, phenotype and paratype. Genotype is the influence of the genes, or in other words, karma, our inheritance from past actions. Phenotype is the education we receive from our family, friends, teachers, etc. Paratype is related to the circumstances of life.

"The personality is time. The personality lives in its own time and does not reincarnate. After death, the personality also goes to the grave. For the personality there is no tomorrow. The personality lives in the cemetery, wanders about the cemetery or goes down into its grave. It is neither the astral body nor the ethereal double. It is not the Soul. It is time. It is energetic and it disintegrates very slowly. The personality can never reincarnate. It does not ever reincarnate. There is no tomorrow for the human personality." - Samael Aun Weor, *The Perfect Matrimony*

"Our personality has to become more and more passive..." - Samael Aun Weor, from the lecture "Knowing How to Listen"

"The human personality is only a marionette controlled by invisible strings... Evidently, each one of these I's puts in our minds what we must think, in our mouths what we must say, and in our hearts what we must feel, etc.Under such conditions the human personality is no more than a robot governed by different people, each disputing its superiority and aspiring to supreme control of the major centers of the organic machine... First of all, it is necessary, urgent and imperative that the Magnetic Center, which is abnormally established in our false personality, be transferred to the Essence. In this way, the complete human can initiate his journey from the personality up to the stars, ascending in a progressive, didactic way, step by step up the Mountain of the Being.As long as the Magnetic Center continues to be established in our illusory personality we will live in the most abominable psychological dens of iniquity, although appearing to be splendid citizens in everyday life... These values which serve as a basis for

the Law of Recurrence are always found within our human personality."-
Samael Aun Weor, *The Great Rebellion*

Poisonioonoskirian Vibrations: If the sexual energy is not used for reproduction of the race and it is not transmuted either, but there is only
abstinence, a forced celibacy and nothing else, that sexual energy then will
devolve, degenerate. Devolution of the sexual secretions produces malignant vibrations called Poisonioonoskirian Vibrations.

Prakriti: "Prakriti, the Divine Mother, is the primordial substance of
nature. Several substances, different elements and sub-elements exist
within the universe, but all of these are different manifestations of a
single substance. The Great Mother, the Prakriti, the Primordial Matter,
is the Pure Akasha contained within the entire space. [...] Millions and
billions of universes are being born and dying within the bosom of the
Prakriti. Every cosmos is born from the Prakriti and is dissolved within
the Prakriti. Every world is a ball of fire that becomes ignited and extinguished in the bosom of Prakriti. Everything is born from the Prakriti;
everything returns to the Prakriti. She is the Great Mother." - Samael Aun
Weor, *The Esoteric Treatise of Hermetic Astrology*

"...during the mahamanvantara [cosmic day], as a consequence of the
activity of the first, second and third Logoi, the Prakriti expands and
builds up from herself in three aspects. The three modes of the Prakriti
are: first, the Unmanifested Prakriti; second, the Prakriti in nature; third,
the Prakriti as queen of the infernos and death." —Samael Aun Weor

"'Prakriti' means that which is primary, that which precedes what is made.
It comes from 'Pra' (before) and 'Kri' (to make). It resembles the Vedantic
Maya. It is the one root of the universe. It is called Pradhana or the chief,
because all effects are founded on it and it is the root of the universe and
of all objects. Pradhana or Prakriti is eternal, all-pervading, immovable. It
is one. It has no cause, but is the cause of all effects. Prakriti is independent and uncaused, while the products are caused and dependent. Prakriti
depends only on the activity of its own constituent Gunas (metaphysical
properties). [...] Prakriti is the basis of all objective existence. Prakriti does
not create for itself. All objects are for the enjoyment of the spirit or soul.
Prakriti creates only when it comes into union with Purusha, like a crystal
vase with a flower. This work is done for the emancipation of each soul.
As it is the function of milk to nourish the calf, so it is the function of
Prakriti to liberate the soul." — Swami Sivananda

"Prakriti does all action. It is the Gunas that operate. Owing to ignorance
the body is mistaken for the Self. Egoism of man asserts at every step, nay,
at every second. Just as the motion of the clouds is falsely attributed to the
sun, so also the movements of the body and the Indriyas are falsely
attributed to the Self. The Self is always silent and is the witness of all
actions. He is Nishkriya or Akarta. You will find in the Gita: "All actions
are wrought by the qualities born of nature only. The self, deluded by
egoism, thinketh: 'I am the doer.' But he, O mighty-armed, who knoweth

the essence of the divisions of the qualities and functions, holding that the qualities move amid the qualities, is not attached." Ch. III-27, 28." — Swami Sivananda

"Prakriti or Nature is that state in which the three Gunas exist in a state of equilibrium. When this equilibrium is disturbed, creation begins and the body, senses and mind are formed. The man who is deluded by egoism identifies the Self with the body, mind, the life-force and the senses, and ascribes to the Self all the attributes of the body and the senses. In reality the Gunas of nature perform all actions." — Swami Sivananda

"Whosoever wants to be born again, whosoever wants to achieve Final Liberation, must eliminate the three Gunas of the Prakriti from their nature." - Samael Aun Weor, *The Esoteric Treatise of Hermetic Astrology*

Root Races: "Every planet develops seven root races and seven subraces. Our planet Earth already developed five root races; it needs to develop two more root races. After the seven root races, the planet Earth, already transformed by cataclysms over the course of millions of years, will become a new moon." - Samael Aun Weor, *The Kabbalah of the Mayan Mysteries*

The seven root races of this planet Earth are:

1. Polar protoplasmatic
2. Hyperborean
3. Lemurian
4. Atlantean
5. Aryan (present)
6. Koradi (future)
7. (Seventh) (future)

Sahaja Maithuna: (Sanskrit) Sahaja, "natural." Maithuna, "sacramental intercourse"

Samadhi: (Sanskrit) Literally means "union" or "combination" and its Tibetan equivilent means "adhering to that which is profound and definitive," or ting nge dzin, meaning "To hold unwaveringly, so there is no movement." Related terms include satori, ecstasy, manteia, etc. Samadhi is a state of consciousness. In the west, the term is used to describe an ecstatic state of consciousness in which the Essence escapes the painful limitations of the mind (the "I") and therefore experiences what is real: the Being, the Great Reality. There are many levels of Samadhi. In the sutras and tantras the term Samadhi has a much broader application whose precise interpretation depends upon which school and teaching is using it.

"Ecstasy is not a nebulous state, but a transcendental state of wonderment, which is associated with perfect mental clarity." - Samael Aun Weor, *The Elimination of Satan's Tail*

Second Birth: To be "born again," thereby becoming a "Twice-born."

The creation of the soul as taught by Jesus to Nicodemus:

"There was a man of the Pharisees, named Nicodemus, a ruler of the Jews: The same came to Jesus by night, and said unto him, Rabbi, we know that thou art a teacher come from God: for no man can do these miracles that thou doest, except God be with him. Jesus answered and said unto him, Verily, verily, I say unto thee, Except a man be born again, he cannot see the kingdom of God. Nicodemus saith unto him, How can a man be born when he is old? can he enter the second time into his mother's womb, and be born? Jesus answered, Verily, verily, I say unto thee, Except a man be born of water and of the Spirit, he cannot enter into the kingdom of God. That which is born of the flesh is flesh; and that which is born of the Spirit is spirit." - John 3:1-6

"In Gnosticism and esotericism, one understands that the fabrication of the solar bodies and the incarnation of the Being are known as the Second Birth." - Samael Aun Weor, *The Esoteric Treatise of Hermetic Astrology*

"No one can reach the Second Birth, be reborn again (as it stated in the Gospel of the Lord), as long as they continue living with the psychology of the inferior, common, everyday humanoid." - Samael Aun Weor, *The Great Rebellion*

Second Death: A mechanical process in nature experienced by those souls who within the allotted time fail to reach union with their inner divinity (i.e. known as self-realization, liberation, religare, yoga, moksha, etc). The Second Death is the complete dissolution of the ego (karma, defects, sins) in the infernal regions of nature, which after unimaginable quantities of suffering, proportional to the density of the psyche, in the end purifies the Essence (consciousness) so that it may try again to perfect itself and reach the union with the Being.

"He that overcometh (the sexual passion) shall inherit all things; and I will be his God (I will incarnate myself within him), and he shall be my son (because he is a Christified one), But the fearful (the tenebrous, cowards, unbelievers), and unbelieving, and the abominable, and murderers, and whoremongers, and sorcerers, and idolaters, and all liars, shall have their part in the lake which burneth with fire and brimstone: which is the second death. (Revelation 21) This lake which burns with fire and brimstone is the lake of carnal passion. This lake is related with the lower animal depths of the human being and its atomic region is the abyss. The tenebrous slowly disintegrate themselves within the abyss until they die. This is the second death." - Samael Aun Weor, *The Aquarian Message*

"When the bridge called "Antakarana," which communicates the divine triad with its "inferior essence", is broken, the inferior essence (trapped into the ego) is left separated and is sunk into the abyss of destructive forces, where it (its ego) disintegrates little by little. This is the Second Death of which the Apocalypse speaks; this is the state of consciousness called "Avitchi." - Samael Aun Weor, *The Zodiacal Course*

" The Second Death is really painful. The ego feels as if it has been divided in different parts, the fingers fall off, its arms, its legs. It suffers through a tremendous breakdown." - Samael Aun Weor, from the lecture The Mysteries of Life and Death

Secret Enemy: "The Nous atom is sometimes called by the occultist the white or good principle of the heart. We will now speak of its opposite: the dark atom or Secret Enemy. In many ways its activities are similar to the Nous atom; for it has legions of atomic entities under its command; but they are destructive and not constructive. This Secret Enemy resides in the lower section of the spine, and its atoms oppose the student's attempts to unite himself to his Innermost. The Secret Enemy has so much power in the atmosphere of this world that they can limit our thoughts and imprison our minds... The Secret Enemy works in every way to deny us any intelligence that would illuminate our minds, and would seek to stamp man into a machine cursed with similarity and a mind lacking all creative power... Man easily degenerates when in the power of the Secret Enemy; it preys upon the burning furnace of his desires, and when he weakens he is lost and sometimes cannot regain contact with his Innermost for two or three lives wherein he works out the karma of his evil desires." - M, *The Dayspring of Youth*

Semen: In the esoteric tradition of pure sexuality, the word semen refers to the sexual energy of the organism, whether male or female. This is because male and female both carry the "seed" within: in order to create, the two "seeds" must be combined. In common usage: "The smaller, usually motile male reproductive cell of most organisms that reproduce sexually." English semen originally meant 'seed of male animals' in the 14th century, and it was not applied to human males until the 18th century. It came from Latin semen, 'seed of plants,' from serere, 'to sow.' The Latin goes back to the Indo-European root *se-, source of seed, disseminate, season, seminar, and seminal. The word seminary (used for religious schools) is derived from semen and originally meant 'seedbed.' That the semen is the source of all virtue is known from the word "seminal," derived from the Latin "semen," and which is defined as "highly original and influencing the development of future events: a seminal artist; seminal ideas."

"According to Yogic science, semen exists in a subtle form throughout the whole body. It is found in a subtle state in all the cells of the body. It is withdrawn and elaborated into a gross form in the sexual organ under the influence of the sexual will and sexual excitement. An Oordhvareta Yogi (one who has stored up the seminal energy in the brain after sublimating the same into spiritual energy) not only converts the semen into Ojas, but checks through his Yogic power, through purity in thought, word and deed, the very formation of semen by the secretory cells or testes or seeds. This is a great secret." - Sri Swami Sivananda, *Brahmacharya* (Celibacy)

Sexual Magic: The word magic is derived from the ancient word magos "one of the members of the learned and priestly class," from O.Pers. magush, possibly from PIE *magh- "to be able, to have power." [Quoted from Online Etymology Dictionary].

"All of us possess some electrical and magnetic forces within, and, just like a magnet, we exert a force of attraction and repulsion... Between lovers that magnetic force is particularly powerful and its action has a far-reaching effect." - Samael Aun Weor, *The Mystery of the Golden Blossom*

Sexual magic refers to an ancient science that has been known and protected by the purest, most spiritually advanced human beings, whose purpose and goal is the harnessing and perfection of our sexual forces. A more accurate translation of sexual magic would be "sexual priesthood." In ancient times, the priest was always accompanied by a priestess, for they represent the divine forces at the base of all creation: the masculine and feminine, the Yab-Yum, Ying-Yang, Father-Mother: the Elohim. Unfortunately, the term "sexual magic" has been grossly misinterpreted by mistaken persons such as Aleister Crowley, who advocated a host of degenerated practices, all of which belong solely to the lowest and most perverse mentality and lead only to the enslavement of the consciousness, the worship of lust and desire, and the decay of humanity. True, upright, heavenly sexual magic is the natural harnessing of our latent forces, making them active and harmonious with nature and the divine, and which leads to the perfection of the human being.

"People are filled with horror when they hear about sexual magic; however, they are not filled with horror when they give themselves to all kinds of sexual perversion and to all kinds of carnal passion." - Samael Aun Weor, *The Perfect Matrimony*

Solar Bodies: The physical, vital, astral, mental, and causal bodies that are created through the beginning stages of alchemy/tantra and that provide a basis for existence in their corresponding levels of nature, just as the physical body does in the physical world. These bodies or vehicles are superior due to being created out of solar (Christic) energy, as opposed to the inferior, lunar bodies we receive from nature. Also known as the Wedding Garment (Christianity), the Merkabah (Kabbalah), To Soma Heliakon (Greek), and Sahu (Egyptian).

"All the masters of the White Lodge, the angels, archangels, thrones, seraphim, virtues, etc., Etc., Etc. Are garbed with the solar bodies. Only those who have solar bodies have the Being incarnated. Only someone who possesses the Being is an authentic human being." - Samael Aun Weor, *The Esoteric Treatise of Hermetic Astrology*

Tantra: Sanskrit for "continuum" or "unbroken stream." This refers first (1) to the continuum of vital energy that sustains all existence, and second (2) to the class of knowledge and practices that harnesses that vital energy, thereby transforming the practitioner. There are many schools of Tantra, but they can be classified in three types: White, Grey and Black. Tantra has long been known in the West as Alchemy.

"In the view of Tantra, the body's vital energies are the vehicles of the mind. When the vital energies are pure and subtle, one's state of mind will be accordingly affected. By transforming these bodily energies we transform the state of consciousness." - The 14th Dalai Lama

Triveni: (Sanskrit) A feminine word. Literally, "Triple-braided, the place where three holy rivers meet, place of confluence of the rivers Ganges, Yamuna, and subterranean Sarasvati."

> "The Nadis of each side Ida and Pingala are the left and right sympathetic cords crossing the central column from one side to the other, making at the Ajna with the Sushumna a threefold knot called Triveni; which is said to be the spot in the Medulla where the sympathetic cords join together and whence they take their origin—these Nadis together with the two lobed Ajna and the Sushumna forming the figure of the Caduceus of the God Mercury which is said by some to represent them... Ida starts from the right testicle and Pingala from the left testicle. They meet with Sushumna Nadi at the Muladhara Chakra and make a knot there. This junction of three Nadis at the Muladhara Chakra is known as Mukta Triveni. Ganga, Yamuna and Sarasvati dwell in Pingala, Ida and Sushumna Nadis respectively. This meeting place is called Brahma Granthi. Again these meet at the Anahata and Ajna Chakra. In the macrocosm also you have a Triveni at Prayag where the three rivers Ganga, Yamuna and Sarasvati meet." - Swami Sivnanada, *Kundalini Yoga*

Turiya: (Sanskrit, literally "fourth") The fourth and highest of the four states of consciousness, transcending the states of vigil ("wakened"), dreaming, and deep sleep. The state of turiya is described in the Mandukya Upanishad as "Invisible, otherworldly, incomprehensible, without qualities, beyond all thoughts, indescribable, the unified soul in essence, peaceful, auspicious, without duality, is the fourth stage, that self, that is to be known." In other words, this is the point of view of Atman / Chesed. "The fourth state is without parts and entanglements; Not bound to this world, It is auspicious and non-dual. Thus the form of AUM is verily the Self itself. He who knows thus enters into his own Self by himself."

Vajroli: (Sanskrit, from vajra: "thunderbolt, lightning, diamond, adamantine") Practices in Hindu and Tibetan Yogas, albeit with an incredible amount of variation and opposing uses.

Vedas: (Sanskrit véda "knowledge") The oldest and most sacred scriptures of Hinduism.

Vital body: (Also called Ethereal Body) The superior aspect of the physical body, composed of the energy or vital force that provides life to the physical body.

> "It is written that the vital body or the foundation of organic life within each one of us has four ethers. The chemical ether and the ether of life are related with chemical processes and sexual reproduction. The chemical ether is a specific foundation for the organic chemical phenomena. The ether of life is the foundation of the reproductive and transformative sexual processes of the race. The two superior ethers, luminous and reflective, have more elevated functions. The luminous ether is related with the

caloric, luminous, perceptive, etc., phenomena. The reflective ether serves as a medium of expression for willpower and imagination." - Samael Aun Weor, *The Gnostic Bible: The Pistis Sophia Unveiled*

In Tibetan Buddhism, the vital body is known as the subtle body (lus phramo). In Hinduism, it is known as pranamayakosa.

White Brotherhood or Lodge: That ancient collection of pure souls who maintain the highest and most sacred of sciences: White Magic or White Tantra. It is called White due to its purity and cleanliness. This "Brotherhood" or "Lodge" includes human beings of the highest order from every race, culture, creed and religion, and of both sexes.

Yoga: (Sanskrit) "union." Similar to the Latin "religare," the root of the word "religion." In Tibetan, it is "rnal-'byor" which means "union with the fundamental nature of reality."

"The word YOGA comes from the root Yuj which means to join, and in its spiritual sense, it is that process by which the human spirit is brought into near and conscious communion with, or is merged in, the Divine Spirit, according as the nature of the human spirit is held to be separate from (Dvaita, Visishtadvaita) or one with (Advaita) the Divine Spirit." - Swami Sivananda, *Kundalini Yoga*

"Patanjali defines Yoga as the suspension of all the functions of the mind. As such, any book on Yoga, which does not deal with these three aspects of the subject, viz., mind, its functions and the method of suspending them, can he safely laid aside as unreliable and incomplete." - Swami Sivananda, *Practical Lessons In Yoga*

"The word yoga means in general to join one's mind with an actual fact..." - The 14th Dalai Lama

"The soul aspires for the union with his Innermost, and the Innermost aspires for the union with his Glorian." - Samael Aun Weor, *The Revolution of Beelzebub*

"All of the seven schools of Yoga are within Gnosis, yet they are in a synthesized and absolutely practical way. There is Tantric Hatha Yoga in the practices of the Maithuna (Sexual Magic). There is practical Raja Yoga in the work with the chakras. There is Gnana / Jnana Yoga in our practices and mental disciplines which we have cultivated in secrecy for millions of years. We have Bhakti Yoga in our prayers and Rituals. We have Laya Yoga in our meditation and respiratory exercises. Samadhi exists in our practices with the Maithuna and during our deep meditations. We live the path of Karma Yoga in our upright actions, in our upright thoughts, in our upright feelings, etc." - Samael Aun Weor, *The Revolution of Beelzebub*

"Yoga does not consist in sitting cross-legged for six hours or stopping the beatings of the heart or getting oneself buried underneath the ground for a week or a month. These are all physical feats only. Yoga is the science that teaches you the method of uniting the individual will with the Cosmic Will. Yoga transmutes the unregenerate nature and increases energy, vitality, vigour, and bestows longevity and a high standard of health." - Swami Sivananda, *Autobiography*

"Brahmacharya [chastity] is the very foundation of Yoga." - Swami Sivananda

"The Yoga that we require today is actually ancient Gnostic Christian Yoga, which absolutely rejects the idea of Hatha Yoga. We do not recommend Hatha Yoga simply because, spiritually speaking, the acrobatics of this discipline are fruitless; they should be left to the acrobats of the circus." - Samael Aun Weor, *The Yellow Book*

"Yoga has been taught very badly in the Western world. Multitudes of pseudo-sapient Yogis have spread the false belief that the true Yogi must be an infrasexual (an enemy of sex). Some of these false yogis have never even visited India; they are infrasexual pseudo-yogis. These ignoramuses believe that they are going to achieve in-depth realization only with the yogic exercises, such as asanas, pranayamas, etc. Not only do they have such false beliefs, but what is worse is that they propagate them; thus, they misguide many people away from the difficult, straight, and narrow door that leads unto the light. No authentically initiated Yogi from India would ever think that he could achieve his inner self-realization with pranayamas or asanas, etc. Any legitimate Yogi from India knows very well that such yogic exercises are only co-assistants that are very useful for their health and for the development of their powers, etc. Only the Westerners and pseudo-yogis have within their minds the belief that they can achieve Self-realization with such exercises. Sexual Magic is practiced very secretly within the Ashrams of India. Any true yogi initiate from India works with the Arcanum A.Z.F. This is taught by the great Yogis from India that have visited the Western world, and if it has not been taught by these great, initiated Hindustani Yogis, if it has not been published in their books of Yoga, it was in order to avoid scandals. You can be absolutely sure that the Yogis who do not practice Sexual Magic will never achieve birth in the superior worlds. Thus, whosoever affirms the contrary is a liar, an impostor." - Samael Aun Weor, *Alchemy and Kabbalah in the Tarot*

Index

Crucified, 88, 151, 177, 194

Crucifixion, 176, 210, 220

Cruel, 12, 74, 82, 99, 194

Crystallization, 35, 56, 151, 161, 165, 168, 178, 192

Cteis, 177, 208-209

Cubic, 151-152, 177-178, 195

Cult, 4, 65, 116, 173, 214, 228

Cup, 32, 143, 145-146, 177, 183

Cupbearer, 184

Cybele, 116, 209

Cycle, 54, 61, 105, 143

Cycles, 66, 97, 106, 143

Cyclical, 80

Cyclones, 29, 31

Cynicism, 104, 149

Czars, 155

Damocles, 20

Daniel, 39

Dante Alighieri, 82, 91

Darwin, 77

David, 95, 206

De-gravitate, 3

Death, 13, 20, 35-36, 38-39, 45, 47, 49, 54, 59, 62-64, 66-67, 82-84, 91, 100, 145, 155, 157, 159, 189, 191, 203, 206, 209, 218-220, 227, 232-233, 235-236

Debts, 186

Decapitated, 194

Defect, 175, 178, 210, 212, 229

Defects, 174, 212, 214, 226, 235

Degenerate, 146, 233

Degenerated, 13-14, 32, 37, 68, 78, 89, 104, 161, 218, 226, 237

Degenerates, 236

Degeneration, 8, 12, 68, 78-79, 216, 223, 227

Degenerations, 88

Degenerative, 78, 80

Degree, 12, 72, 104, 109, 117, 149, 179, 194, 204, 207-208

Degrees, 59, 71, 128, 131-132

Delilah, 127

Delphi, 117

Deluge, 6, 88

Demigods, 65

Democritus, 93

Demon, 43, 208

Demonic, 56, 158, 175, 224

Demons, 27, 138, 140, 208, 221

Designed, 224

Desire, 56, 93, 190, 208, 221, 223, 227, 237

Desired, 146

Desires, 159, 180, 192, 200, 208, 219, 221, 227, 236

Destinies, 13, 99

Destiny, 59, 223

Deva, 43, 187, 210

Devil, 53, 56, 225

Devils, 21, 53, 104, 221

Devolution, 45-46, 48-50, 54, 69, 76-80, 126, 186, 233

Devolved, 9, 80

Devolving, 49-50, 69, 78-80, 143, 219

Dhammapada, 81

Dharma, 186, 191, 203, 227

Dharma Megha, 186

Diamond, 195, 238

Diana, 35, 100, 209

Dimension, 48, 58, 200, 205, 229

Dimensions, 57-58, 158, 207, 219

Diogenes, 93

Dioscorides, 93

Dioscuri, 116

Direct Path, 187, 202

Discipline, 193, 207, 240

Disintegrates, 59, 232, 235

Disintegration, 54, 59, 62, 69, 206

Dissolution, 53, 173, 235

Dissolved, 37, 53, 93, 205, 233

Dissolving, 174, 225

Divine Comedy, 24, 41, 50, 63, 81-82, 89, 178, 205, 214

Divine Couple, 184, 215

Divine Mother, 34-37, 55, 174-175, 180, 183-184, 209, 214, 222, 228, 233

Divine Spirit, 171, 239

Division, 103, 200, 224

Divorces, 68, 139

Fallopian, 105
Falls, 84, 146
Families, 50, 173, 214, 228
Family, 13, 186, 199, 232
Fanatical, 14, 226
Fanaticism, 104, 149
Fanatics, 63, 68, 77
Fascinated, 13
Fast, 51-52, 97, 179, 231
Fatal, 14, 17, 45, 53, 99, 149, 217
Fatality, 149
Fate, 8-9, 37, 125
Father, 4, 95, 128, 132, 138, 168-169,
    194, 218-219, 225, 230
Father-Mother, 211, 237
Fathers, 99
Fault, 16-18, 117
Fear, 32, 56, 72, 163, 195, 199, 235
Fears, 67
Fecundation, 62, 106, 128, 215
Fecundity, 143
Feel, 14, 74, 150, 163, 198, 217, 232
Feeling, 88, 189, 214
Feelings, 43, 239
Feels, 158, 235
Feet, 38, 155, 177-179, 184, 194, 228
Fell, 2, 12, 82, 179, 191, 195, 228
Female, 103-104, 106, 109, 114-115,
    148, 155, 161, 209, 212, 224,
    236
Feminine, 36, 103-106, 134, 137,
    161, 170, 172, 192, 205, 214,
    224, 226, 231, 237-238
Feng, 189, 191-192
Fertile, 35
Fertilized, 5
Fetus, 106
Fiber, 119-120, 133
Fidelity, 56, 74, 206
Field, 78, 106, 132, 168, 180
Fields, 38, 43, 128, 184
Fierce, 93
Fiery, 116, 148, 221
Fifteen, 173, 189
Fifth, 7, 9, 32, 52-53, 58, 73, 100,
    123, 129, 131, 133, 168-169,
    190, 200, 202, 229, 231

Fifth Initiation of Fire, 168, 202
Fifth Patriarch, 190
Fifty, 154, 201
Final Judgment, 37-38, 61, 63
Final Liberation, 55, 234
Fire, 2, 4, 18, 20, 25, 30, 32, 35, 38,
    53, 55-56, 91-94, 99-100,
    109, 115-117, 119, 121-122,
    125-129, 132-133, 139-140,
    143-145, 149, 151, 168-169,
    175, 177-180, 184, 195, 200,
    202-203, 205-206, 212, 214,
    221-222, 225, 230-231, 233,
    235
Fires, 54, 222
Firmament, 184
First, 6-9, 12, 14, 32, 35, 38-39, 45,
    48, 52, 57, 73, 77, 82, 88, 91-
    92, 95, 99-100, 103, 114, 116,
    122, 126, 129, 131-132, 150-
    151, 158, 163, 168, 170, 172,
    174, 177, 179, 185-186, 189,
    191, 203-205, 208, 211-212,
    215, 219-220, 224-225, 229,
    231-233, 237
First Logos, 204, 225
First World War, 39
Fish, 32, 171, 178, 197, 215
Fissures, 17-18, 103
Five, 51-53, 58, 73-74, 100, 107, 122-
    123, 127-128, 132, 147, 151,
    154, 157, 183, 191, 194, 205,
    207, 209, 234
Five Centers, 51-52, 73, 122
Flags, 30, 45, 74
Flame, 116, 205, 213, 219
Flames, 2, 55, 82, 133-134, 180, 210
Flaming, 20, 92, 94, 116, 128, 156,
    168, 184
Floating, 84, 93, 99, 111
Flood, 2, 4, 23
Florentine, 81-82
Flowers, 119, 121, 123, 128, 179
Flowing, 67
Flows, 5, 31, 127-128, 226
Fluid, 105, 117
Fluidic, 165

203, 208, 211-213, 215-216,
218, 221, 225, 231, 237
Humanoid, 235
Humans, 32, 62, 75
Humble, 183, 186
Humiliation, 152
Humility, 228
Hurricanes, 29-32, 54, 189, 218
Hydrogen, 22-26, 29, 87, 161-162,
165-166, 168-169, 215-216
Hydrogen Si-12, 161, 165, 168, 215
Hydrogens, 35, 161, 215
Hyperboreans, 32, 234
Hyperion, 85
Hypersolid, 58
Hyperspace, 58
Hypertrophy, 105
Hypervolume, 58
Hypnotic, 117, 157-158, 221
Hypnotized, 57, 68, 157-158
I. A. O., 116
I. E. O. U. A. N., 177
Ice, 29, 31, 125, 179
Ida, 95, 109-110, 115, 120, 122, 133-
134, 138, 143, 232, 238
Idea, 29, 41, 52, 56, 65-66, 77, 168,
186, 240
Ideas, 189, 236
Ideations, 212
Igneous, 31, 115, 119, 121, 126, 132-
133, 137-138, 214, 222
Igneous Serpent, 115, 119, 137-138,
214, 222
Ignis, 116
Ignorance, 164, 201, 210, 218, 233
Ignorant, 45, 193, 223, 227
Ignore, 7-8, 17, 58, 68, 161, 164
Iliad, 4
Illuminated, 3, 36, 42-44, 82, 149,
207
Illuminating Void, 191
Illumination, 37, 134, 203
Illusion, 67, 100, 192, 207, 226
Illusory, 122, 187, 189, 192, 200, 232
Imagination, 43, 133, 183, 227, 239
Imagine, 57, 71, 119, 222
Immolated, 13-14, 195

Immortal, 139, 155, 171-173, 206
Immortality, 200-201, 203, 228
Impression, 121-122, 208, 215
Impulse, 80, 115, 161, 165, 209
Impulses, 52, 72-73, 97, 106
Inca, 4, 6
Incarnate, 84, 172-173, 186, 206-
207, 235
Incarnated, 67, 131, 171, 204, 206-
207, 230, 237
Incontinency, 45
Incretion, 103
India, 6-7, 30, 112-114, 193, 200,
206, 210, 212, 240
Indian, 17-18, 209-210
Indian Ocean, 17-18
Individual, 56, 199, 201-202, 206,
209, 213, 219, 221, 225, 239
Individuality, 57, 62, 75, 171, 201,
209
Individuals, 47, 53, 55, 62, 84, 105,
120
Indo-American, 4, 7
Indo-European, 200, 212, 236
Indo-Germanic, 200
Inertia, 42
Inferior, 41, 51, 57, 60, 63, 91, 108-
109, 143, 150, 165, 171, 185,
201, 205, 216, 219, 228-229,
235, 237
Inferior Abyss, 205
Inferior Manas, 165, 228
Infernal Worlds, 24, 26, 38, 43-45,
50, 54, 60-61, 63-66, 68-69,
82-83, 89, 91, 126, 139, 149,
152, 174, 186, 192, 205, 216
Inferno, 41-43, 89, 125, 139, 179-180
Infernos, 35-36, 53, 55, 82, 138, 175,
178-180, 221, 233
Infinite, 2, 13-15, 26, 30, 42, 50, 53,
56, 66, 71, 74, 143-145, 147,
156, 163-164, 190, 195-196,
201, 208, 210, 215
Infrared, 44
Infrasexuality, 89, 150, 161, 216-217,
240
Inhales, 80

Masters, 2, 32-33, 65, 88, 141, 191-193, 203-204, 206-207, 216, 237
Mastery, 152
Masturbation, 89, 155, 212, 216, 218, 224
Mater, 174
Material, 9, 25, 53, 56, 120, 162, 212, 219, 221, 223, 229, 231
Materialism, 2, 68, 77
Materialistic, 43, 77
Materiality, 41, 43
Materialization, 49
Materialized, 35
Maternal, 80, 106
Mathematical, 156, 163, 174
Mathematics, 164, 166
Matricides, 13, 217
Matrimonies, 68
Matrimony, 11, 113, 207, 214-217, 219, 224, 229-230, 232, 237
Matter, 7, 19, 24-27, 35, 42, 47-48, 83, 85, 87, 100, 109, 119, 125-126, 151, 157, 162, 183, 191, 199, 205, 215, 221, 231, 233
Matthew, 39, 65, 81, 84, 175, 217, 223
Max Heindel, 7
Maya, 84, 100, 192, 204, 233
Mayan, 1, 4, 220, 234
Mechanical, 2, 23, 46, 67-68, 77, 80, 83, 87, 222, 235
Mechanically, 56
Mechanism, 23-24, 87
Mechanistic, 155
Mechanization, 43, 80, 88
Medic-magicians, 105
Medical, 71, 106
Medicine, 13, 47-48, 107
Medics, 87, 105
Medieval, 48, 92, 100, 147, 231
Meditate, 227, 229
Meditation, 36, 126, 133-134, 189-190, 192, 197, 203, 210, 229, 239

Medulla, 107-109, 111, 121, 133, 202-203, 217, 222, 238
Medullar, 114, 129, 133-134, 137-139, 222
Medusa, 93
Memories, 6, 207
Memory, 88, 134, 172, 180, 220
Menstruation, 87, 106
Mental Body, 129, 163-166, 168-169, 203, 228-229
Metals, 4, 41-42, 47, 184, 199
Metamorphoses, 48, 184
Metempsychosis, 63
Method, 199, 224, 226, 239
Methods, 163, 224
Mexican Army, 47
Mexico, 5, 15, 17, 29-30, 116
Micro-laboratories, 71-72, 106
Micro-organism, 229
Microbe, 144
Microcosm, 42, 204-205
Microcosmic, 71, 115, 231
Milarepa, 88, 202, 210
Milk, 106, 233
Milky, 153-154, 156, 159, 171
Milky Way, 153-154, 156, 159, 171
Mind, 3, 25, 30, 35, 43, 47, 52, 77-78, 163-166, 174-175, 180, 189-192, 199, 201, 203-205, 226-229, 232, 234, 236-237, 239
Mind-stream, 230
Minds, 3, 26-27, 71, 78-79, 164-166, 201, 203, 227, 232, 236, 240
Mineral, 24, 41-43, 45, 47-50, 54, 64, 66, 69, 83, 89, 204, 211, 219
Minerals, 41-42, 210
Minerva, 100
Mithra, 98
Mohammed, 19, 84, 92, 183, 196, 202, 213, 216, 230
Molecular, 25-26, 43, 49, 52, 57, 60-62, 82, 91, 159, 167, 175, 218
Molecular World, 49, 57, 91, 167, 218
Moment, 11, 14-15, 19-20, 23, 26, 52, 56, 62, 74, 106, 125, 134,

Organic, 51, 59, 71, 87-88, 126, 221, 232, 238
Organisms, 13, 236
Organizations, 12, 140
Organize, 225
Organized, 144
Organizing, 12
Organs, 51, 105-106, 109-110, 125, 138, 161, 177, 213, 216, 230
Orgasm, 138, 212-213
Orichalcum, 4
Orifice, 108-109
Origin, 4, 7, 18, 29, 77, 80, 92, 109, 116, 125, 146, 178, 208, 211, 214, 216, 230, 238
Originate, 67, 73, 75, 155
Originated, 6, 93, 223
Originates, 62, 74, 105, 115, 202
Originating, 5, 73
Origins, 4, 146, 231
Ors, 71
Osiris, 145, 230
Ostrite, 100
Ouspenski, 66, 163
Ova, 103
Ovaries, 103, 105, 109
Ovum, 105, 135
P T R, 100
Pacific, 17-19, 26, 30-32
Padma, 186
Padmasambhava, 114, 202, 210
Padmasana, 114
Padme, 61
Pain, 41, 52, 58, 125, 179, 189, 201, 210, 214, 218
Painful, 43, 50, 53-54, 63, 67, 146, 149, 234-235
Painters, 68, 79, 99
Paleolithic, 79-80
Paleontology, 77
Palestine, 155
Pallas, 116
Palm, 3, 166
Palm Sunday, 166
Pan, 85, 116
Panchanga, 156
Pantheon, 59

Parable, 36
Paracelsus, 48, 211
Paradise, 43, 99, 159, 165
Paradises, 187
Paradisiacal, 128
Parapsychology, 47
Parasympathetic, 72
Parents, 86, 100, 208
Paricutin, 30
Paris, 11
Paropamisan Mountains, 199
Parsis, 116
Particle, 47, 172, 214
Particles, 24, 47, 73
Passion, 193, 195, 213, 216, 227, 235, 237
Passionate, 89, 106, 127, 178-179
Passions, 82, 128, 159, 217, 227
Passive, 72, 209, 232
Patar, 100, 177
Paths, 173, 177-178, 187, 223
Patient, 157-158, 198
Patriarch, 95, 190
Patriarchs, 93, 152
Paul, 1-2, 213
Pausanias, 116
Peace, 2, 186, 191, 198, 201, 205, 238
Pearl, 6
Pearland, 6, 8
Pedicles, 108
Pellicle, 88
Pendulum, 87
Pentalpha, 147
Pentecost, 214
Pentecostal, 116, 139
Penthesilea, 93
Perceive, 43, 119, 207
Perceived, 43, 133, 211
Perceives, 57, 119, 208
Percent, 57, 67, 88, 165, 168, 177-178, 212
Percentage, 212
Perceptible, 58, 206
Perception, 58, 119, 207-208, 227
Perceptions, 47, 109, 119
Perceptive, 239

About the Author

His name is Hebrew סמאל און ואור, and is pronounced "sam-ayel on vay-or." You may not have heard of him, but Samael Aun Weor changed the world.

In 1950, in his first two books, he became the first person to reveal the esoteric secret hidden in all the world's great religions, and for that, accused of "healing the ill," he was put in prison. Nevertheless, he did not stop. Between 1950 and 1977 – merely twenty-seven years – not only did Samael Aun Weor write over sixty books on the most difficult subjects in the world, such as consciousness, kabbalah, physics, tantra, meditation, etc., in which he deftly exposed the singular root of all knowledge — which he called Gnosis — he simultaneously inspired millions of people across the entire span of Latin America: stretching across twenty countries and an area of more than 21,000,000 kilometers, founding schools everywhere, even in places without electricity or post offices.

During those twenty-seven years, he experienced all the extremes that humanity could give him, from adoration to death threats, and in spite of the enormous popularity of his books and lectures, he renounced an income, refused recognitions, walked away from accolades, and consistently turned away those who would worship him. He held as friends both presidents and peasants, and yet remained a mystery to all.

When one reflects on the effort and will it requires to perform even day to day tasks, it is astonishing to consider the herculean efforts required to accomplish what he did in such a short time. But, there is a reason: he was a man who knew who he was, and what he had to do. A true example of compassion and selfless service, Samael Aun Weor dedicated the whole of his life to freely helping anyone and everyone find the path out of suffering. His mission was to show all of humanity the universal source of all spiritual traditions, which he did not only through his writings and lectures, but also through his actions.

Your book reviews matter.

Glorian Publishing is a very small non-profit organization, thus we have no money to spend on marketing and advertising. Fortunately, there is a proven way to gain the attention of readers: book reviews. Mainstream book reviewers won't review these books, but you can.

The path of liberation requires the daily balance of three active factors:

- birth of virtue
- death of vice
- sacrifice for others

Writing book reviews is a powerful way to sacrifice for others. By writing book reviews on popular websites, you help to make the books more visible to humanity, and you might help save a soul from suffering. Will you do your part to help us show these wonderful teachings to others? Take a moment today to write a review.

Donate

Glorian Publishing is a non-profit publisher dedicated to spreading the sacred universal doctrine to suffering humanity. All of our works are made possible by the kindness and generosity of sponsors. If you would like to make a tax-deductible donation, you may send it to the address below, or visit our website for other alternatives. If you would like to sponsor the publication of a book, please contact us at (844) 945-6742 or help@gnosticteachings.org.

Glorian Publishing
PO Box 110225
Brooklyn, NY 11211 US
Phone: (844) 945-6742

VISIT US ONLINE AT gnosticteachings.org